THE BOOK OF
WHEN?

A DICTIONARY OF
TIMES AND SEASONS

Compiled and edited by
Rodney Dale

INDEX

To my wife, family and friends

This edition first published in 2004 by CRW Publishing Limited,
69 Gloucester Crescent, London NW1 7EG
This edition published for Index Books Ltd 2005

ISBN 1 904919 20 0

Text copyright © Rodney Dale 2004

Typeset and designed in Bliss by Bookcraft Limited, Stroud, Gloucestershire
Printed and bound in China by Imago

Introduction

I keep six honest serving men
(They taught me all I knew);
Their names are What and Why and When
And How and Where and Who.

Rudyard Kipling

In the delightful garden at Probus in Cornwall there is on a lawn a wall in the shape of Cornwall, and on the raised bed it encloses are placed labelled samples of the many types of rock to be found in the Duchy. It was this geological display that, in 2002, set me thinking about a work that would encompass all human knowledge, starting with the materials from which our universe is made, and proceeding to the rich variety of the flora and fauna inhabiting it, and going on to specific people and achievements ... and so on and so on until there emerged the series of which you are now reading the first book.

The Book of When? deals with that endlessly fascinating subject: Time. Not in too philosophical a way, I hasten to say; rather does it look at the application of time: through calendars, and festivals, and commemorations, and phrases that imply something to do with time. It is not a book of dates, but it does of course include many dates which have some bearing on my approach.

Part 1 of the *Book of When?* is an A-to-Z 'encyclopædic index'; the headwords arranged in alphabetical order, some with definition and explanation, others cross-references. Thus the first part has both the function of an encyclopædia (in its explanatory mode) and that of an index (as an acknowledgement of a word or term, and a direction to its fuller appearance).

Part 2 takes the year 1996, and looks at it day by day. Not all public holidays (for example) – or movable feasts (by definition) – will fall on the same day every year, but I had to make a choice and the reason for choosing that particular year is that it is a leap year beginning on a Monday, and is more familiar to us than the next candidate: 2024.

Part 3 deals with calendars as the practical solutions developed by various civilisations and cultures to the problem of reconciling the irreconcilable: the relative times taken by the Sun, the Moon, and the Earth to perform their cycles.

And so to the book itself. It will be used by many different people in many different ways and, however I present it, there will surely be those who would like something presented differently for their particular uses. Any suggested improvements brought to my attention will receive full consideration, and I will welcome your contributions, preferably by e-mail.

Rodney Dale
Haddenham, Cambridgeshire 2004
info@fernhouse.com

Acknowledgements

Many people have helped to bring this book into being, and I would particularly like to thank Matthew Pettitt who started the ball rolling when I first had the idea way back in the last century – in the last millennium, even! Since then, a number of people have continued the work: Zoë Dale (no relation), Charlotte Edwards (particularly), Lindsay Goddard, Mark Hatcher, Gina Keene and Georgia Parkes.

Others have confirmed facts, made comments, and generally facilitated the work: Stephen Adamson, Anne Challis, Jezz Davies, Christopher Dunn, Meredith MacArdle, Michael and Valerie Grosvenor Myer, Roger Pratt, Steve Puttick, Mike Waggett, and Nick and Sue Webb.

A book such as this stands or falls by its design, and I would like to thank John Button of Bookcraft Ltd, and typesetter Matt Gavan, for an especially creative relationship. Proofreader Graham Frankland's contribution to the reader's wellbeing has been more than helpful – having said which my shoulders accept the usual author's burden as the place where the buck stops.

And for their faith, patience, and ever-cheerful encouragement, Marcus Clapham, Clive Reynard and Ken Webb – in other words, CRW.

A note on transliteration

My information is drawn from a variety of sources; it is inevitable then that there may be some inconsistency in transliteration from other languages. I hope that those erudite enough to note this will, through that erudition, be able to cope with it.

Abbreviations used in this book

=	generally indicates a translation
ab	abbot
Abp	archbishop
abs	abbess
ACT	Australian Capital Territory (Australia)
aet	aged
aka	also known as
AS	Australian slang
b	born
Bp	bishop
bro	brother
C	century
c	about
CofE	Church of England
con	confessor
d	died
DO	Roman Catholic Holy Day of Obligation
et al	and others
HK	Hong Kong
inter alia	among others
K	king
M	martyr(s)
nr	no relation
NSW	New South Wales (Australia)
NT	Northern Territory (Australia)
NZ	New Zealand
OE	Old English

PH	public holiday
PNG	Papua New Guinea
Pr	Prince
pron	pronounced
pt	part
Q	queen
Qld	Queensland (Australia)
qv	which see
RC	Roman Catholic
RS	rhyming slang
S	South, Saturday
S	Sunday
SA	South Australia (Australia)
sis	sister
SS	Saints
St	Saint
Tas	Tasmania (Australia)
UK	United Kingdom of Great Britain and Northern Ireland
US	United States of America
V	virgin
vi	see below
Vic	Victoria (Australia)
vs	see above
WA	Western Australia (Australia)

Part 1
Times and Seasons A–Z

A note on alphabetical order
In the following pages and for the purposes of keeping important material together, some of the highlighted panels may be slightly out of alphabetical order with the main text entries.

Ab (Av)

Fifth month of the sacred, and eleventh month of the civil, Jewish year. Derived from the Babylonian month of Abu, it corresponds roughly to the Gregorian July–August, and has 30 days. The Fast for the Destruction of the Temples (586BCE and 70CE) is observed on 9 Ab – see Jewish Calendar.

Aban

Eighth month of the Persian year.

Abbasid(e)s

A powerful dynasty of caliphs that ruled Islam from 750 to 1258CE descended from Muhammad's uncle al-Abbas 652CE.

Abbot of Misrule

See misrule.

Abbots Bromley (Horn Dance)

One of the rare European animal dances surviving from remote times, it dates back to at least August 1226. Originally danced at the Barthelmy Fair in the Staffordshire village of Abbots Bromley, it now takes place on Wakes Monday: the first Monday after 4 September (unless 4 September is a Sunday, in which case the Dance is on 12 September). The side comprises 12 men: the six Deermen, who carry the reindeer antlers (on iron frames, and weighing between 16 and 25 pounds); the other six are the stock figures: the Hobbyhorse, the Fool, Maid Marian, and the Bowman, and the two musicians who respectively play the melodeon and the triangle. The horns are normally kept in the church, and drawn at 8am on the day of the Dance, which covers some 10 miles and a dozen locations. For nigh on 200 years, the Lead Deerman has been a member of the Fowell family, and he is responsible for choosing the rest of the side.

Abelites

A 4th-Century CE North African Christian sect whose members were allowed to marry, but not to have sexual relations; they kept going by adopting children.

Abhidhamma Day

Held on the full moon of the seventh month of the Burmese lunar year starting in April (corresponding to the full moon day in October), this is the day when the Buddha is said to have gone to the Tushita Heaven to teach his mother the Abhidhamma.

Abstinence, Days of

1   Those on which eating meat is forbidden.
2   In the Anglican church, abstinence = fasting, during the 40 days of Lent, the four Ember days, the three Rogation days, all Fridays except Christmas Day, and the eves of certain festivals.
3   In the RC church, abstinence, fasting, and days of abstinence vary in different countries. Generally, all Fridays, Wednesdays in Advent and Lent, Ember days, and the eves of Christmas, Easter, Pentecost, SS Peter and Paul, Assumption and All Saints are days of abstinence.

Abu

A Babylonian month from which the name of the Jewish month of Ab is derived.

Abundant year

See **Jewish calendar**.

AC

Ante Christum (before Christ), a Latin form of BC.

Academic term

The period during which an academic institution is in session. In England, there are at present three terms separated by the three holidays occasioned by Christmas, Easter, and the summer, giving a term:holiday ratio of about 3:1. See **semester; semesterisation**. Some establishments have a Long Vac Term, to enable students to pursue coursework in the Long Vacation between May exams and the start of the Autumn Term in October.

Academic year

That which begins with the Autumn Term (September–October).

Act of Parliament Clock

See **Clock Tax**.

Adam Style

The neo-classical style of architecture and interior decoration introduced by the Scottish architects and designers Robert Adam (1728–92) and his brother James (1730–94) based on then recently-discovered Græco-Roman remains.

Adar

Twelfth month of the sacred, and sixth month of the civil Jewish year. Derived from the Babylonian Addaru, it corresponds to the Gregorian Feb–Mar; it has 29 days. The Fast of Esther is observed on 13 Adar, and the Feast of Purim (Lots) on 14 Adar – see **Jewish Calendar**. In a leap year, there are two Adars: 1st Adar or Adar Rishon with 29 or 30 days, and 2nd Adar, Adar Sheni or Ve-Adar with 30 days. In leap years, the observances fall in 2nd Adar.

Addaru

Babylonian month from which the Jewish month of Adar is derived.

Addled Parliament

Sat in the reign of James I from 5 April to 7 June 1614; so called for its sterility (as in addled egg), as it was dissolved without passing a single Act.

Adonia

The eight-day feast of the beautiful youth Adonis, doomed lover of Aphrodite, was celebrated in Alexandria, Assyria, Cyprus, Egypt, Greece, Judaea, Persia and Rome. Like his precursors the Sumerian Tammuz (after whom the Jewish month is named) and the Babylonian Marduk, his was a virgin birth, and the feast celebrated his death and rebirth three days later. No wonder that the festival merged into what is now celebrated in the Christian world as Easter.

Advent

The four weeks before Christmas, beginning on St Andrews Day (30 November), or the Sunday nearest to it. Advent Sunday may therefore fall on any day between 27 November and 3 December. Since C6, Advent has been thought of by Christians as a preparation for the Second Coming.

In marketspeak, Advent has become the most intensive part of 'the run-up to Christmas', when retail stores become obsessed with the comparison between sales figures for the current year against the previous year, invent elaborate explanations for the deterioration and, later, announce that it wasn't so bad after all.

Æon

1 A very long time.
2 In geology, the longest division of time, comprising two or more eras.
3 10^9 years.

Age

1 How old something is.
2 Colloquially, a long time as in: 'It's an age since we met'.
3 A word used to denote a period distinguished by particular charac-teristics, such as 'the Middle Ages', 'the Jazz Age' or 'the Age of Aquarius'.
4 The opposite of youth.
5 In geology, a subdivision of an epoch.
6 In arts and crafts, the natural or accelerated process of maturation.

Age of Enlightenment

Or, in Britain, Age of Reason; the C18 rise of a broader and more questioning philosophy based on reason and scientific enquiry, rather than on authoritarian orthodoxy gave rise to the Enlightenment. The seeds were sown in the C17 as the understanding and acquisition of scientific knowledge gained pace, and scholars such as Descartes, Newton and Pascal began to question the established order of things. Well-known British figures are:

1642–1727	Sir Isaac Newton (physicist)
1650–1715	Thomas Savery (steam engineer)
1663–1729	Thomas Newcomen (steam engineer)
1674–1741	Jethro Tull (agriculturalist)
1677–1717	Abraham Darby (ironmaster)
1693–1776	John Harrison (chronologist)
1704–1780	John Kay (weaving engineer)
1709–1784	Samuel Johnson (man of letters)
1711–1763	Abraham Darby II (ironmaster)
1711–1777	David Hume (philosopher)
1716–1772	James Brindley (civil engineer)
1720–1778	James Hargreaves (spinning engineer)
1723–1790	Adam Smith (economist)
1724–1792	John Smeaton (civil engineer)
1728–1779	James Cook (explorer)
1728–1799	Joseph Black (physicist)
1728–1808	John Wilkinson (ironmaster)
1728–1809	Matthew Boulton (engineer)
1730–1795	Josiah Wedgwood (potter)
1731–1802	Erasmus Darwin (physician)
1732–1792	Sir Richard Arkwright (spinning engineer)
1733–1804	Joseph Priestley (chemist)
1734–1794	Edward Gibbon (historian)
1736–1803	Francis Egerton, 3rd Duke of Bridgewater (engineer)
1736–1819	James Watt (engineer)
1748–1814	Joseph Bramah (engineer)
1749–1823	Edward Jenner (physician)
1750–1791	Abraham Darby III (ironmaster)
1753–1827	Samuel Crompton (spinning engineer)
1754–1839	William Murdock (civil engineer)
1757–1834	Thomas Telford (civil engineer)
1771–1831	Henry Maudslay (engineer)
1771–1833	Richard Trevithick (engineer)

Age of consent
The age at which a girl's consent to sexual intercourse, and hence marriage, is legal; in England and Scotland it is 16.

Age of discretion
In law, the age when a child is deemed to have sufficient discretion to be prosecuted for its misdemeanours; in English law this is 14 years.

Age of Elegance
1   The beautiful face of C17–18, as portrayed by Joshua Reynolds (1723–92) or Thomas Gainsborough (1727–88), for example.
2   Anything so dubbed: 'Fashion has entered a new age of elegance ...'

Age of the Popes
C12, according to the historian Henry Hallam (1777–1859).

Age of Reason
1   See Age of Enlightenment.
2   For Roman Catholics, the end of the seventh year when a child begins to assume moral responsibility, the obligation of confession, *etc*.

Age set
Many primitive societies are ordered so that groups of people (usually males) pass through a procession of grades in each of which they are expected to perform various tasks reflecting their abilities such as physical strength, experience and wisdom. There may be 'streams' of warriors, and of elders with political or ritual specialities. Compare this with the introduction of managerial and technical 'ladders' in industry which recognised at last that not everyone worthy of promotion has to be 'manager material'.

Aging
The degenerative process in an organism that starts with birth and ends with death. It may be a genetically-governed process, or it may be due to changes in metabolism and the effects thereof – or a combination of the two. The aging process is reasonably constant for any given type of organism.

AH
Anno Hegirae (Latin = in the year of the Hegira) – the flight of the Prophet Muhammad from Mecca to Yathrib (later Medina) on 6 July 622CE, the start of the Muslim calendar.

Alexandra Day
26 June, on which day red roses are sold in aid of Queen Alexandra's Hospital Fund. It was inaugurated in 1912, the fiftieth year of the residence in England of the Danish Queen Alexandra (1844–1925), wife of King Edward VII.

Alexandrine Age

That during which the Alexandrian school of literature, science and philosophy (c300BCE–640CE) held sway as the world centre of learning.

Al Kadr

Title of Chapter 97 of the Holy Koran; the night on which Muhammad received his first revelation from Gabriel; in the Muslim calendar, the night of 24 Ramadan on which angels are said to descend to earth, and Gabriel to reveal the decrees of God to man.

All Fool's Day

(All Fools' Day) Up to midday on 1 April, when practical jokes are played upon those who thereby become 'April Fools'. The custom, unknown in the UK until C18, may be connected with the festivities of the Spring Equinox. It echoes the fooling of the ancient Indian Spring feast of Holi. It may have arisen as a result of the beginning of the year moving from 1 April to 1 January. In France, an April Fool is the reputedly easy-to-catch *poisson d'avril* (April fish), and in Scotland the reputedly foolish gowk (cuckoo). 'April Fool' is also used as a noun, much as 'En Suite' is now used to denote a bathroom and WC installed for the exclusive use of a bedroom. Perhaps the most widely remembered and quoted April Fool of recent times is the Richard Dimbleby spaghetti-tree spoof on BBC's *Panorama* in 1957.

All-Hallows' Day

See All Saints' Day.

All-Hallows' Eve – or Halloween (or Hallowe'en)

31 October, the night in the Celtic calendar when the witches and warlocks emerged. At that time, bonfires were lit to repel visitors from the spirit world, and this custom may in more recent times have been deferred until 5 November – see Guy Fawkes night. But the unholy visitations are still remembered at Hallowe'en when children of all ages dress up as witches, in-lit eviscerated pumpkins girn on the scene, and trick-or-treaters knock on doors, making a mockery of the rule that sweets should never be accepted from strangers. In the Christian church (which seems somehow to embrace the above frivolity), All Hallows celebrates the lives of all the saints and is, in some countries, a public holiday.

Alliensis, Dies

19 July in Gregorian dating, commemorating the disastrous defeat of the Roman army, cut to pieces by the Gauls at the river Allia in 390BCE.

All Saints' Day

Christian festival on 1 November previously known as All Hallows; 'hallows' is from the Old English *halig* a holy man, a saint. All the saints are remembered on All Saints' Day; it dates from 835CE, but originated in 608CE, when Pope Boniface IV dedicated the Pantheon at Rome to the Church of the Blessed Virgin and All Martyrs. The festival of All Saints was then held on 1 May; it was changed to 1 November in 834CE. All Saints' Day is an RC day of obligation, and in some Christian countries it is a public holiday. Superstitions associated with the pagan festival of 1 November were associated in Scotland with Hallow E'en (Allhallows Eve), the vigil of All Saints.

All Souls' Day

In the RC church, 2 November is reserved for prayers for the souls of the faithful departed in purgatory. It originated in the Abbey of Cluny in 998CE, was omitted from the English Prayer Book at the Reformation, and restored in 1919. It is known as the Day of the Dead in France and Italy. It is a public holiday in some Latin American Countries.

Almanac (Almanack)

A yearly calendar of days and months, phases of the moon, sunrise and sunset times, tides, anniversaries and so on.

am, a.m.

ante meridiem (Latin = before noon); thus a time between a midnight and the following midday.

AM

Anno mundi (Latin = in the year of the world) indicating the year of the Jewish calendar (*qv*). AM5756 (or 756 for short) started on 25 September 1996; the Jewish calendar (*qv*) is deemed to have begun in 3760BCE.

Ambrosian era

In musical history, the C4–6CE, named after the belligerent Bishop Ambrose of Milan (*c*340–97) who established four musical scales, and plainsong, and brought order to liturgical music until it was replaced by the Gregorian Chant in the sixth century.

Ambrosian nights

Evenings of convivial discourse held in Ambrose's Tavern, Edinburgh, Scotland (1822–35) led by John Wilson (*alias* Christopher North), James Hogg, and other literary lights.

America

The continent was discovered by Europeans on Friday 12 October 1492 when Christopher Columbus (1451–1506) and his party arrived at uncertain islands off the east coat of what was named Amrerica after the Italian Amerigo Vespucci (1451–1512) who provisioned at least one of Columbus's expeditions.

Anachronism

Something in the wrong chronological relationship with other things and events as depicted in fiction or inaccurate historical accounts. An oft-quoted anachronism is 'The clock hath stricken three' in the Scottish Play by Shakespeare, but television docudramas offer examples by the shedload, especially in the nuances of the dialogue.

Anapanasati Day

At the end of one rains retreat (Vassa), the Buddha was so pleased with the progress of the assembled monks that he encouraged them to extend their retreat for yet another month. On the full-moon day marking the end of that fourth month of retreat, Buddha presented his *Discourse on Mindfulness of Breathing* (anapanasati).

Ancestor Day

See Ulambana.

Ancien régime

The 'old order of things'; the system of government under the Bourbon monarchy, so described by the French revolutionaries.

Anecdotage

Facetious word for that state of old age when the subject tends to tell the same stories over and over again.

Angelus

An RC devotion, in honour of the Annunciation, at 6am, midday and 6pm at the sound of the Angelus bell. The office begins: 'Angelus Domini nuntiavit Mariae'.

Anno Domini; AD

1 (Latin = in the year of our Lord) Indicates that a quoted year or century falls within the Christian era. The idea was introduced in the first half of the sixth century by the monk Dionysius Exiguus. See also CE.

2 The term is also used facetiously to explain one's creaking joints and general deterioration.

Anno regni regis/reginae

Latin = in the year of the reign of our king/queen. See Regnal years.

Annunciation, Feast of the

25 March, also called Lady Day; an immovable feast.

Annus Horribilis

(*cf* Annus Mirabilis) The Horrible Year: 1992, according to HM Queen Elizabeth II, in which so many unpleasant things happened to the

Anniversaries

Certain materials or artefacts are traditionally (or commercially) attached to particular wedding anniversaries, as follows:

1	Cotton	Paper	Plastics	Clocks
2	Paper	Cotton	Calico	China
3	Leather	Glass	Crystal	
4	Fruit	Flowers	Linen/Silk	Appliances
5	Wood	Silver		
6	Iron	Sugar	Sweetmeats	
7	Wool	Copper	Brass	Desk Sets
8	Bronze	Pottery	Appliances	Linen
9	Copper	Pottery	Willow	Leather
10	Tin	Aluminium	Diamond	
11	Steel	Jewellery		
12	Silk	Linen	Pearl	
13	Lace	Textiles	Fur	
14	Ivory	Gold		
15	Crystal	Timepieces		
20	China	Platinum		
25	Silver			
30	Pearl	Diamond		
35	Coral	Jade		
40	Ruby	Garnet		
45	Sapphire			
50	Gold			
55	Emerald	Turquoise		
60	Diamond	Gold		
70	Platinum			
75	Diamond	Gold		

In the above table, the traditional materials are on the left, and more modern introductions (which embrace specific artefacts as well as the material from which they might be made) as you move to the right. In general, it appears that the longer whatever it is has been going on, the more expensive the material associated with it; however values of materials change: relatively, some have increased (leather, wood, copper, tin) and others decreased (sugar, wool, china). Presumably the category '(electrical) appliances' was introduced by the Electrical Appliances' Manufacturers' Association or some such. As for the desk set …

British Royal Family, culminating in the fire at Windsor Castle; in *Sun*speak: 'One's Bum Year'.

Annus Luctus

The first year after the death of a husband, during which his widow should not marry for the (somewhat naïve) avoidance of doubt about the parentage of any child born during the first nine months.

Annus Mirabilis

(Latin: The Year of Wonders) – 1666 according to the poem by Dryden of that name (the year of the Great Fire of London, and the victory of the English over the Dutch), or any other year so designated by a narrator – for example 1963 so designated by Philip Larkin.

'Come cheer up my lads, 'tis to glory we steer, To add something more to this wonderful year ...' words and music by Dr William Boyce for David Garrick's pantomime *Harlequin's Invasion* of 1759, a year which saw also the victories at Minden and Quiberon Bay.

Anomalistic month

The 27.55455 days between two successive passages of the moon through perigee.

Anomalistic year

The 365.25964 mean solar days (365 days, 6 hours, 13 minutes, and 53 seconds) between two successive passages of the earth through perihelion.

Anzac Day

25 April, commemorating the landing of the Anzacs (Australia and New Zealand Army Corps) on the Gallipoli peninsula in 1915, when some 7,000 of the 10,000 who took part were either killed or wounded; the Day is a public holiday in Australia and New Zealand.

Aoi Matsuri

Japanese festival held at the Kamo Shrines, Kyoto, on 15 May; there is a procession of people dressed as court nobles of the Heian period, wearing headgear decorated with leaves of the aoi plant (*Asarum caulescens*); the leaves are offered to the deities of the Shrines to secure a bountiful rice harvest.

Apple Day

Nominally 21 October, although the dates of celebrations vary. It was instituted in 1990, and celebrates the fruit in its numerous varieties with displays, tastings, advice on cultivation – and, no doubt, sales.

April

Fourth month of the Gregorian year (*qv*); named from Aphrodite (the Greek Venus) or from the Latin *aperire* (= opening); if the latter, it would be one of the few examples of a month's English name associated with nature; birthstone: diamond.

April Fool's Day
See All Fool's Day.

Aquarius

The 11th sign of the Zodiac (21 January to 18 February). The Age of Aquarius is said to have dawned, especially in flower-power circles, in the 1960s when everything good (peace, brotherhood, etc) seemed about to happen. In fact, the Precession of the Equinoxes (*qv*) is a 25,920-year cycle, so that each zodiacal 'age' is 2,160 years. The consensus is that the Age of Aquarius is not due to 'dawn' until the year 2080CE ±20 years.

Arabian Nights
A collection of C10 oriental tales (introduced to the west at the beginning of the C18), supposed to have been told nightly by the Sultana Scheherazade, bride of the Sultan Schahriah, to (successfully) delay her execution for infidelity; also called 1,001 Nights.

Arakhshama
Babylonian month from which the Jewish month of Marcheshvan is derived.

Arbor Day
In Canada, the US and New Zealand, a day for planting trees; instituted in Nebraska in 1872, it became a legal holiday in 1885. The date varies according to the locality, but in Nebraska is usually 22 April.

Archaeozoic
See Precambrian.

Arcmin
A term sometimes used instead of minutes of arc; a minute of time is equivalent to 15 arcmin.

Armageddon
According to the Revelation of St John the Divine (16:14) the site of the last great battle of that great day of God almighty ... (16:16) at the place that in Hebrew is called Harmagedon (*ie* the mountain district of Megiddo). The concept has been widened to embrace any great slaughter, such as World War I.

Armistice Day

11 November 1918, and subsequently the day on which to commemorate the fallen in World War I. In 1946 its name was changed to Remembrance Day so that it could include those who died in World War II. 11 November is a legal holiday in the US and Canada; there, its name was changed to Veterans' Day in 1954.

ARR

Anno regni regis/reginae.

Art Deco; Nouveau

Decorative styles of art design, art deco referring to the 1920–30 Odeon and Clarice Cliff period, and art nouveau to that of the 1890s and early 1900s: the Paris Métro, and British Patent Office.

Arvo

Australian slang for afternoon, usually elided to 'the sarvo'.

Asalha Puja Day (Dhamma Day)

On the full moon day of the 8th lunar month, Buddhists pay homage to the Buddha's first teaching: the turning of the wheel of the Dhamma (Dhammacakkappavattana Sutta) to the five ascetics at the Deer Park (Sarnath) near Benares city, India, where the senior ascetic Kondanna attained the first level of enlightenment (Sotapanna).

Ascension Day

Holy Thursday, the fortieth day after Easter (thus falling between 30 April and 3 June) on which, according to Christian legend, Christ ascended from earth to heaven. Ascension Day is a public holiday in many Christian countries.

Ascensiontide

The 10 days between Ascension Day (Holy Thursday, the fortieth day after Easter) and Whitsun Eve.

Ashadh

Fourth month of the Hindu year.

Ashvin

Seventh month of the Hindu year.

Ash Wednesday

The first day of Lent, which can be any Wednesday between 4 February and 10 March. Its name recognises the RC custom (perhaps introduced at the end of the C6 by Pope Gregory the Great) of scattering consecrated ash of palms from the previous Palm Sunday on the heads of penitents (nowadays Christians may mark their foreheads with ashes in the sign of the Cross).

Astrologer

One who purports to be able to guide a subject by an interpretation of the positions of the heavenly bodies at the time of that subject's birth, and their movements during the subject's life. It is difficult to provide a plausible mechanism whereby such an effect might work, other than the possibility of the subject's view of the world being shaped by the conditions obtaining when his or her consciousness developed. If this were to happen at, say, six months after one's birth, then it would be expected that those born in the winter would have a generally sunny view of life, and those born in the summer would have a generally cold and muffled view. But the way the perceived environment (not to mention interpersonal relationships) affects one's general interpretation of the way things are must depend on many factors. It must be said, however, that astrologers tend to agree on their readings, even though the way they might affect an individual may be so ambiguous as to be only in the eye of the beholder. A list of astrological characteristics might read:

Aries	aggressive, competitive, dominant, impatient, noisy
Taurus	amicable, loyal, reliable, self-motivated
Gemini	dilettante, loquacious, straightforward
Cancer	caring, considerate, easy to get on with, reliable
Leo	attention-seeking, creative, popular
Virgo	helpful, organised, quiet, self-effacing
Libra	charming, eloquent, equable, good teamworker, sociable
Scorpio	considerate, disciplined, hard-working, intense, secretive, strong-willed
Sagittarius	disorganised, forgetful, generous, good-humoured, gregarious, messy
Capricorn	ambitious, cynical, persevering
Aquarius	ingenious, organising, stubborn, unpredictable
Pisces	creative, imaginative, inspirational, thoughtful.

Remember: there are billions of people and only 12 star signs. To test astrology, read the lists of birthdays in the paper and see if different professions cluster at different times. If you're really keen, cut out the horoscopes with covert identification and see which seem to apply best to you and yours. See Zodiac.

Assumption, Feast of the

... of the Blessed Virgin Mary, 5 August, an RC Feast of Obligation (instituted in the C6) to remember her death, and the reuniting of her body and soul in heaven. It is a public holiday in Greece and most Roman Catholic countries.

AST

Atlantic Standard Time, 4 hours slow on GMT; see Time Zones.

Atomic clock

The idea of using atomic or molecular vibrations to control the frequency of an electronic oscillator was put forward in 1946. The first 'atomic' clock was built it 1948 by Harold Lyons. It used the vibrations of ammonia molecules to provide a standard ten times more accurate than those of the quartz crystal. Molecules of ammonia are injected into a cavity between metal electrodes charged to a high voltage. The ammonia molecule is not symmetrical and, according to whether a given molecule has a high or a low energy content, so it aligns itself one way or another in the electric field. By appropriate manipulation of the charges, the high-energy molecules can be separated from their fellows and fed into a cavity resonator, where they control the frequency of vibration of an electrical signal with very high accuracy. The signal may then be treated as in the quartz clock, and made to drive a system for measuring the passage of time.

Atonement, Day of

See Yom Kippur.

AUC

(From Latin *Ab urbe condita* or *Anno urbis conditae* = 'from the foundation of the city (of Rome)' or 'In the year of the city's foundation'); The date from which the Roman calendar was supposed to have begun (753BCE).

August

Eighth month of the Gregorian year (*qv*); named after the Roman Emperor Augustus in 8BCE; birthstone: peridot or sardonyx.

Augustan Age

Supposedly the golden age of Latin literature, corresponding with the reign of the Roman Emperor Augustus (27BCE to 14CE), during which flourished Latin poets such as Horace, Livy, Ovid and Virgil. The concept was extended to specify the Augustan age of French literature (C17) and the Augustan age of English literature (C18).

Aurignacian

A culture flourishing some 36,000 years ago, characterised by heavy flint and other stone tools, and artefacts of polished bone, not to mention remarkable cave paintings (*eg* at Lascaux). It may have come from the middle east; it was first recognised in 1860 at Aurignac in the French Department of Haute-Garonne.

Australia Day

(Commemoration Day) The first Monday after January 26, commemorating the arrival of the first settlers in New South Wales on 26 January 1788, when Capt Arthur Phillip, later the first Governor of New South Wales, stepped ashore at Sydney Cove and founded a colony of 1,030 people, 736 of whom were convicts. (Transportation of convicts, often for the pettiest of crimes, ended in 1865.) It was first celebrated as Foundation or Commemoration Day in NSW in 1818; from the establishment of the Commonwealth in 1901 it has been a holiday nationwide on the day if a Monday, or the first Monday after.

Autumn

The third season of the year, between Summer and Winter; from the September equinox to the December solstice in the Northern hemisphere, and from the March equinox to the Summer solstice in the Southern hemisphere. Also called 'fall' in older English and current American; 'back end' in northern English speech.

Autumnal Equinox

1 When the Sun crosses the plane of the equator away from the relevant hemisphere, and day and night are of equal length. In the Northern hemisphere it occurs about 23 September, and 21 March in the Southern hemisphere.
2 In astronomy, the point on the celestial sphere in Virgo at which the ecliptic intersects the celestial equator.

Av

See Ab.

Avalokitesvara's (Kuan Yin) Birthday

This festival on the full moon day in March celebrates the Bodhisattva ideal represented by Avalokitesvara, the perfection of compassion in the Mahayana traditions of Tibet and China.

Awa Odori (Awa Dance)

Japanese festival held at Tokushima on 12–15 August, when groups of men and women parade along the main streets of Tokushima, dancing and singing the song *Yoshikono-bushi* to the accompaniment of shamisen, flutes, and drums.

Awkward Age
Epithet adduced for the transition from child to adult, especially by parents as an excuse for any embarrassing behaviour; better perhaps to remember the adage 'never apologise; never explain'.

Ayara
Babylonian month from which the name of the Jewish month of Iyyar is derived; it means 'bud'.

Azar
Ninth month of the Persian year.

Back end
A widely-used term for Autumn in the north of England.

Bahman
Eleventh month of the Persian year.

Baisakhi
The Hindu New Year Festival celebrated by exchanging gifts, feasting, praying and bathing in sacred waters; in the Gregorian calendar it falls in April–May. At the same time, Sikhs commemorate those killed by British troops at the holy city of Amritsar in 1919.

Baktun
According to the religion-oriented calendar of the Maya people who flourished in Mexico and Central America during the 200s–800s CE, a cycle of 400 years, each year 360 days made up of eighteen twenty-day 'weeks'. It may be totally coincidental, but 400 such years contain 144,000 days – a number that in souls, years, or other units is significant in several different religions.

Balolo moon
The annelid balolo (or palolo or paolo) worm (*Eunice viridis*) flourishes among coral reefs in the Pacific; its sexual activity, when its rear end containing sperm or ova detaches and swims to the surface to release the gametes, is governed by the phases of the moon. There is a small rising in October (Vula i balolo lailai), and a much larger one in November (Vula i balolo levu), when the islanders put to sea to collect the delicacy. See Fijian calendar.

Bannock
Round, flat griddle cake of oatmeal or barley eaten in Scotland around May Day; originally 'Bannoch Belltainn' baked in the Beltane (*qv*) fire, it later shed its knobs and acquired a cross on one side like a hot cross bun; moreover, Scottish children took to rolling the bannock down hillsides in the manner of an Easter egg.

Banyan Day

An English nautical phrase to describe a day on which the rations contained no meat.

Barebones Parliament

That of 140 godly members approved by Oliver Cromwell which sat between 4 July and 11 December 1653; it was named (happy coincidence) after one of its members, Praise-God Barebon.

Barnaby Bright

Old name for St Barnabas' Day; 11 June, once the longest day.

Barons' War

1 The English civil war (1215–17) precipitated by King John's failure to abide by the terms of Magna Carta.
2 The English civil war (1264–67) fought between the baronial supporters of Simon de Montfort and those of Henry III, who refused to accept limitations to his authority.

Baroque Period

The European style of art and architecture that followed the High Renaissance and Mannerism, and lasted from about 1600 to 1740. It was particularly popular in Italy, France and Spain in Catholic churches and public buildings, and was encouraged as part of the Counter-Reformation to appeal to the emotions of a population that was still largely illiterate. It was also highly suitable for silently supporting the idea of divine right of kingship, and so was adopted by many monarchs, particularly Louis XIV of France. Foremost exponents included the sculptor Gian Lorenzo Bernini, and the painters Peter Paul Rubens and Pietro Berrettini da Cortona.

Bartholomew Fair

An annual fair held at Smithfield on St Bartholomew's Day (24 August), from 1133 to 1752, and then (after calendar reform) on 3 September until its last year: 1855. It moved from Smithfield to Islington in 1840; its successor was the Caledonian Market ('The Stones') which closed in 1939, but lives on as the New Caledonian Market in Bermondsey, South London.

Bartholomew, Massacre of St

Catherine de Médicis ordered the slaughter of French Huguenots; it began on St Bartholomew's Day (24 August) 1572, in Paris and the provinces; as many as 70,000 may have been slain.

Bank holidays

By English Common Law the days that mark the birth and death of Christ (Christmas Day and Good Friday) are public holidays.

By custom, the Bank of England at the beginning of the last century was closed on at least 40 saints' days and anniversaries. In 1830 such bank holidays were cut to 18 and in 1834 to only four. In 1871 Parliament passed the Bank Holidays Act, introduced by Rt Hon Sir John Lubbock, MP, 4th baronet – later Lord Avebury – and this statute regulated bank holidays as follows: *England and Wales;*

New Year's Day	1 January, but if this falls on a Saturday or Sunday, the next Monday – by Statute.
Good Friday	by Common Law.
Easter Monday	by Statute.
May Day	from 1978, Monday 1 May, or the first Monday after 1 May.
Spring Holiday	the last Monday in May.
Late Summer Holiday	the last Monday in August (earlier, August Bank Holiday).
Christmas Day	25 December – by Common Law.
Boxing Day	or St Stephen's Day 26 Dec, but if this falls on a Sunday, 27 December – by Statute.

Scotland

New Year's Day	1 January, but if this falls on a Sunday, the next day – by Statute – and the day following – by Statute.
Good Friday	by Statute.
The first Monday in May	by Statute.
The first Monday in August	by Statute.
Christmas Day	25 December – by Statute.

In addition most Scottish cities and towns have a spring and autumn holiday fixed by local custom.

Northern Ireland

March 17	St Patrick's Day – but if this falls on a Sunday, the next day – by Statue.
Good Friday	by Statute.
Easter Monday	by Statute.
Easter Tuesday	but note banks in fact remain open on this public holiday – by Statute.
12 July	Battle of the Boyne Day – but if this falls on a Sunday, the next day.

| Christmas Day | 25 December – by Statute. |
| Boxing Day | or St Stephen's Day 26 Dec, but if this falls on a Sunday, 27 December – by Statute. |

In addition to the above public and bank holidays the Sovereign has power under Section 4 of the 1871 Act to proclaim a public holiday in any district, borough, town, city, county or throughout the whole country. Such occasions were on her Coronation Day in 1953 and her Jubilee Day in 1977, and most recently her Golden Jubilee in 2002. If a Bank holiday is inexpedient it may be replaced by another date by Proclamation.

Bastille Day
Commemorates 14 July 1789, when the French Revolution began with the storming of the Bastille fortress in Paris, built in C14, used as a state prison in C17 and 18, and seen by the mob as a symbol of the incompetent, corrupt and despotic Bourbon monarchy.

BBC time pips
See **Time Signal**.

BC; BCE
Qualifying a date, signifies Before (the birth of) Christ, as determined by the Council of Nicaea 325CE; it may be rendered with cultural neutrality as BCE (Before the Common Era), just as CE is an alternative to AD.

Bean king, queen
The child who plays the monarch on Twelfth night, he or she is chosen by the act of finding the bean in the Twelfth Night cake.

Belle époque
In French, the time immediately before World War I, regarded as a time of elegance and prosperity; in English, it might be equated with the Edwardian Era (*qv*).

Beltane
May Day in Scotland; one of the ancient Celtic quarter days, associated particularly with sacrificial fire and animals; it may have been held to protect cattle before they were put out for summer grazing. The fire ritual persisted in Ireland until early C19, when cows were made to leap over a fire to protect their milk from being pilfered. See **Bannock**.

BH
Bank Holiday.

Bells

On board ship, a system of announcing the time in half-hours for all to hear. Eight bells, sounded as four paired chimes, represents 4, 8, and 12 o'clock both day and night. The next half-hour – 4.30, 8.30, and 12.30, am and pm – is one bell; the following half-hour – 5, 9, and 1 o'clock – is two bells; and so on. In this way, the hours are immediately audible as complete pairs of chimes; half-hours always have one final unpaired chime.

The Watches are as follows:
1200–1600 Afternoon Watch
1600–1800 First Dog
1800–2000 Last Dog (not Second Dog)
2000–0000 First Watch
0000–0400 Middle Watch
0400–0800 Morning Watch
0800–1200 Forenoon Watch

	Morning	Forenoon	Afternoon	First Dog	Last Dog	First	Middle
1 bell	0430	0830	1230	1630	1830	2030	0030
2 bells	0500	0900	1300	1700	1900	2100	0100
3 bells	0530	0930	1330	1730	1930	2130	0130
4 bells	0600	1000	1400	1800	2000	2200	0200
5 bells	0630	1030	1430			2230	0230
6 bells	0700	1100	1500			2300	0300
7 bells	0730	1130	1530			2330	0330
8 bells	0800	1200	1600			0000	0400

All Watches are of four hours, except for the two Dog Watches of two hours each, a system designed to obviate the same people taking alternate Watches from being on the same Watch every day ('dog' is derived from 'dodge'). As the New Year dawns, 16 bells (rather than eight) are struck to usher it in.

Bhadrapad

Sixth month of the Hindu year.

Biennial

Once every two years, or lasting for two years. Biennial plants spend their first year growing ready for the second year's flowering.

> ### Biedermeier Period
>
> Of or suggesting a style of furniture and interior decoration popular among the middle classes in Austria, Germany and Scandinavia in the 19th century (*fl* 1816–48). The fictional character Gottlieb Biedermeier, master of bourgeois bad taste, was created by the German poet Ludwig Eichrocht (1827–92). Biedermeier painting aimed at naturalism, apparently reflected by the English Pre-Raphaelite Brotherhood who – wittingly or not – took over when Biedermeier ended.

Big Sea Day

Old-time custom in New Jersey when, on the second Saturday in August, the farmers and their families drove to the sea-shore to picnic and to bathe in their everyday clothes.

Bimestrial

Once every two months; lasting for two months.

Biorhythms

In the 1970s–80s, the 'newest scientific discipline' of Biorhythmics came to the fore; 'the computerised study of biological clocks – built-in natural cycles that powerfully influence our behaviour.' According to the theory, there were three chief co-existing rhythms that swung from positive to negative about a time axis in the manner of sinewaves. The physical wave has a frequency of 23.5 days, the emotional 28 days and the intellectual 35 days. If all these cycles start on day zero, they will not all reach zero again for 6,580 days, or just over 18 years. During that period, there will be every combination of the three rhythms relative to one another, and hundreds of examples were gathered demonstrating the apparent relationship between events in the lives of the famous and infamous and the states of their biorhythms. The chief application seemed to be to demonstrate the power of the computer to open-mouthed visitors to exhibitions, and to sell books about biorhythms. The whole 'discipline' seems to have today fallen by the wayside, and biorhythms are no longer a central topic of conversation.

Birdlime

(RS) time; hence 'bird' for a prison sentence.

Bissextile

A leap year, so called because every four years the Romans counted the sixth day before 1 March twice; see Roman calendar.

Birth stone

A gemstone associated symbolically with the month of one's birth:

January	Garnet
February	Amethyst
March	Bloodstone or Aquamarine
April	Diamond
May	Emerald
June	Pearl, Agate, Moonstone or Alexandrite
July	Ruby or Cornelian
August	Sardonyx or Peridot
September	Sapphire or Chrysolite
October	Opal or Tourmaline
November	Topaz
December	Turquoise or Zircon

Black day
An unlucky day, see below.

Black Friday
1 6 December 1745, the day on which London heard that the Young Pretender had reached Derby.
2 11 May 1866, the day on which the bank Overend, Gurney and Co caused financial panic by suspending payments.
3 24 September 1869, in the USA when many speculators were ruined by the government's release of gold into the open market.
4 15 April 1921, (black for the British Labour Movement), when the threatened General Strike was cancelled.

Black Monday
1 14 April 1360; Edward III was besieging Paris, and the day so dark and cold that many men and horses died. It fell in the week after Easter (Easter day was 5 April), and although it was a Tuesday, the Monday after Easter Monday came to be called 'Black Monday' in remembrance.
2 27 February 1865; there was a fearsome gale resulting in terrible havoc in Melbourne, Australia.

Black Parliament
That which sat between 1529 and 1536, in the third decade of the reign of Henry VIII, when the Church of England came into being.

Black Saturday

4 August 1621, in Scotland, when there was a violent storm during the sitting of parliament when episcopacy was forced upon the people.

Black Thursday

6 February 1851, when there was a terrible bush fire in Victoria, Australia.

Blink

See Units of Time.

Bloody Monday

Every Monday, according to the jaded.

Bloody Sunday

1   13 November 1887, the dispersal of a socialist demonstration in Trafalgar Square which had been prohibited by the Commissioner of Police led to baton charges being made.
2   22 January 1905, A deputation of workers marched to St Petersburg to present a petition to the Tsar. They were attacked by troops and hundreds were killed.
3   30 January 1972, the dispersal of anti-internment marches in Bogside, Londonderry, by British troops when 13 civilians were killed.

Bloody Thursday

The Thursday in the first week of Lent, the day after Ash Wednesday, was once so called.

Bloomsday

16 June 1904, the day on which Stephen Dedalus and Leopold Bloom wander round Dublin and finally meet, in James Joyce's *Ulysses* (1918). It was the very day on which Joyce and Nora Barnacle (later Mrs Joyce) first walked out together.

Blue Monday

The Monday before Lent.

Blue moon

The third full moon in a season where there are four, and during a twelve month period when there are thirteen; 'once in a blue moon' thus means 'very rarely' (though perhaps the phrase conveys a greater rarity than the frequency of the lunar phenomena just described).

Bolt from the blue

A sudden, unexpected event.

Booths, Feast of

See Sukkot

Boxing Day

An alternative name in some countries for St Stephen's Day, 26 December, *qv*.

Box-Day

A Scottish legal custom established in 1690 whereby pleadings could be filed by placing them in a box for private examination by a judge; there were box-days in spring and autumn, and at Christmas.

Boy bishop

St Nicholas of Bari was reckoned to be pious from his earliest days, and was so named; a custom arose as a result that on his day (6 December) a boy should be chosen from a local or cathedral choir to act as a mock Bishop for three weeks, until Holy Innocents' Day (28 December); this practice was followed also at some public schools. Henry VIII abolished the custom in 1541, revived under Edward VI in 1552, and abolished for ever by Elizabeth I (she thought). The custom has been revived; at St Nicholas's Church, Tuxford, Nottinghamshire, on 6 December 2002, retired Bishop John Finney 'enthroned' 9-year-old Louis Maybe as boy bishop 'to help young people feel more included'. Louis Maybe handed his regalia on to 11-year-old Amanda Brewer the following year, making her the first girl bishop.

BP

Before the present, a useful device when discussing a particular period, but it must be clear when 'the present' is in the context, especially if the work is likely to be revived later.

Brazen Age

The final age of the decline and fall of a civilisation, following the golden and silver ages, when culture is replaced by force of arms.

British Summer Time

See Greenwich Mean Time.

Bronze Age

A period of civilisation between the Stone Age and the Iron Age; the term does not refer to one particular period, as different cultures reached it at different times. Some present-day cultures are still effectively in the Bronze Age, and good luck to their unspoilt life. In round figures, the Bronze Age dates between 4,000 and 1,200 BCE in the Middle East and between 2,000 and 500 BCE in Europe.

Brose Day/Night

An Orkney and Moray feast held in February, named after the oatmeal or pease porridge broth which was a favourite dish, sometimes with added fat.

Brumaire

(Mists); second month of the French Revolutionary Calendar, *qv*.

Burns Night

The Anniversary of Robert (Rabbie) Burns's Birthday on 25 January 1759. Burns Night celebrations have assumed a set form the world over; a meal is served consisting of cock-a-leekie soup, and haggis with champit neeps and bashit tatties (chicken and leek broth, and haggis with mashed turnip and mashed potatoes). The haggis is 'piped in' (escorted to the table by someone playing the bagpipes) and Burns's *To a Haggis* is recited. This consists of eight stanzas, each of seven lines, beginning:

Fair fa' your honest, sonsie face,
    Great Chieftan o' the Puddin-race!
Aboon them a' ye tak your place,
    Painch, tripe, or thairm:
Weel are ye wordy of a grace
    As lang's my arm.

And ending:

Ye Pow'rs wha gie us a' that's gude
    Still bless auld Caledonia's brood,
Wi' great John Barleycorn's heart's bluid
    In stoups or luggies;
And on our boards, that king o' food,
    A gud Scotch Haggis!

Three toasts – to the monarch, to the memory of the poet, and 'To the Lassies' – are drunk, followed by the grace:

Some ha'e meat and canna eat,
    And some wad eat that want it;
But we ha'e meat, and we can eat,
    And sae the Lord be thank it.

The meal is followed by dancing, songs, and readings of Burns's poems, accompanied by copious draughts of whisky, and the evening ends with the song *Auld Lang Syne*.

BST
See Standard Time.

Buckley's (chance)
(AS) never; possibly 1. From William Buckley, a convict who absconded from Port Philip and went native between 1803 and 1835 when he gave himself up; he died in 1856; possibly 2. From the Melbourne firm of Buckley and Nunn.

Buddha Day
See Vesak.

Buddhist New Year
This falls at different times depending on the country of origin or ethnic background of those involved. Theravadin countries (Burma, Cambodia, Laos, Sri Lanka, and Thailand) celebrate the new year for three days from the first full moon day in April. In Mahayana countries the new year starts on the first full moon day in January. Chinese, Koreans and Vietnamese celebrate in late January or early February according to the lunar calendar; the Tibetans usually celebrate about one month later.

Budhawar
(Wednesday); day of the Hindu week.

Butter Week
See Cheese Week.

Caesar, Julius
Roman general, statesman and calendar reformer, born 100 or 102BCE, and assassinated on the Ides (15) of March 44BCE; see Roman calendar.

Cainozoic Era
See Cenozoic Era.

Calendars
A method for subdividing a year, of which there are many different variations: see Part 3.

Calends/kalends
In Ancient Rome, the *calends* were originally the public proclamations that were made by the officers known as *pontifices* stating exactly when the nones for the month were to be celebrated – on the fifth or seventh day of the month, the term came itself to refer to the beginning of the month – an important day because, by Roman law, it was the day on which interest on loans became due ... which is why many people's salaries and wages are still payable by the *calendar* month (the month that begins at the calends); see Roman calendar.

Call

1 Actors' warning of the amount of time left before 'beginners'. The usual call times are half-hour ('the half'), fifteen minutes, five minutes, and beginners
2 Reminder of entrance during the performance
3 A notice of a rehearsal or performance posted on the callboard
4 Treasury call = pay-day in the professional theatre.

Cambrian Period

The oldest geological Period during the Palaeozoic or Primary Era. The first Period of the Era, immediately following the Precambrian or Archaeozoic Era, it was followed by the Ordovician Period and corresponded roughly to between 590 and 505 million years ago. The system of rocks dating from the period is the oldest in which fossils can be used for dating, and contains the earliest forms of shelled life. By the end of the period, primitive invertebrate marine creatures – notably trilobites and bivalved brachiopods – were common. The period is named after the country of Wales, called by the Romans *Cambria* (*cf Cymru*, the Welsh for Wales, found also in English place names and surnames as Cumbria, -gomery, and so forth), an area in which rocks of the Period are prominent; see Geological Time Divisions.

Canada Day

July 1; observed as a public holiday in Canada in commemoration of the proclamation of dominion status in 1867.

Canberra Day

Commemorates 12 March 1913 when the federal capital of Australia came into being; the foundation stone was laid on the Capitol Hill and the Governor-General's wife announced that the city would be named Canberra.

Cancer

(Latin = the Crab); fourth sign of the zodiac; 22/23 June – 22/23 July; sixth northern (septentrional) sign – first summer sign – first descending sign; see Zodiac.

Candlemas Day

2 February, formerly the Feast of the Purification of the Virgin Mary.

Canicular Period

The ancient Egyptian cycle of 1461 years, or 1460 Julian years.

Canicular Year

The ancient Egyptian year computed from one heliacal rising of the dog star to the next.

Canonical Age

In the church, an age (in years) deemed by Canon Law after which an individual is allowed to do or be something; in the CofE, a deacon must be 23, a priest 24 and a bishop 30; in the RC church, a novice must be 16, one who fasts must be 21, a deacon 22 and a bishop 30.

Canonical hours

The different parts of the Divine Office which follow, and are named after, the hours of the day. In England, the phrase means more especially the times of the day within which persons can be legally married – between 8am and 6pm.

In RC parlance, the seven times of day reserved for prayer and worship, as decreed by canon law, are: Mat(t)ins, also called Lauds; Prime; Tierce; Sext; Nones; Vespers; Compline (or Complin).

Cantate Sunday

The fifth Sunday after Easter.

Carboniferous Period, lower and upper

In America, commonly known as Mississippian and Pennsylvanian. Rocks dating from the earlier period are mostly marine shales representing the deep sediments formed by tiny, dead, shell-covered organisms and corals long turned to limestone; there are also some black shales that contain life forms such as trilobites. The later period was one in which club mosses and horsetails flourished amid warm freshwater lagoons, fossilizing where they fell to produce the world's present reserves of coal – after which the whole period is named. A time of considerable volcanic activity, glaciation took over towards the end, especially in the Southern Hemisphere near the modern equator; see also Geological Time Divisions.

Cardinal Solar Points

When rents and other dues are paid: Christmas, Lady Day, Midsummer Day and Michaelmas.

Care Sunday

The fifth Sunday in Lent.

Carlin(g) Sunday

The fifth Sunday in Lent, when carlin(g)s (peas cooked in butter) were eaten.

Carolean
Descriptive of a style (in architecture, furniture design, or clothing) pertaining to the times of Charles I (1625–49) and of Charles II (1660–85).

Carolean/Carolingian/Carlovingian
The dynasty named from *Carolus Magnus*. They ruled France (751–987), Germany (752–911) and Italy (744–887). So called because many of the more important kings and emperors were called Charles.

Catterning
See Clementing.

Cavalier Parliament
That which sat from 1661 to 1679, after the Restoration of Charles II; also known as the Long or Pensioner Parliament, the latter from the pensions it awarded to its own.

CDT
Central Daylight Time, adopted by parts of Canada and the USA, 6 hours slow on GMT; see Time Zones.

CE
See Common Era.

Cé (dedicé, millicé)
See Units of Time.

Celestial pole
Either of the two points on the celestial sphere round which the daily rotation of the stars appears to take place.

Cenozoic (Cainozoic) Era
Most recent geological Era that includes the present day; its name corresponds to the progressions inherent in the names of the previous eras: Palaeozoic 'ancient life', Mesozoic 'middle life', and thus Cenozoic 'new (or modern) life'; see Geological Time Divisions.

Centenarian/centenary/centennial
One who has passed his or her 100th birthday/celebrated 100 years after the original event/the one-hundredth anniversary itself.

-cento
As a suffix, used to denote the century of origin of styles in art and other cultural achievements in Italy between AD 1200 and 1800. Duecento corresponds to AD 1200s (thirteenth century)

Trecento	1300s (fourteenth century)
Quattrocento	1400s (fifteenth century)
Cinquecento	1500s (sixteenth century)
Seicento	1600s (seventeenth century)
Settecento	1700s (eighteenth century)

The terms above represent the Italian for 'two hundred', 'three hundred', 'four hundred', and so on and, in each case, rely on an understood prior term *mille* 'one thousand'.

Century
A group of 100 things, especially 100 years.

CET
Central European Time, 1 hour fast on GMT.

Chaitra
First month of the Hindu year.

Chalcolithic
Of the Bronze Age, a stage of human culture in which tools and weapons were made of copper or bronze. Referring to no specific period of human history, the word derives from the two Greek elements meaning 'copper/bronze' and 'stone' respectively.

Chanukkah
See Hanukkah.

Char(e) Thursday
Another name for Maundy Thursday.

Cheese Week
Bulgarian and Greek children help to prepare for Lent during this week by trying to eat food dangled on strings from the ceiling.

Cheshvan
See Marcheshvan.

Chichibu Yo Matsuri (Chichibu Night Festival)
Japanese festival held to honour the deities of the Chichibu Shrine, Chichibu, Saitama Prefecture, when fireworks are let off, and there is a parade of floats carrying musicians and singers.

Chief
The best part, or prime (obsolete meaning); hence 'the chief of the day'.

Childermas
See Holy Innocents.

Chiliad

A group of 1000; a period of 1000 years, a term derived from the ancient Greek *chilioi* = thousand.

Chinese New Year

The Chinese New Year is signalled by the New Moon marking the first day of the new year, and ends with the full moon 15 days later, when the Lantern Festival is celebrated at night with lantern displays and children's lantern parades. The New Year's Eve and New Year's Day celebrations are a family affair, a time of reunion and thanksgiving. The celebration was traditionally highlighted with a religious ceremony in honour of Heaven and Earth, the gods of the household and the ancestors of the family, remembered with great respect as those responsible for laying the foundations of the family as it is today. A New Year's Eve dinner remembers the ancestors who, together with the living, take part in Weilu = surrounding the stove.

Chinese Year Cycle

The well-known cycle of Chinese years follows; for more information, see **Part 3**.

1 Snake	2 Horse	3 Sheep	4 Monkey
5 Chicken	6 Dog	7 Pig	8 Rat
9 Ox	10 Tiger	11 Rabbit	12 Dragon

Ching Ming Festival

The Chinese Festival of Pure Brightness which happens around the 5th of April on the 106th day after the winter solstice. It is a festival which centres upon visits made by families to the graves of their ancestors. After this ritual there is often a picnic on the site when the living, so to speak, share a feast with the dead.

Christian Era

The period dating from the official birth of Jesus.

Christmas Box-Day

A Christmas box is a gratuity given on Boxing Day, the day after Christmas Day (26 December).

Christmas Day

This celebration of the birth of Jesus to Mary at Bethlehem in c4 BCE has been celebrated by Christians from earliest times. However, there is no proof that this historic event took place on 25 December. Although Orthodox Churches celebrate Christmas on 25 December, their festivities take place in January.

Christmas Eve

24 December, the day before Christmas Day, traditionally kept as a strict fast. It is a public holiday in a few Christian countries.

Chronicle

An early 12th century chronicle from the creation to 1117 written by Florence, a monk of Worcester.

Chronology

Concerned with time; a chronology is often found in a biographical or historical study, where key dates are brought out to a table for easy reference.

Chronon (tempon)

The time taken for electromagnetic radiation to cover a distance equal to the radius of an electron – about 10^{-23} s; see **Units of Time**.

Chronotype

Description of when a person is at his or her best; a lark (early to bed, early to rise) or an owl (late to rise, late to bed), or somewhere in between.

Chung Yeung Jit

Also known as Chung Gau (= double nine; also = for ever); a Chinese festival held on the ninth day of the ninth month of the Chinese calendar; the day on which Chinese people tend their ancestors' graves, sacrifice special paper money and paper winter clothing, and then enjoy a picnic of food and wine made from chrysanthemums, symbols of good health and longevity.

It commemorates also the occasion during the Han Dynasty (221–206BCE) when Fei Chang-fei, a Taoist soothsayer, advised the scholar Huan Jing to escape to the hills with his family to avoid an impending disaster. Off went Huan Jing with his family, taking supplies of food and chrysanthemum wine. When they returned home their livestock had succumbed to a plague and they realised that the soothsayer had saved their lives.

Church Fast Days

According to the *Didache*, a church manual written at the beginning of the second century: 'Your fasts must not be identical with those of the hypocrites. They fast on Mondays and Thursdays; but you should fast on Wednesdays and Fridays'.

Circannian/circannual

Recurring once every year or so, or recurring in a cyclic pattern completed in a year or so – especially in relation to the human body cycles dependent on the length of day or the amount of sunlight received, and especially in relation to body rhythms of animals that hibernate or aestivate on an annual basis.

Circadian

Circadian: recurring every twenty-four hours or so, or recurring in a cyclic pattern completed in twenty-four hours or so – especially in relation to body rhythms such as regular digestive processes, peaks and troughs in mental alertness, and some consequent behavioural manifestations (such as defecation and sleep patterns). However, the Circadian pattern is driven by hormones that vary cyclically, and it is opposed by the homeostatic system that increases the body's need for sleep the longer it is awake. This implies that caffeine as a means of keeping awake is more effective as the day goes on and the caffeine levels in the brain fall.

Civilisation

The process of becoming civilised, theoretically developing a relatively high level of culture and technology, though it seems that this may encourage assumptions of religious or moral correctitude from which may grow belligerent feelings toward those who do not appear to share the same values.

Clepsydra

A water clock: a device for measuring the passage of time that relies on the constant flow of water (or occasionally some other liquid, rarely mercury) through a stricture. Even the ancient Egyptians had some device of this kind. The term is the Latin form of the Greek for 'water clock'.

The clepsydra measures time as a constant flow, rather than variably as a sundial does. The ancient Egyptians were preoccupied with death and resurrection, and the behavior of the Sun (dying each evening) provided constant work for their priests who wished to ensure its continuing morning reappearance. During the day, the Sun itself could cast a shadow to mark the passage of time; in the hours of darkness the clepsydra performed that function.

The principle of the clepsydra is simple: water flows (or drips) from a hole in a reservoir. The level of the water drops, and the passage of time can be read from marks inside the reservoir. Alternatively, the water flows from the reservoir into another vessel, and the passage of time is read from the rising level of the surface. Another method is to place a perforated bowl in the reservoir, and observe the bowl sinking as the water leaks in; alternatively, a calibrated air-filled vessel may sink as the air leaks out.

Classical Period

In music, 1750–1850; see musical periods.

Clementing

A Staffordshire begging custom, on St Clement's Day, similar to the Hallowe'en Trick or Treat; *cf* catternning in South Staffordshire, North Herefordshire and Worcestershire on St Catherine's Day.

Clock

An old name for church bells; more usually, a device for measuring time.

The origins of the first mechanical clocks in Europe are not known, though it is likely that they were devised to mark the Divine Offices in monasteries. This may have led to some confusion, since the word 'clock' is derived from the root we see in French 'cloche', a bell, reflecting the early 'clocks' in which a bell marked the passage of time. Equally, when the Latin word 'horologium' is used in a mediaeval text, it might mean a clepsydra, sundial, mechanical clock or bell. However, the bell of the reported 'horologium' or 'clock' may have been struck by a monk watching a clepsydra, hour-glass, candle or other measuring device, and thus the description was not necessarily of a wholly-automatic device. It has been suggested that a dearth of reliable human timekeepers may have spurred the development of the mechanical clock; on the other hand, there must always have been those keen on research and invention, and devising a means for mechanical timekeeping is an ideal task for exercising ingenuity.

The birth of the mechanical escapement clock is unrecorded, though it is likely that many craftsmen were experimenting with such devices in various centres of the 13th century. A mechanical clock is said to have been built by the monks of Dunstable Priory, Bedfordshire, in 1283. This predates other recorded clocks by several decades. An astronomical clock with automata and a dial set up in Norwich Cathedral is recorded in the Sacrist's Rolls for 1325.

Clock tax

In 1797, the British Government sought to raise money by imposing an annual clock tax – five shillings for public and domestic clocks, ten shillings for watches carried on the person, and two shillings and sixpence for timekeepers falling outside of the first two categories. The difficulties of collecting the tax are obvious, and it caused such a decline in the clockmaking industry that thousands were put out of work. Fortunately, good sense prevailed; the tax was repealed in 1798, and some compensation paid to the industry. The legacy of the clock tax is the 'Act of Parliament Clock', a large-faced timepiece widely bought and displayed by hoteliers and innkeepers of that time for the benefit of their customers.

Close season

A period during which a given activity is prohibited, usually applied to huntin', shootin' and fishin'. Thus in England, Wales and Scotland the following must not be taken between the given dates:

Birds

Black game	11 December	19 August except as below
	11 December	31 August in Somerset, Devonshire & The New Forest
Capercaillie	1 February	30 September
Grouse*	11 December	11 August
Partridge*	2 February	31 August
Pheasant*	2 February	30 September
Ptarmigan*	11 December	11 August (Scotland only)
Snipe	1 February	11 August
Wild Duck	21 February	31 August (below high water mark)
Wild Geese	21 February	31 August (below high water mark)
Woodcock	1 February	30 September (except in Scotland)

*Not on Sundays or 25 December in England and Wales

Fish

Trout	1 October	28(29) February
Salmon	1 November	31 January
Coarse Fish	15 March	15 June

Deer	England and Wales		Scotland	
Fallow				
Male	1 May	31 July	1 May	31 July
Female	1 March	31 October	16 February	20 October
Red				
Male	1 May	31 July	21 October	30 June
Female	1 March	31 October	16 February	20 October
Roe				
Male	1 November	31 March	21 October	31 March
Female	1 March	31 October	1 April	20 October
Sika				
Male	1 May	31 July	21 October	30 June
Female	1 March	31 October	16 February	20 October
Red/Sika hybrids				
Male	21 October	30 June		
Female	16 February	20 October		

Club Parliament
Held in Northampton in 1426 when, forbidden to bear arms, its members came equipped with the C15 equivalent of baseball bats; also known as the Parliament of Bats.

Coal Measures
A geological Stage during the Upper or Pennsylvanian division of the Carboniferous Period of the Palaeozoic Era in what is now the United States. It is named after its characteristic alternating strata of coal and clayey sandstone.

Columbus Day
In Spain commemorates the day in 1492 – 12 October – when Columbus and his men sighted the New World.

Common Era
See Christian Era.

Commonwealth
Term commonly applied to the British Commonwealth, the free association of most nations of the former British Empire. A term also given to the period beginning 1649, after the British monarchy was replaced by the Lord Protector.

Commonwealth Day
The second Monday in March.

Concession
A relaxation of the norm as a recognition of age (or youth, or impecuniosity); one of the few perks of growing old.

Concluding Festival
See Shavuot.

Confederate War Dead Day
Observed on 19 January in Texas, April 26 in Alabama, Florida, Georgia, and Mississippi; 10 May in North and South Carolina; and 3 June (Jefferson Davis's birthday) in Louisiana and Tennessee.

Contemporaneous
Something occurring at the same time as something else; thus a policeman giving evidence from his notebook may say (or be asked if) his notes are 'contemporaneous'.

Contemporary
1 Something occurring at the time under discussion (Sir Francis Drake was a contemporary of Queen Elizabeth I).
2 Something occurring in the present (I despair of contemporary politics).
3 In the modern style (her flat is full of contemporary furniture).

4   Someone of about one's own age (he and I are contemporaries).
5   In journalism, a rival publication.

Convention Parliament

1   That of 1660 convened by General Monk for the Restoration of Charles II.
2   That of January 1689, to offer the throne to William and Mary as joint sovereigns.

Copper Age

A less-well-attested name for the Chalcolithic or Bronze Age, the stage in a human culture in which tools and weapons were made of copper or bronze, but referring to no specific period of human history; thus some peoples may still be in their Copper (or Bronze) Age.

Corning

See Mumping.

Corn showing

A Herefordshire custom, called 'walking the wheat' in adjacent Monmouthshire, when farmers and bailiffs walked their fields on the afternoon of Easter Day, carrying plum-cakes and cider to eat and drink to the success of their crops. The practice seems to have died out at the end of C19.

Corpus Christi

Held in devotion to the Eucharist (Holy Communion), this festival is celebrated on the Thursday after Trinity Sunday and is a public holiday in many Catholic countries. It may fall on any date between 21 May and 24 June.

Cosmic year

The time the Sun takes to complete one orbit within the (revolving) Galaxy, thought to be about 200 million years. There have been only about twenty-three cosmic years, or solar orbits, since the Solar system came into existence, and only about 70 cosmic years or galactic revolutions, since the Galaxy itself was created.

Cretaceous Period, Upper and Lower

Dating from a geological Period, the last Period of Mesozoic Era, lasting from about 146 million to about 65 million years ago, and marked by the dominance of dinosaurs; see Geological Time Divisions.

Crispin's Day, St

25 October, the day of battle of Agincourt in 1415.

Cron

See units of time. Suggested by JS Huxley (1957): 1 chron = 10^6 years; 1 millichron = 1 millennium.

Creation dates

Many attempts have been made to establish a date for the creation of the world. The Holy Bible presents a tempting chronology wherefrom it should be possible to work back to Adam and Eve, who appeared on the sixth day of the Great Work. Archbishop James Ussher (1581–1656) was born in Dublin, where he was a scholar and fellow of Trinity College, and became Archbishop of Armagh in 1625. His magnum opus was his *Annals of the Old and New Testament* (1650–54), which revealed that the world was created in the morning on 23 October 4004BCE. This lay between the traditional Jewish Start date of 3761BCE, and the Byzantine suggestion of 5509BCE.

Cru

In viticulture, a term denoting the year in which wine was made, or whether the grapes involved were those of the first harvest ('premier cru') or a later harvest.

CST

Central Standard Time, 6 hours slow on GMT, adopted in central parts of Canada and the USA.

Cuckoo Calendar

A rhyme describing an idealised sequence of cuckoo behaviour; there are various versions that all say more or less the same thing:

In April come he will
In May he sings all day
In June he changes tune
In July he prepares to fly
In August go he must.

Curtain Call

After the play proper has ended, the cast reappears to acknowledge the audience's applause; if ever there's a time to judge nicely when to leave 'em howling for more, this is it.

Custom

What a person is in the habit of doing or does regularly; a typical mode of behaviour; the reason for a particular practice may be lost in the mists of time.

Cycle

A period during which a recurring series of events or numbers takes place; whatever it is may recur many times in the same order.

Dachstein

Geological Division or Stage during the Triassic Period of the Mesozoic Era, between 248 and 213 million years ago. It is named after the mountains in the Austrian Alps that were formed at this time; see **Geological Time Divisions**.

Daimonji Okuribi (Daimonji bonfire)

Japanese festival held at Nyoigatake (Daimonjiyama) on 16 August to mark the end of the Bon Festival with an enormous okuribi (send-off bonfire (to bid farewell to the souls of ancestors)), laid out in the shape of the Chinese character dai ('great') lit on the slopes of the mountain Nyoigatake.

Danian

A Stage during the early Palaeocene Epoch of the Cenozoic Era, but sometimes held instead to be an extremely late stage of the Upper Cretaceous Period just inside the Mesozoic Era. Named after the country Denmark, the rock formation so described is found also in France and Belgium; see **Geological Time Divisions**.

Dark Ages

A term applied to the (early) Middle Ages, because of the lack of contemporary written sources to tell us what was happening. The period between the end of the Roman civilisation (around 450–500CE) and about 1000CE or, according to some authorities, until the beginning of the European Renaissance (around 1400–1450CE), during which scientific discoveries were few and far between, and cultural advances equally scanty, probably as a result largely of religious intolerance.

Darkie Day

A Christmastide custom in Padstow, Cornwall, when fishermen and their wives black up and sing plantation songs to raise money for charity; an obvious target for those who believe in Political Correctness.

Darwin

See **units of time**.

Day

It is noticeable that we are seldom concerned that there is no difference between the word for a 24-hour period, and that for the part of the former when activity usually takes place, at least part of which is carried out in natural light.

The sidereal day is the mean time taken for the earth to complete one revolution on its axis. The solar day is the mean time interval which elapses between when the sun is in a predetermined position, e.g. overhead, and its return to the same position. Clearly, because the Earth is in orbit round the sun as well as turning on its own axis, the two are not the same; there are 365.24 solar days and 366.24 sidereal days in a year. There are 86,400 seconds in a mean solar day and 86,164.0906 seconds in a sidereal day, a difference of 235.9094 seconds, or just under 4 minutes.

The longest day (day with the longest interval between sunrise and sunset) is the day on which the *solstice* falls and in the northern hemisphere occurs on 21 June, or increasingly rarely on 22 June. The latest sunset, however occurs on 13 or 14 June but sunrise is still getting earlier by sufficiently large a margin to make the duration of night shorter until Midsummer's Day. At Greenwich (South London) daylight may last up to 16 hours and 39 minutes, though the longest duration sunshine is 15 hours and 48 minutes, recorded at nearby Kew (West London) on 13 June 1887. The shortest day occurs either on 21 or 22 December, when daylight at Greenwich may last only 7 hours and 50 minutes. The evenings, however, begin lengthening imperceptibly on 13 or 14 December when each sunset is about 2 seconds later than that on the previous day.

Day
Tenth month of the Persian year.

Day of Atonement; of Awe
See Jewish calendar.

Day of Arafat
Islamic Festival falling on 9 Dhû'l Hijja.

Day of Assembly
An Islamic Festival celebrated every Friday.

Daylight Saving
Adjusting the clock in order to make optimum use of the hours of daylight.

Days of Grace, of Obligation, of the Dupes
The three days over and above the time stated in a commercial bill.

Day-time
That part of a (24-hour) day that is not night-time.

Dazaifu Usokae (Dazaifu Bullfinch Exchange)
Japanese festival held at Dazaifu on 7 January, when visitors to the shrine participate in a group exchange of carved wooden bullfinches.

Disguised shrine officials introduce metal models, which are believed to bestow good luck on recipients.

Decade
A group of ten, particularly a ten-year period.

Décadi
Tenth day of the French Revolutionary week; see French Revolutionary Calendar.

December
Twelfth month of the Gregorian year; named in the Julian calendar from the Latin *decem* (= ten); birthstone turquoise or zircon.

Decennial
Of ten years; occurring every ten years; lasting for ten years.

Decoration Day
See Memorial Day.

Defective year
See Jewish calendar.

Degré
See Units of Time.

Degree (photographic)
The Scheiner and DIN systems for indicating the speed of photographic film both use degrees; see Film Speed.

Dendrochronology
The study of the growth of tree rings, each of which gives information on a tree's growth and hence the environmental conditions during the associated solar year. The growing bank of dendrochronological information, and the assistance of the computer, provide another dating weapon in the armoury of the archaeologist and the historian.

Depression
The period of economic stagnation, mass unemployment, and hardship worldwide in the early 1930s.

Devil's Parliament
Met at Coventry in 1489 (in the fourth year of the reign of Henry VII, the first Tudor king) to pass the Acts of Attainder against the Yorkist leaders (the last of whom on the throne had been Richard III, killed at the Battle of Bosworth Field in 1485).

Dhamma Day
See Asalha Puja Day.

Devonian Period

Geological Period between the Palaeozoic or Primary Era, before the Carboniferous Period, roughly between 408 and 360 million years ago. It is often known as the Age of Fishes; much of the earth's surface was covered with salt or brackish water and the dominant forms of life were fishes of all kinds, corals and seaweeds. By the end of the Period, fish had begun to develop lungs, leading to the emergence of amphibian forms. See Geological Time Divisions.

Dharma

The doctrine of universal truth common to all individuals, as proclaimed by the Buddha. Dharma, the Buddha himself, and the sangha (community of believers) make up the triratna ('three jewels') as the prime statement of Buddhist belief. In Hinduism, the dharma is the moral and religious law that governs individual conduct. It is one of the four ends of life, to be followed according to one's class, status and position in life.

Dhû 1 and 2

Short for Dhû Al-Qa'da (Muslim month 11) and Dhû Al-Hijja (Muslim month 12).

Dhû'l Hijja

Twelfth month of the Muslim calendar qv; it marks the Hajj (pilgrimage to Mecca).

Dials at Whitehall

How King Charles II's timekeeper, set up in 1669, worked, is not clear. Britten writes: 'This curious erection had no covering; exposure to the elements and other destroying influences led to its speedy decay and subsequent demolition.' However, it is elsewhere reported that this fancy construction of glass globes became the focus of the well-known rake John Wilmot, 2nd Earl of Rochester, and his companions as they returned from some drunken gathering. Stung by the impudence of the multiphallic construction ("What? Dost thou stand here to f*ck time?"), they laid about it with their sticks and smashed it to smithereens. The king was not amused.

Dhû'l-Qa'da
Eleventh month of the Muslim calendar, *qv*.

DIN system
Deutsche Industrie Norm method of indicating the speed of photographic film; see Film Speed.

Distaff's Day, St
7 January, so called because it was the day the women returned to their distaffs or daily occupations following the end of the Christmas festival on Twelfth Day.

Diwali
Celebrating the end of the monsoon. The Hindu Festival of Lights honouring Laksmi, the goddess of wealth, when merchants open new accounts, and the festivities include feasts, exchange of gifts, decorating houses and wearing new clothes; in the Gregorian calendar, it falls in October–November. At this time, Sikhs celebrate the release from prison of Guru Hargobind.

Dog days
Days of great heat in the northern hemisphere, observed at the heliacal rising of Sirius, the Dog Star. Their duration (according to observations of the Greater or Lesser Dog Star, Sirius or Procyon) have been stated by different observers to be between 30 and 54 days; the accepted period is 3 July to 15 August (43 days).

Dog watch
One of two two-hour watches, a split four-hour watch, so that there is an odd number (7) of watches in 24 hours by which means watchkeepers avoid having to be on the same watch day in, day out.

Domesday
(Or doomsday = a day of reckoning); hence the Domesday (or Doomsday) Book, a record of a survey of English lands made by order of William I in the year 1086, so that he could assess the extent of his possessions and the value for taxation purposes of those of his tenants in chief. Royal commissioners collected details of each manor, shire by shire, giving an almost complete (and historically invaluable) picture of the England of the time.

Dominion Day
Celebrated in Canada on 1 July.

Dotage
A state or period of mental decline in old age; see also Anecdotage.

Double Summer Time

BST + 1 hour, or GMT + 2 hours was brought in from 1941 to 1945, and in 1947. During the war, it was supposed to make life safer in the black-out; the 1947 experiment was not repeated – see **Summer Time**.

Dreamtime

Native Australian term for the forgotten days of their ancestors. A golden age recorded in the legends of certain Australian Aboriginal peoples as the time when their first ancestors were created (alche-ringa); now used colloquially to denote something remote, or out of touch with the present.

Drunken Parliament

The stotious Edinburgh assembly of January 1661.

DST

See **Double Summer Time**.

Dublin Time

See **Time Zones**.

Dudman and Ramhead

Dudman and Ramhead are two forelands 23 sea miles apart; the phrase 'when Dudman and Ramhead meet' therefore refers to some-thing which will never happen.

Dulheggia, Dulkaada

Alternative spellings for the Islamic months of Dhû'l Hijja and Dhû'l-Qa'da (*qv*).

Dumping

Cumberland and Westmorland sport of decorating and rolling Easter eggs.

Dunmow Flitch

The expression 'eating Dunmow bacon' was formerly used of happily married couples, especially those who had lived long together and never quarrelled. The allusion is to a custom said to have been insti-tuted by Lady Juga Baynard in 1104 and restored by Robert Fitzwalter in 1244. It was that any person going to Dunmow, in Essex, and humbly kneeling on two sharp stones at the church door, might claim a flitch (side) of bacon if he could swear that for 12 months and a day he had never had a household brawl or wished himself unmarried. Allu-sions to the tradition are frequent in literature from C17 and the custom was revived in the second half of C19. Today the Flitch Trials are held at Little Dunmow (Essex) in mid-June every Leap Year.

Duodi
Second day of the French Revolutionary week; see **French Revolutionary Calendar**.

Dupes, Day of the
In French history, 11 November 1630, when Marie de'Medici sought to overthrow Louis XIII's minister, Cardinal Richelieu.

Dussehra
Hindu Festival celebrating the goddess Durga during the period of Navrati (nine nights); in the Gregorian calendar, it falls in September–October.

Du'ûzu
A Babylonian month named after a god from which the name of the Jewish month of Tammuz is derived.

Dwynwen
The feast of the Welsh patron saint of love, held on 25 January.

Dynasty
A house or succession of hereditary rulers, or generations of a powerful family, or the time during which they rule; a powerful group or family that maintains its position for a considerable time.

Dyzemas Day
Tithe day; Latin *Decima* = a tenth part, a tithe.

Easter
There has long been a festival recognising the vernal equinox, the time of rebirth; in pre-Christian times it honoured a goddess of dawn, Eastre. In the Christian legend, the death and resurrection of Christ is commemorated at Easter; early Christians linked the date to the Hebrew calendar, saying that the Resurrection took place on the first day of the week following Passover, which in turn occurs on the first full moon after the vernal equinox. Easter Day (the Sunday) was decreed by the Council of Nicaea (325CE) to be the first Sunday following the full moon that appears on or after 21 March – unless that full moon appears on a Sunday, in which case Easter is celebrated on the following Sunday. Since 1963, the Vatican has wisely been in favour of a fixed date for Easter; if only everyone else involved would agree.

Easter Eggs
Like many Easter rituals, the giving of Easter Eggs is based on pre-Christian festivals of fertility and spring. Eggs symbolise new life, and the first Easter Eggs were painted hens' eggs. Because it was forbidden to eat eggs during Lent, but the hens didn't stop laying, their eggs were boiled and saved for Easter.

Easter Eve
   See Holy Saturday.

Easter Saturday
   The Saturday after Easter, not to be confused with Holy Saturday, the day between Good Friday and Easter Sunday.

Easter Sunday
   The celebration of the Resurrection of Christ falls on the first Sunday after the full moon that happens on or following the 21 March. If the full moon falls upon a Sunday, Easter is celebrated upon the following Sunday. The day following Easter Sunday (Easter Monday) is often a public holiday in Christian countries.

Ecclesiastical Calendar
   That pertaining to the Church, which still begins on the old New Year's Day, Lady Day, 25 March.

Eclipse

By a dispensation of providence, the Sun and the Moon appear from the Earth to be very similar in diameter. Thus, if the Moon is interposed between the Earth and the Sun, the latter is eclipsed, partially or totally. On the other hand, if the Earth is interposed between the Sun and the Moon, it's more than big enough for an eclipse of up to 104 minutes totality.

Eclipses of the Sun and Moon are measured by their duration (how long the eclipse lasts) and their extent (what proportion is eclipsed). The duration of a partial eclipse may be no more than a few seconds; a total eclipse may last for more than 28 minutes from start to finish, with totality for a maximum of 7 minutes 31 seconds. The extent of occultation of a partial eclipse is measured in 'digits'; a digit is half the apparent diameter of the Sun or Moon.

EDA
   Estimated Day of Arrival (were one, for example, rowing across the Atlantic).

EDT
   See Time Zones.

Edwardian age/era
   Period from (22 Jan) 1901 to (6 May) 1911, during which King Edward VII occupied the British throne. (There had not been an Edward on the throne since 1553.) The Edwardian Period is generally regarded as a

period of relaxation after the Victorian era and, in retrospect, seems to have come to an end with the start of the First World War (31 August 1914). In France, the period is referred to as La Belle Époque.

Egg Feast; Egg Saturday
The Saturday before Shrove Tuesday, so called because the eating of eggs was forbidden during Lent, and it was therefore wise to finish one's stocks beforehand.

Egg timer
See sand glass.

Egyptian Days
According to the Egyptian astrologers, certain days were 'unlucky' for doing business; there were two in each month, but the last Monday in April, the second Monday in August, and the third Monday in December were deemed to be especially unlucky.

Eid-Al-Adha
Islamic Festival of Sacrifice commemorating the prophet Abraham's readiness to sacrifice his son Ishmael to Allah whereupon, to mark Abraham's devotion, Allah suggested that he should sacrifice a lamb instead; falls on 10–12 Dhû'l Hijja.

Eid-Al-Fittr
Feast of Breaking Fast – A Muslim festival marking the end of Ramadan, celebrated by feasting and visiting graves; it falls on 1 Shawwâl.

Eighth Day of Conclusion
See Shemini Atzeret.

Eighth Day, The Feast of, or Solemn Assembly of The
See Sukkot.

Elephant Festival, The
Held on the third Saturday of November to commemorate Buddha's analogy of training a wild elephant by harnessing it to a tame one to illustrate the benefits of a new Buddhist having a special friendship with an experienced one (early example of a buddy or mentor).

Eleven days, Give us back our
See Gregorian calendar.

Eleven Years' Tyranny
The period from 1629 to 1640 when Charles I governed without summoning a parliament.

Elizabethan age/era

1   Almost always refers to the reign of Queen Elizabeth I (17 November) 1558 to (23 March) 1603.

2   Occasionally, the period from the accession of Queen Elizabeth II on 6 February 1952, sometimes referred to as the 'New Elizabethan' age.

Elul

Sixth month of the sacred and twelfth month of the civil Jewish calendar. Its name is derived from the Babylonian Ulûlu (Purification), and it corresponds roughly to the Gregorian months of August–September; it has 29 days. 1–29 Elul is Teshuvah, repentance.

Embargo

A prohibition, commercially on the movement of ships or goods; in the world of PR, a restraint on publishing a story before a given time.

Ember Week

There are four such weeks in the year, more or less quarterly; those following the first Sunday in Lent, Whit Sunday, Holy Cross Day (14 September) and St Lucy's Day (13 December). During these weeks, the Wednesday, Friday, and Saturday (Ember days) were days of fasting and abstinence, and the following Sunday (that after the Saturday) a day of ordination.

Embolismic

Pertaining to intercalation, the insertion of one or more days into a calendar; in the Jewish Calendar an embolismic year consists of thirteen lunar months, an ordinary year of twelve. Gregorian (and other) leap years are also embolismic.

Emergent year

The year or date at which an era is deemed to begin: the year 0 (or 1) of a calendar. In the Gregorian calendar, the emergent year is taken as being the non-existent year between 1BCE and 1CE. And yet some still hold that a century ends on 31 December YY99 rather than 31 December YY00.

Empire Day

Instituted after the South African War, to focus schoolchildren on their duties and responsibilities (would that it were now so), particularly their role as citizens of the British Empire. 24 May was chosen to remember the birthday of Queen Victoria who had died the year before.

Empire Style
The artistic design vocabulary of furniture, decoration, costume, *etc* in Napoleonic France in the first two decades of C19; it followed the excesses of the Revolution in the previous decade, and reflected Napoleon's grandiose dreams.

EN28601
The European equivalent of ISO8601(*qv*).

End of the World
In Judaism, the application of gematrial techniques shows that the world is intended to last for 6,000 years. According to others, the world comes to an end from time to time, but immediately re-emerges with no perceptible shudder.

Entre deux Guerres
The period between the two World Wars; *cf* Entre deux Mers.

Eogene
A geological time, a collective name for the Palaeocene, Eocene, and Oligocene Epochs of the Tertiary period in the Cenozoic Era, corresponding roughly to between 65 and 25 million years ago. During this Epoch there was a general warming of the Earth's surface and atmosphere. By the end, tropical and subtropical vegetation abounded in many forms still found today; see Geological Time Divisions.

Eolithic or Protolithic
The dawn (eos) of the Stone (lithos) Age; the time of the first attempts to fashion tools and weapons from stone.

Eon
A unit of time equal to 10^9 years; the US spelling of Æon.

Eozoic
An imprecise term to try to describe the geological time at which life forms first appeared on Earth. The term Precambrian, or Archaeozoic, Era is more authoritative; see Geological Time Divisions.

Epact
1   The 11 days (12 in a leap year) by which the solar year is longer than the lunar year: 365 (or 366) days, as opposed to 354.
2   The number of days in the lunar month that have already passed at the beginning of the solar year (1 January), used in determining the date of Easter for that year.

Epagomenal
Adjective describing a period of a day or days inserted into the calendar; in leap years, 29 February is an epagomenal day.

Ephemeris second
See units of time.

Ephemeris time
In 1956, the International Bureau of Weights and Measures adopted a standardised measure of time based upon the ephemeris second, which was derived from the precise time taken by the Moon and the planet Earth each to complete one orbit during the solar year 1900. Ephemeris time differs by several seconds from Universe or Newtonian time, which varies because the Earth's rate of rotation varies.

Epiphany
6 January: the Festival of the Epiphany celebrates the manifestation of the infant Jesus to the Magi or 'wise men'; 5 January is the Vigil of Epiphany.

Epoch

1   The start of a new or distinctive Period (the Epoch of the Muslim calendar in Gregorian terms is 16 July 622CE).
2   (Astronomy) A precise date to which information pertaining to a celestial body is referred.
3   A long period of time associated with some characteristic happening (the Devonian Epoch).
4   (Geological) Division of time within the Cenozoic (the most recent) Era during either of the geological Periods known as the Tertiary and the Quarternary. Similar divisions occur also in two of the other three Eras, but are not generally called Epochs (and are for the most part divisions of relevant Periods into 'Upper', 'Middle', and 'Lower' parts); see Geological Time Divisions.

Epping Forest Stag Hunt
A Hunt held on Easter Monday.

Equation of Time
The difference between mean solar time (as shown on a sundial) and apparent time (as shown on a clock). It has a maximum positive value of about 14.5 minutes in February and a maximum negative value of about 16.5 minutes in November. It is equal to zero four times a year: at the solstices and equinoxes.

Equinox

The time of year when the Sun appears to cross the Celestial Equator and day and night are of equal length. There are two equinoxes every year, in the spring, and autumn. The vernal (spring) equinox in the Northern Hemisphere corresponds exactly to the autumnal equinox in the Southern, and vice versa. The two times of year at which the lengths of day and night are conversely *least* similar are the solstices.

Era

A series of years beginning from some epoch or starting-point as:

	BCE
The Era of the Chinese	2697
The Era of Abraham (1 October)	2016
The Era of the Greek Olympiads	776
The Era of the Foundation of Rome	753
The Era of Nabonassar (Babylon)	747
The Era of Alexander the Great	324
The Era of the Selucidæ	312
The Era of the Maccabees	166
The Era of Tyre (19 October)	125
The Era of Julian	45
The Era of Actium (1 January)	30
The Era of Augustus (27 June)	27

	CE
The Christian Era	1
The Era of Diocletian (29 August)	284
The Era of Armenia (9 July)	552
The Era of the Hegira (16 July)	622
The Era of Yezdegird (Persian – 16 June)	632
The Era of American Independence (4 July)	1776
The Era of the French Republic (22 September)	1792

Era, Geological

Major division of the geological history of the planet Earth. According to most authorities, there are four Eras: the Precambrian, the Palaeozoic, the Mesozoic, Cenozoic, or present Era. In their turn, the Eras are divided into Periods of various durations corresponding to the geological events that took place; see Geological Time Divisions.

Erlang

or Traffic Unit; in telephony, a unit of traffic density $e = CT$, where C is the number of calls per hour and T is the average time of each call. The

unit was adopted in 1946, named after the Danish mathematician A K
Erlang (1879–1924).

Esfand

Twelfth month of the Persian year.

Esther, Fast of

In the Jewish calendar, observed on 13 Adar or, in a leap year, 13 Adar
Sheni. See **Taanit Esther**.

ETA/D

Estimated time of arrival/departure.

Eternal Life

In religious terms, death.

Etesian

1   A Mediterranean wind which rises annually about the dog days,
    and blows for about 40 days.
2   Something that happens annually, from Ancient Greek *etesios* =
    yearly.

Evil May Day

1 May 1517, a day of serious rioting in London.

Exaltation of the Cross

An RC feast held on 14 September to commemorate the restoration of
the true cross to Calvary in 629.

Expectation Week

Between Ascension and Whit Sunday, when the Apostles continued
praying 'in earnest expectation of the Comforter'.

Fairs

At one time, there were great periodical markets upon which people
would converge from miles around; the annual Bartholomew Fair (*qv*),
or the horse fairs and goose fairs still remembered in certain parts of
the country. The word now usually conjures up a travelling amuse-
ment fair, or a trade fair (which is really an exhibition directed at
encouraging orders associated with a particular trade).

Fall

A descriptive English term for the time of year when leaves fall from
the trees, now supplemented on the east side of the Atlantic Ocean by
the word Autumn, but retained on the west side.

Farvardin

First month of the Persian year.

Fasts and fasting

A complete abstention from food and drink, but the word may also be applied to a limitation of diet. Many religions have a period of fasting as part of their custom: Christian Lent and Muslim Ramadan, for example.

Fast of 10 Tebet

In the Jewish calendar, a Minor Fast commemorating the day upon which Nebuchadnezzar began his siege of Jerusalem.

Fast of 17 Tammuz

In the Jewish calendar, this Minor Fast commemorates the breaching of the walls of Jerusalem by the Romans (c70CE), Moses' breaking of the tablets of the Law, Apostomos the Greek burning the Torah, and the day the regular daily sacrifice in the temple ceased. It begins the Three Weeks of National Mourning to 9 Av, during which the pious abstain from all enjoyment.

Fast of 20 Sivan

In the Jewish calendar, a Fast commemorating the day in 1171 when 51 Jews were burned at the stake in Blois, France.

Father's Day

A day devoted to fathers in the annual calendar, falling on the third Sunday in June. Britain imported the occasion from the United States, where it was devised in 1910 in Spokane, Washington, as a counterpart to Mother's Day. It has never won the popularity of the old festival, however.

Father Time

Personification of time, often shown carrying a scythe with which to determine our lives (in some unspecified way) when we reach our allotted span. Alternatively, he may at midnight on 31 December hand over the old year to a babe-in-arms who personifies the new year; in this case, his rate of aging is remarkable. The conventional figure is represented by the engraver William Hogarth (1697–1764) in *Time Smoking a Picture* – to make it look old, a satire on the connoisseurs of the day who, it appears, would buy anything as long as it looked old.

Feast, The

See **Sukkot**.

Feast of Dedication

See **Jewish calendar**.

Feast of Esther

See **Jewish calendar**.

> ## Feast or Festival
>
> A day or days for designated religious observances; for example, every Sunday is a feast day. RC and Greek churches have many feasts; CofE few. Apart from Sundays, there are the four quarter days:
>
> Annunciation; Lady Day: 25 March
> Nativity of St John the Baptist: 24 June
> Michaelmas: 29 September
> Christmas Day: 25 December
>
> and
>
> Circumcision, Naming of Jesus or New Year's Day: 1 January
> All Hallows' Day: 1 November
> Any Saint's day one cares to commemorate.
> The movable feasts are those that are dependent on the date of Easter, itself dependent on the behaviour of the moon.

February
Second month of the Gregorian year (*qv*); named from Februa, the Roman festival of purification; birthstone: amethyst.

Festival of 1 Elul
In the Jewish calendar, a day that marks the remembrance of the beginning of the Third Plague in Egypt.

Festival of Lights
See Hanukkah.

Festival of Lots
See Purim.

Fig Sunday
An old name for Palm Sunday, when figs were eaten in commemoration of Jesus's blasting of the barren fig tree.

Fin de siècle
This term has come to imply decadent, with particular reference to the end of the 19th century. The term is French = end of (the) century.

Financial Year
In the UK, the year ending 31 March. The taxation year ends on 5 April as a consequence of the transition to the Gregorian Calendar (*qv*). Since there are no concessions to the day of the week on which 5 April falls, the weeks of the financial year differ from one year to the next. US equivalent: Fiscal Year.

Film speed

A measure of the sensitivity (to light) of a photographic emulsion, a figure which can be used to work out the correct exposure for taking a photograph in given conditions.

The H&D system was proposed in 1891 by F Hurter (1844–98) and VC Driffield (1848–1915) who established a graph of density against the relative logarithm of the exposure time; the central part of the curve is linear, wherefrom the H&D speed is found.

The Weston number, the ASA system, and the BSI speed number use the same principle as the H&D system.

The ASA (American Standards Association) speed is defined as 0.8/E, where E is the exposure of a point 0.1 density units greater than the fog level on the characteristic curve of the emulsion. It has superseded the BSI (British Standards Institution) system.

The DIN (Deutsche Industrie Norm) system gives an indication of speed in degrees based on the minimum exposure needed to form a detectable image on the emulsion.

The Scheiner scale was devised by J Scheiner (1858–1913) in 1898, and taken up by the Secco Film Company of Boston MA the following year. There are two versions, the European and the American.

Fingan Eve
    21 December, when fires are lit on cliff-tops in the Isle of Man.

Fire Festivals
    The four ancient Celtic quarter days (Samhain, Imbolc, Beltane and Lughnasadh) are known as fire festivals.

First Born, Fast of
    See Taanit Behorim.

First day of year, pre-1752
    March 25.

First Foot
    The first visitor at a house after midnight has ushered in New Year's Day, especially in Scotland; it is considered lucky if the first footer is carrying symbols of warmth, wealth and food (a handsel), usually a piece of coal, some salt (once more valuable than today) and cake; he or she is rewarded with refreshment such as the Het Pint (a mixture of beer, whisky, eggs and sugar). There are local names for first footing, such as the Yorkshire Lucky Bird, and the Manx Quaaltagh.

First Fruits, Festival of
See Shavuot.

Fiscal year
More common US term for financial year.

Flag Day
1   In the USA 14 June, the anniversary of the adoption of the Stars and Stripes.
2   In the UK, a day upon which tins are rattled at passers by to collect money for designated good causes.

Floating Bowls
See Loy Krathong.

Floralia
Festival of Flora, the Roman goddess of flowers, which was held from 28 April to 3 May.

Floréal
(Flowers); eighth month of the French Revolutionary Calendar *qv*.

Floriade
A Dutch garden festival lasting all summer held every 10 years from 1972.

Fortnight
Two weeks; a contraction from the Old English for 'fourteen nights'. In Shakespeare's time, a week was known also as a *sennight* – a contraction from the Old English for 'seven nights'. Both these expressions are so ancient as to refer to a time when it was easier to talk about nights than to talk about days, as the latter had no set hours.

Forty days/forty years
In ancient Israel (and therefore the Bible), a mystical period regarded (in both cases) as a long time and one with overtones of greatness – although the number 40 had no such meaning *per se*.

Fourfold Assembly
See Magha Puja.

Four-minute Men
Those who run a mile in under four minutes, the first of whom was Dr (now Sir) Roger Bannister (*b*1929) at an athletics meeting at Iffley Road, Oxford in 1954; his time was 3m 59.4s.

Fourth of June
King George III's birthday and speech day at Eton College.

French Revolutionary calendar

Adopted by the National Convention on 5 October 1793, retrospectively as from 22 September 1792, and in force in France till 1 January 1806. It consisted of 12 months of 30 days each, with 5 intercalary days called Sansculottides. Every fourth or Olympic year was to have six such days; see Part 3.

Friday the 13th

A particularly unlucky Friday. In fact, any month beginning on a Sunday must contain a Friday 13th, and Table 3 in the introduction to the Gregorian Perpetual Calendar shows when such months occur in the 14 different sorts of year. And, as you would expect, there are as many Friday 13ths (48) in the 28-year cycle as any other specified day. There are various theories as to why the day has been thought to be unlucky, but different cultures have different opinions on such superstitions. Perhaps the best that can be said about it is that when the papers have column inches to fill, there's always someone who stays in bed on Friday 13th to keep out of harm's way, only to suffer a collapse of the ceiling, or a runaway lorry ploughing through the wall.

Frimaire

(Frosts); third month of the French Revolutionary Calendar *qv*.

Fructidor

(Fruits); twelfth month of the French Revolutionary Calendar *qv*.

Furry Dance

Part of the spring festival held at Helston, Cornwall, on 8 May. The name has been incorrectly rendered as the 'floral dance', and thus perpetuated by the popular song with the curious drone.

Gamma (photography)

In photography and television, a measure of the contrast in a reproduced image (made by comparing its luminance/brightness with that of the original).

Gandhi Jayanti

Hindu celebration of the birth of Mahatma Gandhi (2 October).

Ganesh Chaturthi

Hindu Festival in honour of the elephant-headed god Ganesh; in the Gregorian calendar it falls in August–September.

Ganga Dussehra

Hindu celebration in honour of the goddess Ganga; in the Gregorian calendar, it falls in May–June.

Gay Nineties

The last decade of C19, characterised by whirling couples in ballrooms (which in fact formed a minuscule part of what was happening at the time).

Gedaliah, Fast of

See Tsom Gedaliah.

Gemini

(Latin = the Twins); third sign of the zodiac; 21/22 May – 21/22 June; third northern (septentrional) sign – third spring sign – sixth ascending sign; see Zodiac.

Génie, La Fête du

Talent Day; see French Revolutionary Calendar.

Geochronology or geochronometry

Dating fossils and rocks by applying analytical techniques.

Geological stratum

Any of the observable layers (beds) into which sedimentary rocks are divided. The word 'stratum' is imprecise, but is used as a general term to describe a feature imagined rather than observable.

George, St

St George is the patron saint of England, and his day is 23 April. Although the feast is rarely celebrated nationally, football supporters have breathed new life into St George's Cross, a red plus on a white background. William Shakespeare died, and is supposed to have been born, on 23 April, though the latter may be but a patriotic assumption supported by the known day of death.

Georgian age/era

Period from 1714 to 1830, during which four kings named George occupied the British throne – see Regnal Years.

The period is particularly noted for its style of architecture and furniture.

Since 1830, there have been two more kings named George on the throne of Britain: George V reigned from 6 May 1910 to 20 January 1936, and George VI from 11 December 1936 to 6 February 1952, but neither period is generally thought of as Georgian.

Germinal

(Seed time); seventh month of the French Revolutionary Calendar *qv*.

Generation

The people in a family or group that were born, raised and educated at roughly the same time. But since people are not born in clumps, there is a gradation of generations in the general population, and generations are best thought of within families, though even then they may become disjointed when siblings' birth dates become widely spaced. Generations generally advance at between three and four per century.

The population of England has grown roughly as follows:

1600	4.8m
1700	6.0m
1800	8.9m
1900	32.5m
2000	49.9m

At any given time, the foundations for the future population are being laid down. So consider a child born in the year 2000, who will have, at four generations per century:

1900	16	great-great-grandparents
1800	256	6 × greats grandparents
1700	4,096	10 × greats grandparents
1600	65,536	14 × greats grandparents

If we treat everyone as coming from a unique line, today's population of 49.9m would imply a 1600 population of 49.9 × 65,536 = 3,270,196.5m. This is clearly an absurd calculation, and the apparent discrepancy is explained by couples having more than one child, cousins marrying, and so on.

We can get some idea of the rate of procreation over the years by assuming (somewhat breathtakingly) that the total population at any given time is half male and half female, and that each couple bears children, all of whom go on to have children of their own. This yields the (simplistic) information that the progress of average number of children per family was as follows:

C17	2.12 children
C18	2.22
C19	2.78
C20	2.24.

Geological Time Divisions

Era	Period	Epoch	began × 10^6 years ago	Stages
Cenozoic	Quaternary	Holocene	0.01	
		Pleistocene	1.6	
	Tertiary	Pliocene		Astian
			5.3	Plaisancian
		Miocene		Pontian
				Tortonian
				Helvetian
				Burdigalian
			23	Aquitanian
		Oligocene		Chattian
			34	Stampian
		Eocene		Bartonian
				Lutetian
			53	Ypresian
		Palaeocene		Thanetian
				Montian
			65	Danian
Mesozoic (Secondary)	Cretaceous	Upper		Senonian
				Turonian
				Cenomanian
		Lower	135	Albian
				Aptian
				Barremian
			144	Neocomian
	Jurassic	Upper (Malm)		Portlandian
				Kimmeridgian
			173	Oxfordian
		Middle (Dogger)		Callovian
				Bathonian
				Bajocian
			183	Aalenian
		Lower (Lias)		Toarcian
				Pliensbachian
				Sinemurian
			213	Hettangian
	Triassic			Rhaetian
				Keuper
			248	Muschelkalk
Palaeozoic (Primary)	Permian			Thuringian
				Saxonian
			286	Autunian

Carboniferous	Upper (Pennsylvanian)		Stephanian
			Westphalian
	Lower (Mississippian)	360	Dinantian
Devonian			Famennian
			Frasnian
			Givetian
			Eifelian
			Coblentzian
		408	Gedinnian
Silurian			Ludlowian
			Wenlockian
		438	Llandoverian
Ordovician			Ashgillian
			Caradocian
			Llandeilian
			Llanvirnian
			Arenigian
		505	Tremadocian
Cambrian			Potsdamian
			Croixian
			Acadian
			Albertan
			Georgian
		590	Waucobian
PreCambrian (or Archaeozoic or Proterozoic)		4600	

Gion Matsuri

Japanese festival held in honour of the deity Gozu Tenno at the Yasaka Shrine, Kyoto, on 17 July, when there is a parade of two varieties of floats: those with large wheels and a tall pole, carrying musicians, and those carried on shoulders, presenting famous historical or mythical tableaux.

Gion Okera Matsuri

Japanese festival held at Yasaka Shrine, Kyoto, on 31 December (New Year's Eve) when a sacred fire of the medicinal herb okera (*Atractylis ovata*) believed to prevent sickness is lit; through the early hours of 1 January visitors take home some of that fire to cook the first meal of the year.

Girl Bishop

See Boy Bishop.

Glorious First of June

1 June 1794, when the Channel Fleet under Lord Howe gained a decisive victory over the French under Admiral Villaret Joyeuse.

Glorious Twelfth

12 August, the day grouse-shooting begins; less glorious for the grouse; see Close Season.

GMAT; GMN; GMT

Greenwich Mean Astronomical Time; — Noon; — Time.

Gnomon

The structure on a sundial, the shadow of which sweeps across the dial to indicate the time of day. The word is from ancient Greek *gignoskein* (= to know); hence the gnomic utterance, nothing to do with gnomes (Helvetian or horticultural).

Golden Afternoon

4 July 1862 when Revd Robin Duckworth (then a fellow of Trinity College, Oxford) and Revd Charles Lutwidge Dodgson (1832–98; *alias* Lewis Carroll), the Oxford mathematician, rowed a boat in company with the ten-year-old Alice Pleasance Liddell and her sisters Lorina Charlotte (13) and Edith (8) up the River Thames from Folly Bridge (near Oxford) to the village of Godstow, upon which trip the foundations for the classic that emerged as *Alice's Adventures in Wonderland* (1865) were laid.

Golden Age

Those days when whatever is under discussion was at its peak – sometimes a civilisation (the Golden Age of Sumeria, of Greece, etc); sometimes an activity (the Golden Age of Motoring, of Literature, etc). It may be a mental concept of some time past that has assumed a Golden aura, whose downside is conveniently forgotten. In progressive terms, it may be followed by Silver and Bronze Ages.

Golden Number

The number of the year in the Metonic Cycle (*qv*), which may therefore be any number from 1 to 19 inclusive.

Golden Wednesday

21 April 2004 when a cassette in the Barclays cash machine at Woolner, Northumberland, 'The Gateway to the Cheviots', was filled with £20, rather than £10, notes.

Good Friday
The Friday preceding Easter Day, which may be any Friday between 20 March and 23 April. This Christian commemoration of the Crucifixion is a public holiday in most Christian countries.

Good Parliament
That assembled in the last year of his reign by Edward III (1376), which pursued the unpopular Lancastrians, who nevertheless made it to the throne in 1399.

Goose Fair
A fair formerly held in many English towns about the time of Michaelmas.

Goose-month
The lying-in month for women.

Gowk
The cuckoo, hence a fool or simpleton hunted on 1 April.

Grace Days; Days of Grace
The three days over and above the time stated for payment in a commercial bill. The fourteen allowed on a road-fund licence have long since been retracted. Those handing in an RFL for a refund may regret the passing of the phrase: 'Handing in on the first will not do.'

Grace, Year of
Any year of the Christian era.

Grattan's Parliament
The free Irish Parliament (1782–1800) wherein Henry Grattan's machinations led to the Act of Union between Great Britain and Ireland (1800), an arrangement that lasted until 1922, and whose repercussions show no signs of abating.

Great Dying, The
When the land-masses of the earth were united as Pangea, in the End-Permian Period 250 million years ago, the 'Great Dying' took place; 90 per cent of marine life and 80 per cent of terrestrial life was wiped out as a result, it is thought, of a meteoric impact in the area now found off the north-west coast of Australia; see **Geological Time Divisions**.

Greek Kalends, deferred to the
(Ad Kalends Graecas), *ie* never because (unlike the Roman calendar) the Greek calendar had no Kalends.

Green Ribbon Day
17 March in Ireland, St Patrick's Day, when the shamrock and green ribbon are worn as the national badge.

Gregorian Calendar

The Julian calendar was introduced by Julius Caesar in 44BCE. The Julian year was, however, 11 minutes 14 seconds too long, which amounts to one day in 128.2 years. As time went on, therefore, the calendar became more and more out of step with the seasons, and in 1582 Pope Gregory XIII introduced to RC countries what has become known as the Gregorian calendar.

Gregory's plan was, first, to leave out an appropriate number of days to pull the calendar back into sync; second, to keep the Julian system (whereby a year whose number is divisible by four is a leap year, which would still give the 11-minute error), but to counteract it by making years ending in 00 non-leap years unless they were divisible by 400. This leads to a discrepancy of only 0.0005days per year, which suggests that 4000CE will not be a leap year – but we'll have to wait and see.

In 1582, 4 October was followed by 15 October. Between then and 1923, most of the world has embraced the Gregorian calendar, leaving out as many days as necessary at the time of adoption.
British Parliament passed in March 1751 the Calendar (New Style) Act, known as Lord Chesterfield's Act (24 Geo II, c 23), declaring that the following First of January should be the first day of the year 1752 for all ordinary purposes. It was also enacted that, because the two calendars were 11 days out of step, Wednesday 2 September 1752 should be followed by Thursday 14 September, giving rise to the cry 'Give us back our eleven days'.

Not surprisingly, many men in the street thought that the government was trying to pull a fast one, and to restore some faith in government, and to avoid trying to explain the inexplicable to those who could or would not see, the end of the tax year was pushed forward eleven days from Lady Day (25 March) to 5 April, where it remains to this day.

However, apparent anomalies of the kind whereby William of Orange, later King William III, left Holland on 11 November 1688 (New Style (NS)) by the Gregorian Calendar and landed in England on 5 November 1688 (Old Style (OS)) by the Julian Calendar were eliminated.

Countries switched from the Old Style (Julian) to the New Style (Gregorian) system as follows:

1582   Italy, France, Portugal, Spain
1583   Flanders, Holland, Prussia, Switzerland, and the Roman Catholic states in Germany
1586   Poland

1587	Hungary
1600	Scotland (except St Kilda until 1912)
1700	Denmark and the Protestant states in Germany
1700–40	Sweden (by gradual process)
1752	England and Wales, Ireland and the Colonies, including North America (11-day lag).
1872	Japan (12-day lag)
1912	China (13-day lag); St Kilda
1915	Bulgaria (13-day lag)
1917	Turkey and the USSR (13-day lag)
1919	Romania and Yugoslavia (13-day lag)
1923	Greece (13-day lag)

See also Part 3.

Green Thursday

The Thursday before Easter, when some Christians believe that green plants and food acquire special healing powers.

Greenery Day

A day on which greenery, or flowers and foliage, are used to decorate celebratory ceremonies occurring at Christmas, Easter, and May Day.

Greenwich Fair

A Fair held on Easter Monday.

Greenwich Mean Time

(Also Universal Time since 1928); a mean time based on noon determined as the mean sun passing over the 0° meridian through Greenwich. It is the standard time adopted by astronomers and was used throughout the British Isles until 18 February 1968, when clocks were advanced one hour and Summer Time became 'permanent'. The new system was designated British Summer Time (as from 27 October 1968), but the arguments against it duly prevailed and the country reverted to Greenwich Mean Time on 31 October 1971.

BST, British Summer Time, one hour in advance of Greenwich Mean Time, is kept between 0200hrs GMT on the day following the third Saturday in March and 0200hrs GMT on the day following the fourth Saturday in October. Other countries adjust their clocks in this way; the shift is called Summer Time (*qv*), or Daylight Saving Time. The idea is to make the times by which we live from day to day more in keeping with changing daylight hours; see Summer Time.

Groundhog Day

Candlemas, 2 February, the earliest designation of which appears in 1841 when James Morris recorded in his diary that, according to German immigrants, 'the Groundhog peeps out of his winter quarters and if he sees his shadow he pops back for another six weeks' nap, but if the day be cloudy he remains out, as the weather is to be moderate'. Thus was the imported tradition of Candlemas (from the earlier pagan feast of Imbolc) transferred from the European badger to the American groundhog, aka woodchuck (*Marmota monax*).

If the sun shines on Groundhog Day;
 Half the fuel and half the hay.

I have yet to discover why, in the film *Groundhog Day* (1993), the TV weatherman played by Bill Murray kept waking up to Groundhog Day anew. It was, however, an effective means of popularising the annual re-enactment of Groundhog Day for the commercial benefit of its participants.

Gregorian Epoch
The epoch or day on which the Gregorian calendar introduced by Pope Gregory XIII began in October 1582.

Gule, The Gule of August
1 August, Lammas Day.

Günz
The first of the Ice Ages that occurred in Europe during the Pleistocene Epoch; see also **Mindel, Riss and Würm**, and **Geological Time Divisions**.

Guruwar
(Thursday); Fifth day of the Hindu week.

Guy Fawkes' Day/Night
Commemorates 5 November 1605 when it appeared that Catholic conspirators planned to blow up James I and the Houses of Parliament in London. The plot was discovered, the men apprehended and tried for treason, and executed. 5 November was set aside as 'a day of thanksgiving to be celebrated with bonfires and fireworks', possibly taking over the pre-Christian fires once lit at Hallowe'en. This would have extra meaning if, as now seems likely, the 'plot' was an elaborate charade designed to discredit Rome. The leader was Robert Catesby (1573–1605), but the name of one of the others – Guy Fawkes (1570–1606) – seems to have caught the public fancy.

Remember, remember, the fifth of November,
  Gunpowder, treason and plot.
There seems no reason why gunpowder treason
  Should ever be forgot.

Until recently, children made Guy Fawkes' Day an excuse for trundling round stuffed effigies (Guys) on broken-down prams demanding 'a penny for the Guy', but this custom seems to have died out since universal paedophilia and H&S paranoia took over, not to mention the urban legend concerning the butcher who was so beset by continual demands for Guy money that he rushed out and stabbed the Guy, which turned out to be a real child dressed in rags. However, the bonfires and fireworks continue to take place, often on a convenient Saturday before or after 5 November, preceded by a parade of Guys, but conducted behind barriers by trained pyrotechnists, provided that they can find a company to insure the event.

Notwithstanding this, the sale of fireworks is not yet properly controlled, and many random explosions take place at around this time (and beyond); presumably the increasing threat of terrorist attack will eventually make all such activity illegal.

Hachinohe Emburi (Hachinohe Rice-Planting Festival)
Japanese festival held at Hachinohe, Aomori Prefecture, on 17–20 December when, hoping for a good crop of rice to come, supplicants mime rice planting using the emburi (a tool for smoothing the mud in rice paddies).

Hakata Dontaku (Hakata 'Holiday')
Japanese festival held at Fukuoka on 3–5 May, when residents dressed as the Seven Deities of Good Fortune parade through the streets accompanied by colourful floats. (Dontaku (holiday) may have come from the Dutch word *zondag* (Sunday).)

Halcyon Days
Times of happiness and prosperity, a meaning derived from the old Sicilian idea that the halcyon bird, or kingfisher (a bird of the *Alcedinidae* family, particularly *Alcedo atthys*), lays its eggs in a nest on the surface of the sea which must, perforce, be calm; generally taken to be seven days on each side of the winter solstice: 14–28 December.

Half, The
In the theatre, half an hour before the first actors are due on stage (*ie* 35 minutes before the show begins). All actors must be in by the Half; traditionally, the audience is allowed into the auditorium at the Half; traditionally at the Half the House Manager blows a whistle in the auditorium.

Half-life
A scientific term referring to an exponential event and defining how long half of whatever it is takes to occur; usually applied to the time taken for half the atoms in a radioactive substance to disintegrate. It's cogent to ask how any particular atom knows when its turn has come, but those who might know tend to turn away when the question is posed. Time measurements of such events may be used as a basis for geological dating.

Half past/after
In telling the time, 30 minutes past the hour. In the English language, 'half three' refers to the previous hour (half *past* three), but the practice is not universal, and in Germanic languages 'half three' means 'half an hour *to* three' – that is, 2.30, or half past two.

Hall Sunday
The Sunday before Shrove Tuesday.

Hallowe'en
31 October, the eve of All-Hallows' Day *qv*.

Hamamatsu Takoage (Hamamatsu Kite-Flying Festival)
Japanese competitive festival dating back to C16 held at Hamamatsu, Shizuoka Prefecture, on 3–5 May; after the kite battles (tako-gassen), there is a procession of floats carrying the giant kites.

Hana Taue (Rice-Transplanting Festival)
Japanese festival held in Shimane and Hiroshima Prefectures in mid-June, a form of Otaue (Great Rice Transplanting) when rice farmers seek a good crop with their traditional songs and banging of drums.

Handsel Monday
The first Monday of the year, when small gifts were given, before Boxing Day took its place.

Hanging day
Another name for Friday as it was once a common day for executing condemned criminals.

Hanoverian
Any of a line of monarchs belonging to the British royal house of Hanover that reigned from 1714 to 1901. See Regnal Years.

Hanukkah
(or Chanukkah) In the Jewish calendar, the Festival of the dedication of the Temple, otherwise known as the festival of lights; it falls on 25 Kislev – 2/3 Tebet; in the Gregorian calendar it falls in December–January.

Hanuman Jayanti
Hindu celebration in honour of the god Hanuman; in the Gregorian calendar it falls in March–April.

Harvest Festival, Hindu
See Pongal.

Harvest, Festival of
See Shavuot.

Harvest Home
General festivities initiated by a farmer when the last of his harvest had been brought in, and such activities were more labour-intensive than nowadays.

Harvest Moon
The full moon nearest the autumn equinox.

Harvest Thanksgiving
On Sunday 1 October 1843 Revd R S Hawker, vicar of Morwenstow, Cornwall, held a service to thank God for the harvest, an innovation that the Church of England picked up and ran with.

Hegira
(Arabic *hejira* – the departure), 16 July 622CE on which the Prophet Muhammad took flight from Mecca to Medina, and which became the first day of the Muslim calendar – 1 Muharram AH; see Muslim calendar.

Heian era
Period in Japan between C9 and C12, in which a strongly artistic culture flourished, centred on the city now called Kyoto.

Heroic Age
Perhaps the precursor of a Golden Age, when the gods came down from their pedestals and mated with ordinary mortals; the Heroic Age of Motoring clearly led to its Golden Age.

Hertz
The SI unit of frequency equal to one cycle per second. Named after Heinrich Rudolf Hertz (1857–94), the German physicist who transformed Maxwell's predictions into the reality of Hertzian – or, as we now call them electromagnetic, or radio – waves.

Heshvan
See Marcheshvan.

High Days and Holidays
Special occasions, a high day being a festival or great occasion.

Hilary Term
The former legal term, and the university term at Oxford and Trinity College Dublin corresponding to the Lent term elsewhere.

Hiring fair
A statute fair, once held annually on Martinmas Day (11 November) in most market towns of England and Wales, when labourers and servants were available to new masters and mistresses.

Hobby horse night
1 January, at Culworth in Northamptonshire a performance involving a horse with a painted covering.

Hock Day; Hock Tuesday
The second Tuesday after Easter Day.

Hocktide
The Monday and Tuesday after Easter.

Hogmanay
In Scotland, the last day of the year, whose celebration lasts into the following year providing an occasion for singing *Auld Lang Syne*, and first-footing.

Hognel Time
A widespread English custom, the detail of which is unknown; what is known is that collecting money to celebrate it is recorded in many parish accounts from C14 onwards. At Bolney in Sussex hognel time lasted until 2 February.

Hola Mohalla
Sikh spring festival of sporting competitions, held at the same time as the Hindu Holi festival.

Holi Festival
31 March, a boisterous Hindu Festival marked by bonfires and throwing red powder; it has been likened to April Fool's Day in the Gregorian calendar, to whose date it is very close.

Holocaust Remembrance Day
See Yom ha-Shoah.

Holy Cross Day
14 September, the feast of the Exaltation of the Cross.

Holy Innocents; Childermas
A feast celebrated on 28 December to commemorate Herod's Massacre of the Innocents – the male children of Bethlehem 'from two years and under'; at one time, it was customary to whip children, and even some adults, in remembrance.

Holy Days of Obligation; Holidays

Days on which RCs are bound to hear Mass and to abstain 'from servile work'. These Feasts of Obligation vary slightly in different counties. In England and Wales they are: all Sundays, Christmas Day, the Epiphany (6 January), Ascension Day (40th day after Easter Sunday), Corpus Christi (Thursday after Trinity Sunday), SS Peter and Paul (29 June), the Assumption of BVM (15 August), All Saints (1 November).

St Joseph (19 March) and St Patrick (17 March) are observed in Ireland and Scotland. The former and the feasts of the Octave Day of Christmas (1 January) and the Immaculate Conception (8 December) are not observed in England and Wales. Epiphany, Corpus Christi, SS Peter and Paul, and St Joseph are not kept in the USA.

Holy Rood Day
14 September, the day of the Feast of the Exaltation of the cross.

Holy Saturday
(or Easter Eve); the last day of Lent; hence any Saturday between 21 March and 24 April; often wrongly called 'Easter Saturday'.

Holy Thursday
1 Old English name for Ascension Day, the Thursday next but one before Whitsun. 2 To others, including RCs, it means Maundy Thursday, *ie* the Thursday before Good Friday.

Holy Week
The last week in Lent.

Horn Dance
See Abbots Bromley.

Horology
The study of the measurement of passing time, and the science of making instruments to effect such measurements. The term derives from Latin words meaning 'telling the hour'.

Hoshana, The Great
See Sukkot.

Hot Cross Buns
To be eaten on Good Friday, the cross being a Christian symbol whose mysterious power would prevent the buns from going mouldy. This mystique led to some considering the bun to be a medicinal cure-all, particularly as a cure for diarrhoea. Their symbolism led to them being banned by Oliver Cromwell.

Hour
A measure of time equal to 3600 seconds, there are 24 hours in a solar day.

Hour glass
See Sand glass.

Huli
See Holi.

Hundred Days, The
The days between 20 March 1815, when Napoleon reached the Tuileries (after his escape from Elba) and 28 June, the date of the second restoration of Louis XVIII.

Hundred Years War
A series of wars fought between England and France between 1337 and 1453, as a result of England's claim to the crown of France; England lost all its French possessions except Calais, and that went in 1558.

Hungry Forties
The 1840s in Great Britain, characterised by poor harvests (and hence expensive bread) and unemployment. With hindsight, we see that the 1820s may have been even worse, the saving grace in the 40s being the development of the railways (providing work), and the repeal of the Corn Laws that kept prices artificially high.

Huronian
A geological Stage within the Precambrian Era (before the Alkonian Stage), typified by the rocks found to the north of Lake Huron in Canada; see Geological Time Divisions

Ice Ages
Term usually applied to the earlier part of the present geological period, when the climate was colder, and the polar ice caps more extensive, than today. It is when the Ice Ages seem to have stopped that the modern geological time – the Holocene epoch – is said to have begun. During each Ice Age much of the sea froze, exposing considerable areas that had previously been seabed. Thus it was that that many of the animals of previous millennia managed to become so widespread, crossing land bridges that do not exist today; see Geological Time Divisions.

Ides
A day in the calendar of ancient Rome that was about half-way through the month, which it thus divided in two. It was normally on the 13th, but in March, May, July and October was on the 15th; see Roman calendar.

Illinoian
Describing the third sequence of ice ages (glaciation) in North America, which occurred during the Pleistocene Epoch and lasted for about 55,000 years from about 230,000 years ago – see **Geological Time Divisions**.

Imbolc
1 February – One of ancient Celtic quarter days, and a precursor of Candlemas and Groundhog Day *qv*.

Immaculate Conception
8 December. Commemorating the (RC) doctrine that Mary was conceived free from the effects of original sin; this festival is a public holiday in some Catholic countries.

Incubation period

1   The time that elapses between an organism laying an egg and its hatching. It varies from a few days for a small bird to several weeks for a large tortoise.

2   In medicine, the time that elapses between infection by a bacterium or virus and the onset of the disease (when the first symptoms show). The incubation periods of some common diseases are:

chickenpox	2–3 weeks
common cold	2–72 hours
diphtheria	2–5 days
gonorrhoea	3–9 days
influenza	1–3 days
malaria	2 weeks
measles	8–13 days
mumps	12–26 days
paratyphoid	1–10 days
poliomyelitis	3–21 days
rabies	2–6 weeks
rubella	14–21 days
scarlet fever	1–3 days
syphilis	2–70 days
tetanus	4–21 days
typhoid	1–3 weeks
typhus	7–14 days
whooping cough	7 days

Independence Day

4 July, a national holiday in the USA whose Declaration of Independence was adopted on 4 July 1776.

Index fossil

Any fossil found commonly enough to be used as an indicator of the date of the rock within which it has been found.

Indian Summer

It was noted in America that the lands of the Native Americans (formerly Red Indians) often experienced a late season of dry, hazy weather; thus such a period came to be described as an Indian Summer.

Industrial Revolution

A term referring to the time of technological and economic changes which transformed Great Britain from a rural agrarian to an urban industrialised state. It is difficult to pinpoint its start, as it was one of those occasions when there seems to be a sudden and widespread upsurge of something new (cf the emergence of Jazz in America at the beginning of C20), and see Age of Enlightenment. The beginnings must have lain in the work of Thomas Savery (end C17) and then Thomas Newcomen, who developed crude but workable steam engines for pumping water from the mines of Cornwall, then from mines further afield to extend their workings, followed by the expansion of the canal system, improved techniques of smelting, the rise of manufacturing, each development pushing the others forward, with the result that people began to move toward conurbations, away from agriculture and into manufacture.

Infradian

Recurring in a cyclic pattern completed in well under 24 hours. The word relates particularly to body rhythms such as regular digestive processes and other such neurologically organised functions.

Ingathering, Festival of

See Sukkot.

Inhour

For a nuclear reactor, a unit of reactivity equal to the reciprocal of the opening time in hours (so that, for example, a 3-hour period of operation gives 1/3 inhour reactivity).

Inst.

Abbreviation – meaning 'of this month' – of the word *instant*. From the mid-1500s to perhaps the 1970s a common method of referring to dates of the current month in formal correspondence, the expression is now rapidly becoming obsolete, and is generally regarded as stylistically questionable (*cf* Ult. and Prox.).

Instant

A proposed unit of time, a grade of the Degré; see **Units of Time**.

Interim

Latin = meanwhile.

International Atomic Time (TAI)

See **Greenwich Mean Time**.

International Date Line

The imaginary great semicircle running from the North Pole to the South Pole that represents the end of one day and the beginning of another. The line of longitude defined as the Greenwich meridian is the line of 0°; the date line is for the most part accordingly the line of 180°. Thus, 12 noon on Sunday at Greenwich corresponds just to the west of the date line to the time of 12 midnight at the end of Sunday, almost the first thing Monday morning; and just to the east of the date line to the time of 12 midnight at the end of Saturday, almost the first thing Sunday morning.

International Standard Date and Time Notation

See **ISO8601** below.

Iron Age

Judging (and naming) a civilisation by its tools, the Iron Age followed the Bronze Age; in the Near East it began about 3,000 years ago, a couple or so centuries later in the Hallstatt Period of the Northern Alps, 2,500 years ago in Ancient Britain and a couple or so centuries later in Scotland.

Israel Independence Day

See **Yom Ha'Atzmaut**.

ISWN

International Standard Week Number; see **ISO8601**.

Iyyar

Second month of the sacred and eighth month of the civil Jewish year. Derived from the Babylonian month of Ayara (a bud) it corresponds roughly to the Gregorian April–May; it has 29 days. Yom H'zikharon (Israel Memorial Day) is observed on 4 Iyyar, Yom ha-Atzmaut (Israel Independence Day) is observed on 5 Iyyar, Pesach Sheni (Second

ISO8601

International Standard for expressing dates and times. The progression works from the longest to the shortest period thus: YYYY–MM–DD HH:MM:SS – year, month, day, hour, minute, second. When dates and times are expressed in full, it is permissible to insert a T between the two sets of figures, especially if the short form is used: YYYYMMDDTHHMMSS. Similarly, the letter Z (= Zulu – phonetic Z) may be appended to the HHMMSS to indicate Universal Time (UTC – Universal Time Co-ordinated, which Greenwich Mean Time officially became in 1972, though GMT lives on).

This system is entirely logical, and essential for computer sorting, but the first half is difficult to get used to and – as we try to replace our mindsets with new experience – open to mistakes, especially in the abbreviated form; is 1/3 (or 1-3, or 0103) 3 January or 1 March? Some Americans and most Britons would choose 3 January, but the rest would choose 1 March.

The Standard also embraces week numbering. Week 01 is that which contains the first Thursday of the year.

An ordinary year that begins on a Thursday has a week 53, and a leap year that begins on a Wednesday or a Thursday also has a week 53.

The first day of a week is deemed to be Monday, and the days are numbered 1–7. So for a leap year starting on a Monday, W084 is Thursday 22 February.

ISO8601 has been adopted as European Standard EN28601.

Pesach, for those who were ritually impure or on a journey during Pesach) is observed on 14 Iyyar, Lag Ba'Omer (the 33rd day of the Count of the Omer) is observed on 18 Iyyar and Yom Yerushalayim (Jerusalem Reunification Day) is observed on 28 Iyyar.

Jacobean age/era

- Period between 1603 and 1625 when James I occupied the English throne. James II occupied the throne for so short a period (1685–88) that his name is hardly associated with any particular style or fashion.

Jagannatha (Ratha-yatra)

The Hindu celebration of Krishna as the lord of the universe; in the Gregorian calendar it falls in June–July.

Jamada I; II

See Jumâda.

Janmashtani
Hindu Festival celebrating the birth of the god Krishna.

January
First month of the Gregorian year (*qv*); named from Janus, the two-faced (derived from the sun and the moon) Roman god who presided over the beginnings of everything, and doorways (hence janitor); birthstone: garnet.

Jarping
Northumberland to Cleveland name for dumping.

Jazz Age
F Scott Fitzgerald (1896–1940) published *Tales of the Jazz Age* in 1922. Jazz emerged at the beginning of C20, and began to spread into the public consciousness 20–30 years later. 'The Jazz Age' carries with it images of The Charleston danced by flappers with long cigarette holders, Art Deco and the like: it was the Golden Age of Jazz, and faded as the 30s ended and World War II began.

Jerusalem
Breaching of the walls: see Tammuz; Reunification: see Yom Yerushalayim; Siege: see Tebet.

Jewish Calendar
Calendar dating from the creation, fixed at 3761 BCE. It consists of 12 months of 29 and 30 days alternately, with an additional month of 30 days interposed in embolismic years to prevent divergence form the months of the solar year. The 3rd, 6th, 11th, 14th, 17th and 19th years of the metonic cycle are embolismic years; see Part 3.

Jewish New Year
See Rosh Hashanah

Jidai Matsuri
Japanese festival held (since 1895) at the Heian Shrine, Kyoto, on 22 October when there is a procession of people dressed in costumes through the ages, some representing historical figures.

Jours Complémentaires, Les
See French Revolutionary Calendar.

Jubilee
Any fiftieth anniversary is called Jubilee, a Silver Jubilee is celebrated every 25 years.

Judica Sunday
The fifth Sunday in Lent.

Judgement, Day of
See Rosh Hashanah.

Julian
Pertaining to Julius Caesar (100–44BCE)

Julian Year
The average year of 365¼ days according to the Julian Calendar.

July
Seventh month of the Gregorian year (*qv*); named from the Roman Emperor Julius Caesar in 44BCE; birthstone: cornelian or ruby.

Jumâda I; II
Fifth and sixth months of the Muslim calendar, *qv*.

June
Sixth month of the Gregorian year (*qv*); named from the Roman god Juno (the queen of heaven); birthstone: agate, alexandrite, moonstone or pearl.

Jurassic Period; Upper, Middle and Lower
A geological Period during the Mesozoic or Secondary Era, between the Triassic and Cretaceous Periods, corresponding roughly to between 213 million years ago and 144 million years ago. The Period is generally considered to comprise three divisions: first the Lower Jurassic (or Lias), and then the Middle (or Dogger) and Upper (or Malm) Jurassic both together also known as the Oolithic. The Lower Jurassic lasted from roughly 213 million years ago to about 183 million years ago; the Middle from roughly 183 million years ago to 173 million years ago; and the Upper from roughly 173 million years ago to 144 million years ago. In the Northern Hemisphere, the Jurassic was a period of mountain-building, coral growth in shallow seas, and an abundance of ammonites and other molluscs. On land the dinosaurs reached their maximum sizes, roaming among the cycads, conifers, and ferns. The name of the period is derived from the Jura mountains, a large crescent-shaped range of limestone plateaux that line the borders of France, Switzerland, and Germany. See Geological Time Divisions.

Just now
Phrase which in some communities signifies time past (I did that just now = I've already done it) in others time present (I'll do that just now = immediately), and in yet others time future (I'll do that just now = very shortly).

Jyeshtha
Third month of the Hindu year.

Julian calendar

The Julian Calendar, introduced by Julius Caesar in 45BCE, on the advice of the Egyptian astronomer Sosigenes, was in use throughout Europe until 1582 when it was 10 days out of step with the seasons. Pope Gregory XIII therefore ordained that 5 October should be called 15 October. The discrepancy occurred because of the Augustinian ruling of AD 4 that every fourth year shall be 366 days and hence include a Leap Day; this introduced an error of 3/4 day per century; see Gregorian Calendar.

The Julian calendar is almost good enough to use today. It is still 11 minutes 14 seconds too long, which, though it may seem a small discrepancy, amounts to 18.72 hours over 100 years. This discrepancy was noticed by those responsible for fixing the date of Easter, following a method of calculation settled by the Ecumenical Council held at Nicaea in Asia Minor in 325CE, but they did nothing about it at the time.

Julian A		Julian B		Gregorian C	
Month	Days	Month	Days	Month	Days
January	31	January	31	January	31
February	29	February	28	February	28
	(30)		(29)		(29)
March	31	March	31	March	31
April	30	April	30	April	30
May	31	May	31	May	31
June	30	June	30	June	30
July	31	July	31	July	31
August	30	August	31	August	31
September	31	September	31	September	30
October	30	October	30	October	31
November	31	November	31	November	30
December	30	December	30	December	31

In Julian A, the months are alternately of 30 and 31 days (saving February, which has always had the honour of holding the leap day). In Julian B, Augustus Caesar decided that if Julius had 31 days (July), so should he (August). In Gregorian C, then as now, the last four months have exchanged numbers of days to avoid having three 31-day months together.

Kalendae
The Roman New Year Feast, 1 to 3 January.

Kalends
See Roman calendar.

Kalpa
In Hindu cosmology, a period in which the universe experiences a cycle of creation and destruction.

Kamakura Matsuri (Snow Hut Festival)
Japanese festival held in Yokote, Akita Prefecture, on 15 February when children build snow huts (kamakura) containing ceremonial altars to honour the Shinto water gods.

Kamikaze
Japanese for 'divine wind' recalling the night in August 1281 when a typhoon repulsed an impending Mongol invasion; towards the end of WW2, the word was applied to Japanese pilots willing to self-destruct, or 'suicide bombers' as we would now call them.

Kanda Matsuri
Japanese festival held at Kanda Shrine, Tokyo, on 15 May when its deities are honoured with a parade of portable shrines (mikoshi), and wagons bearing dancers.

Kanto (Lantern Festival)
Japanese festival held in Akita, Akita Prefecture, on 5–7 August when young men balance long bamboo poles hung with tiers of lanterns (kanto) on their palms, shoulders, and foreheads during nocturnal parades; it is the Akita version of the Tanabata Festival.

Kartik
Eighth month of the Hindu year.

Kasuga Matsuri
Japanese festival held at the Kasuga Shrine, Nara, Nara Prefecture, on 13 March when, in a ceremony said to be unchanged since the 9th century, a series of rites is held in honour of the Shrine's tutelary deity (the clan god of the Fujiwara family); it incorporates yamato-mai, a well-known ritual dance performed by eight young girls holding branches of the sakaki tree.

Kasuga Wakamiya
Japanese festival held at the Kasuga Wakamiya Shrine, Nara, Nara Prefecture, on 17 December, when there is a procession of people dressed as ancient courtiers or feudal warriors, and performances of Japanese classical music and Noh; the festival originated with the Fujiwara family in C12.

Kathina Ceremony (Robe offering ceremony)
Buddhist occasion held on any convenient date after the end of the Vassa Retreat (the three-month rains retreat season (Vassa) for the monastic order); the laity may offer the monks new robes and other requisites.

Khordad
Third month of the Persian year.

Kilowatt-hour; kWh
The kilowatt-hour is the commercial unit by which electricity is sold to the consumer.

Kislev
Ninth month of the sacred and third of the civil Jewish year. Its name is derived from the Babylonian month of Kislîmu, and it corresponds roughly to November–December in the Gregorian calendar; it has 29 or 30 days. Hanukkah (the Feast of Lights), begins on 25 Kislev.

Kislîmu
See Kislev.

kph
Kilometers per hour, a measure of speed indicating the number of kilometers travelled in one hour.

Krishna
The 'dark fortnight' of the Hindu month (see Shukla).

Kuan Yin
See Avalokitesvara's Birthday.

Kurama Hi Matsuri (Kurama Fire Festival)
Japanese festival held at Yuki Shrine, Kuramayama, Kyoto, on 22 October, when the two portable shrines of the Kyoto Yuki Shrine are paraded at nightfall among crowds holding torches; afterwards, large torches are carried about the grounds of the shrine until dawn.

Kumbha Mela
A Hindu Festival held every 12 years, when worshippers bathe in the waters at the confluence of the Ganges and Jumna rivers; in the Gregorian calendar it falls in January.

Laa'l Breeshey
In C18 Isle of Man, 31 January was so called for Brigit's Festival.

Labor Day
A holiday on the first Monday in September in USA and some parts of Canada.

Labour Day

1 May. A public holiday in many countries, although in Jamaica it is on 23 May; see Labor Day.

Lady Day

25 March, so called to commemorate the Annunciation of Our Lady, the Virgin Mary. Since *all* days associated with the Virgin are, strictly speaking, Lady Days, it was earlier called St Mary's Day in Lent. 25 March was also New Year's Day until 1752, when the year was deemed to begin on 1 January.

Lag Ba'Omer

The 33rd Day of counting the Omer: in the Jewish calendar, 49 days before the Feast of the Wheat Harvest (Shavuot); held on 18 Iyyar.

Lailat Al-Isra wa Al-Miraj; Lailat Bara'ah

See Muslim calendar.

Lammas Day

1 August, a Scottish Quarter Day, and in England a half- (or cross-) quarter day, falling as it does between Midsummer and Michaelmas; in Anglo-Saxon England, first fruits were offered on Lammas, and bread for the Lammas Day Eucharist was made from the new corn.

Lancaster, House of

See Plantaganet.

Last Trump

The last trumpet call which, some believe, shall awaken and raise the dead on the Day of Judgement, when all earthly things shall finally come to an end.

Law Terms

There are four Terms in the English legal calendar (dates given are for 1996):

Hilary (11 January–3 April)
Named for St Hilary; 13 January (RC 14 January)
Law sittings usually begin on 11 January and end on the Wednesday before Easter.

Easter (16 April–24 May)

Trinity (4 June–31 July) First Tuesday after Trinity Sunday to the end of July.

Michaelmas (1 October–21 December).

Law, The Rejoicing of
   See **Simhat Torah**.

Lay Days
   Days allowed for loading and unloading a ship under the terms of a charter party (the contract for hiring the whole or part of a ship for the delivery of cargo).

Leap year
   A bissextile year; one of 366 days. The ordinary year has 365 days, but is 365.2422 days long; the calendar therefore lags behind by 0.2422 days in such a year. An extra day is therefore inserted every four years; thus if the number of the year is divisible by 4, it is deemed to be a leap year. However, it will be apparent that this practice adds an average of 0.0078 days too many to each year, and this is adjusted by ruling that years divisible by 100 are *not* leap years, unless they are also divisible by 400, when they *are* leap years. This is because $400 \times 0.0078 = 3.12$; suppressing three days in 400 almost redresses the balance. However, it looks as though, in order to take account of that extra 0.12 day every 400 years, we will need to incorporate a means of losing a day every 3,200 years ($1.2 \times 8 = 0.96$ and $8 \times 400 = 3,200$). But there are variations in the length of the solar year (*qv*), so we'll cross that bridge when it hatches.

Lent
   OE = Lengthening – hence spring, during which takes place the Christian Fast of Lent: 40 days (originally 36 days) beginning on Ash Wednesday and ending at midnight on Holy Saturday, the day before Easter. Lent is observed as a period of reflection, repentance and preparation for Easter – a reminder of Christ's time spent in the wilderness.

Leo
   (Latin = the Lion); fifth sign of the zodiac; 23/24 July – 22/23 August; fifth northern (septentrional) sign – second summer sign – second descending sign; see **Zodiac**.

Lias
   Alternative name for the geological Period otherwise known as the Lower Jurassic Epoch, during the earlier part of the Mesozoic era. The term is an alternative to *lees*, the dregs or grounds at the bottom of a bottle, in this case referring to the clayey bluish layers of sedimentary limestone that make up the rock strata characteristic of this Period; see **Geological Time Divisions**.

Liberation of Africa Day
   25 May; observed in Chad, Mali, Mauritania and Zambia.

Libra

(Latin = the Balance); seventh sign of the zodiac; 23/24 September – 22/23 October; first southern (austral) sign – first autumn sign – fourth descending sign; see Zodiac.

Life expectancy

Statistically, the further length of time (usually in years) that an average person of a particular age in a particular condition is expected to live – a projected lifespan.

Life sentence

A sentence of imprisonment 'for life'. In Britain life is the mandatory sentence for murder, and the maximum penalty for certain serious offences such as arson, manslaughter, and rape. People awarded life sentences are normally detained for at least 20 years. If and when they are released, they remain on licence for the rest of their lives and are subject to recall if their behaviour suggests that they might again be a danger to the public.

Lighting-up time

Refers to the period between half an hour after sunset and half an hour before sunrise when it is compulsory for road vehicles to show white front and rear red lights when in use. In this context, the law recognises local times rather than mean times.

Light year, Light-year

A unit introduced in 1888 and now used in popular astronomical literature to describe stellar distances. 'Proper' astronomers, they often tell us, eschew the light year and use the parsec. The distance travelled by electromagnetic radiation (of which light is but one octave) in one year is 9.4605×10^{15}m or about 0.33 parsec (*qv*).

Lion Sermon

A sermon preached annually on 16 October at St Katharine Cree Church, Leadenhall Street, London.

Little Christmas

Alternative name for Epiphany.

Little Ice Age

A minor reversal in the receding of the last true Ice Age (which lasted until about 10,000BCE). There was a period of slightly increased glaciation from about 3000BCE that continued right up until the 1600s and 1700s CE, when it appeared to peak. At that time, many rivers as far south as in England and the Netherlands froze solid every winter. Since then, the climate has, for the most part, gradually become warmer.

Longest Day
1   Another term for the summer solstice, 21 June, when the hours of daylight are longest (and the night shortest). In the Southern hemisphere, it falls on 22 December.
2   According to the film of that title, D-Day, 6 June 1944.

Long Parliament
1   That of Henry IV sitting from 1 March to 22 December 1406.
2   That summoned by Charles I, that sat from 3 November 1640 to 16 March 1660 (the king was beheaded on 30 January 1649).
3   That which sat from 1661 to 1679 in the reign of Charles II.

Lord Mayor's Day
Originally the Feast of St Simon and St Jude (28 October), but now officially 9 November, although in recent years the Lord Mayor of London has been sworn in on the second Friday in November.

Lord of Misrule
See Misrule.

Lost Sunday
Another name for Septuagesima Sunday, from its having no special name.

Lots, Feast of
See Purim.

Louis Quatorze

French style or fashion of the years 1643–1715 during which King Louis XIV (*quatorze*), the 'Sun King', reigned; the style was a deliberate attempt at an extravagant French national vocabulary of design.

Louis Quinze

French style or fashion of the years 1723–74 during which King Louis XV (*quinze*) reigned; it was a sophisticated reaction, rococo and informal, to the extravagances of Louis Quatorze.

Louis Seize

French style or fashion of the years 1774–92 during which King Louis XVI (*seize*) reigned; although he was terminated by the Revolution, the style continued for some years as if to show that the fault lay in people and not things.

Low Sunday

The Sunday next after Easter.

Loy Krathong (Festival of Floating Bowls)

Takes place on the full moon night of the Twelfth Lunar month in Thailand at the end of the Kathin Festival season, when the rivers and canals are full of water. People bring bowls made of leaves, containing flowers, candles and incense sticks, and float them in the water to banish bad luck. The traditional practice of Loy Krathong was meant to pay homage to the holy footprint of the Buddha on the beach of the Namada River in India.

Lucky Bird

See First Foot.

Lughnasadh

1 August; one of ancient Celtic quarter days.

Lunar day

As far as observers on the Earth are concerned, the lunar day has a duration of 24 hours 50 minutes. From the point of view of the Sun, however, a lunar day lasts for 27 days 7 hours 40 minutes 48 seconds.

Lunar month

The lunar or synodic month, or *lunation*, covers all the lunar phases – that is, it is the time between two consecutive passages of the Moon through conjunction or opposition, equal to 29.53059 days.

Lunar phases

The phases of the Moon are:

New Moon (Moon visible)
Crescent Moon (pointing right)
First quarter (left-half-Moon)
Gibbous Moon (incomplete on right)
Full Moon
Gibbous Moon (incomplete on left)
Third quarter (right-half-Moon)
Crescent Moon (pointing left)
[New Moon (Moon visible)]

Lupercal, Lupercalia

Roman feast beginning on 15 February, when (*inter alia*) the names of eligible young women would be written on slips of paper, which were then picked unseen from jars by eligible young men, who would become their consorts for the feast, or the month – or, indeed, for ever. The Christian church was at pains to eradicate a pagan ceremony, the Lupercal custom was moved back to 14 February, and so St Valentine's Day was born.

Lustrum

In ancient Rome the purification sacrifice made by the censors for the people once in five years, after the census has been taken; hence a period of five years. The term derives from an ancient Roman ritual of purification by washing undertaken at five-year intervals by the city censors immediately after the completion of a national census, and on behalf of the people, who were then deemed to be spiritually cleansed.

M; m

March; May; minute; month – and, indeed, mile and metre.

Machine Age

Somewhat vague term for whatever period its user wishes to so identify.

Mad Parliament

Whose title arose from the French adjective *insigne* (distinguished – or notorious) being mistaken for *insane*; it met at Oxford in 1258 to limit the powers of King Henry III.

Magh

Eleventh month of the Hindu year.

Magha Puja Day (Fourfold Assembly or 'Sangha Day')

A Buddhist festival held on the full moon day of the third lunar month (March) to commemorate the day on which, early in the Buddha's teaching life, he went, after the first Rains Retreat (Vassa) at the Deer Park at Sarnath, to Rajagaha city where 1250 Arahats (enlightened saints, the Buddha's disciples) had returned from their wanderings to pay respect to the Buddha. They assembled in the Veruvana Monastery with the two chief disciples of the Buddha: Ven Sariputta and Ven Moggalana. The assembly is called the Fourfold Assembly because:
1   All 1250 were Arahats.
2   All had been ordained by the Buddha himself.
3   There was no call to assembly.
4   It was the full moon day of the month Magha (March).

Maggie Thatcher Day

10 January on the Falkland Islands.

Magna Carta

Great Charter of liberties extorted by church and barons from King John and signed by him at Runnymede, a meadow on the south bank of the River Thames near Windsor, on 15 June 1215.

Mahashivrati
The Great Night of Shiva; Hindu Festival honouring the god Shiva; in the Gregorian calendar, it falls in January–February.

Makar Sankranti
Hindu Festival marking the Winter Solstice; in the Gregorian Calendar, it falls in January.

Man-day; -hour; -shift; -year
See Person-day etc.

Mangalwar
(Tuesday); Third day of the Hindu week.

Mar's Year
The year of 1715, that of the Earl of Mar's rebellion on behalf of the Old Pretender.

March
Third month of the Gregorian year (*qv*); named from Mars, the Roman god of war, father of Romulus and hence of Rome; birthstone: aquamarine or bloodstone.

Marcheshvan – or Cheshvan or Heshvan
Eighth month of the sacred and second of the civil Jewish calendar. Its name is derived from the Babylonian month Arakhshama; it corresponds roughly to October–November in the Gregorian calendar; it has 29 or 30 days.

Margashirsh
Ninth month of the Hindu year.

Marian Year
Any that reckoned 25 March, the Feast of the Annunciation of the Blessed Virgin Mary, as New Year's Day until the reformation of the calendar in 1752.

Market Day
A prime reason for travelling is to exchange goods – either for other goods (barter) or, later, for money. Focusing trade on one place – a market – is obviously a good idea, and arriving on market day is important. Thus (by definition) every market town has its weekly market day; other markets (for horses and cattle for example) may be regular but less frequent.

Marriage, close seasons for
In days gone by, these were:
1   From Advent to St. Hilary's Day (13 January).
2   From Septuagesima to Low Sunday.
3   From Rogation Sunday to Trinity Sunday.

Martinmas
The feast of St. Martin, 11 November.

Martin Luther King Day
January 15 (USA).

Martin's Summer, St
A late spell of fine weather; *cf* Indian summer.

Matins
In the RC church, the first of the seven canonical hours of prayer (*qv*), originally observed at night, but now often recited with lauds in the early morning. In the Church of England, morning prayer generally.

Matzot, Festival of the
See **Pesach**.

Maundy Thursday (aka Sharp, Sheer, Shere or Shrift Thursday)
Any Thursday between 19 March and 22 April; the day before Good Friday, the commemoration of the Last Supper and when the British Monarch distributes Maundy Money to as many poor men and women as the sovereign's age in years in Westminster Abbey (or nowadays other cathedral). Takes its name from the Latin *dies mandati*, = the day of the mandate, referring to the mandate given by Christ to His disciples to love one another. In the RC church it is marked by the symbolic washing of feet by the priest, in commemoration of Christ washing the feet of the disciples.

May
Fifth month of the Gregorian year (*qv*); named from the Roman goddess Maia, eldest and most beautiful of the seven Pleiades (daughters of Atlas and Pleione); birthstone: emerald.

May Day
The first day of May has long been a day of celebration, as 'Nature's outbreak into beauty excites so joyful and admiring a feeling in the human breast'. In Ancient Rome, the occasion was celebrated as part of the Floralia, or Floral Games, beginning on 28 April and lasting for some days. As a well-known part of the celebration, children dance round the maypole, each holding a coloured ribbon attached to the top of the pole, and weaving in and out as they dance round, in the manner of a machine for braiding decorative electric cables. The proceedings may be enhanced with a village procession and collections for charity. Maypoles were forbidden by Parliament in 1644, a decree enforced by penalties that 'effectually carried out their gloomy desires'. King Charles II was restored to the throne on 29 January 1661, in good time for the populace to give vent to its suppressed May Day jollity; he

joined the new custom of the social élite of promenading in Hyde Park on that day. In England and Wales, May Day officially became a public holiday in 1978; in Scotland, it is a Bank Holiday.

Meal times

There is a case for synchronising meal times in the household, however busy the family, lest manners and good behaviour suffer (assuming that the family is civilised enough to care). 'Break-fast' breaks the fast of the night, and sets the body up for the day ahead, a fact (or fiction) widely recognised by manufacturers of breakfast cereals as a means of selling what may become perilously close to being junk food. Hotels and the like offer the 'full English breakfast' or the 'continental breakfast', both often found in a series of lidded dishes on a central table with hot lights glaring down, the choice for the former to be made from eggs cooked in various ways, bacon (which may or may not be properly crisp), mushrooms, black pudding, tomato (which may or may not be slush from a tin), fried bread, and baked beans; and for the latter simplified to which of the croissants you pick. It may be served between 0700 and 1000, according to the day of the week and the degree of civilisation of the house. This brings us round to 'elevenses' or docky time as we call it in these parts, although docky, or snap, can be taken at any time. Lunch, which some confusingly call 'dinner', is served at about 1300, afternoon tea (with crust-off cucumber sandwiches and the best china) at about 1600, dinner (or 'supper' as those who take dinner at lunch time would have it) at about 2000, although some would have 'high tea' somewhat earlier – say 1900. This might precede going to the play, in which case supper would be served later in the evening after the entertainment was over.

Mean solar day

The average value of a day during a complete solar year (the time between two consecutive transits of the Sun across the meridian).

Mean solar time

Time measured by the hour angle of mean Sun plus twelve hours, also called Universal Time. When it is referred to the Greenwich meridian (longitude 0°), it may be called Greenwich Mean Time (GMT).

Mediaeval Era; Period

A term used to denote that period of European history between the downfall of the ancient classical civilisation of Greece and Rome consequent upon the barbarian invasions (c5C) and the Europe of the Renaissance and Reformation (C14).

Medicinal Days

Ancient medicine adhered to an arcane practice of assigning propitiousness or otherwise to certain days; thus it was believed that, in the course of a disease, its 6th, 8th, 10th, 12th, 16th, 18th, etc day were preferable for treatment to the others. There might be some metabolic explanation with certain conditions; in other cases the observer might see what was expected, and the patient react to the placebo effect – provided that he or she had no knowledge of the Unlucky Days.

Mehr

Seventh month of the Persian year.

Meiji era

(= the era of enlightened rule); in Japan, the years 1868 to 1912CE, during which the Emperor Mutsuhito was on the throne and there was considerable social and political change; Mutsuhito himself so described it.

Memorial Day

In the US, Memorial Day was originally called Decoration Day; it is a day of remembrance for those who have died for the nation. There are many stories concerning its origins, but it predates the British Remembrance Day by several decades, as it was first officially proclaimed on 5 May 1868 by General John Logan, national commander of the Grand Army of the Republic, and first observed on 30 May that year. New York recognised the occasion in 1873, and all the Northern states had joined in by 1890. The name was changed from Decoration Day to Memorial Day in 1882. The South did not recognise the Day until after WW1, when the set of those remembered was enlarged to include *all* American war dead. It is now generally celebrated as a weekend around the last Monday in May. The fund-raising red poppy emblem was introduced by Moina Michael in 1915, and taken up in Britain after WW1 by the Earl Haig Fund. Memorial Day was declared a US national holiday to be held on the last Monday in May in 1971, though there are those who would revert to 30 May to restore its original solemnity. Confederate War Dead Day is held on January 19 in Texas, April 26 in Alabama, Florida, Georgia, and Mississippi; May 10 in South Carolina; and June 3 (Jefferson Davis's birthday) in Louisiana and Tennessee.

Memorial, Day of

See **Rosh Hashanah**

Mensal

An unusual word for 'monthly'.

Merciless or Unmerciful Parliament
That which met in 1388 (halfway though the reign of Richard II) to condemn his friends to death or exile.

Merovingian Era
The French era so named from the royal dynasty of Merovius, Merovech, or Merwig – the Merovingian kings who occupied the French throne from C5 to mid-C8, traditionally regarded by the French as the first Kings of France.

Merry Monday
Old name for the day before Shrove Tuesday; 'eat, drink and be merry ...'

Mesolithic
The Middle Stone Age in Europe – at this stage people lived in small nomadic groups and communities, existing primarily by hunting – especially fishing – and gathering, and using wooden or stone tools and weapons.

Mesozoic or Secondary Era
Geological Era before the present (Cenozoic) and following on from the Palaeozoic. It is divided into the Triassic, Jurassic and Cretaceous Periods, recognised by considerable volcanic activity and mountain building on the Earth's surface. Reptiles flourished and, from the start of the era, dominated the formerly ubiquitous arthropods, brachio-pods, molluscs, and other marine and near-marine animals; by the end of the era, in fact, dominating all sizeable mobile organisms in the form of dinosaurs. Nonetheless, the beginning of the Era also marks the initial evolution of mammal species which, after the end of the Era, were to become dominant in their turn; see **Geological Time Divisions**.

Messidor
(Harvest); tenth month of the French Revolutionary Calendar *qv*.

Metonic cycle
The cycle of nineteen years during which new moons fall on the same days from one cycle to the next.

MEZ
(German) Mitteleuropäische Zeit = Central European Time; see **Time Zones**.

Michaelmas
29 September, the festival of St Michael and All Angels. St Michael was one of the Archangels, the prince of all angels and leader of the celes-tial armies. He is depicted as a handsome young man with wings, wearing white or armour, holding a lance and shield.

Metrical feet

In poetry, the rhythmic elements upon which a poem is structured; the main ones – in the order shown – are:

iamb(us)	di-dah	guitar
trochee or choree	dah-di	fancy
dactyl	dah-di-di	architect
anap(a)est	di-di-dah	Bucharest
spondee	dah-dah	ding dong
amphibrach	di-dah-di	caramba

Others are combinations

amphimacer or cretic	dah-di-dah	fancy that
antibacchius or palimbacchius	dah-dah-di	Tintagel
antispast	di-dah-dah-di	Sir John Gielgud
bacchius	di-dah-dah	it's play time
choreus or tribrach	di-di-di	Zebedee
choriamb	dah-di-di-dah	excellent owl
dibrach or pyrric	di-di	silly
diamb	di-dah-di-dah	it's ten to twelve
dispondee	dah-dah-dah-dah	go to your room
ditrochee	dah-di-dah-di	buy some candy
dochmiac	di-dah-dah-di-dah	there's no time for that
epitrite	di-dah-dah-dah	they've all gone home
ionic majore	dah-dah-di-di	long time coming
ionic minore	di-di-dah-dah	Titicaca
mollossus	dah-dah-dah	come down here
paeon	dah-di-di-di	owl homily
procleusmatic	di-di-di-di	Peter Piper

Michron

The time of vibration of a wave of wavelength 1 micron (one-millionth of a metre). The term derives from the first syllables of the ancient Greek words *mikros* and *chronos*, 'small' and 'time', and is a scientific pun on micron; see **Units of Time**.

Microsecond

One millionth of a second; see **Units of Time**.

Middle Age

If man's span is threescore years and ten, middle age must be around 35 years old; however, it may be thought to encompass the 40s to the

60s, especially if one feels a need to take it seriously. Personally, I've always been in my prime.

Middle Ages

A fuzzy period of European history, between perhaps the decline and fall of the ancient classical civilisations of Greece and Rome, and the emergence of the Renaissance and Reformation; in round terms, C5–C14.

Middle Kingdom

In ancient Egyptian history the XIIth–XIVth Dynasties between about 2130 to 1600BCE.

Mid-Lent Sunday

The fourth Sunday in Lent.

Midnight Mass

Christmas Eve service bridging the midnight between Christmas Eve and Christmas Day.

Midsummer Day

24 June; nativity of St John the Baptist

Milad al-Nabi

An Islamic Festival celebrating the Prophet's Birthday; it falls on 12 Rabîa – 1 Eid.

Minden Day

On 1 August 1759 six regiments of the British Army won the most spectacular victory of the Seven Years War (against the French), sporting wild roses in their caps plucked as they advanced across Minden Heath (north-west Germany). The Day is commemorated by the Minden Regiments (with the exception of the Royal Welch Fusiliers) wearing roses in their caps on 1 August: they were/are The 12th Foot, later the Suffolk Regiment (in which your compiler had the honour to spend his first six weeks of National Service in 1953), later the 1st Battalion Royal Anglian Regiment; The 20th Foot, the Lancashire Fusiliers (the Minden Boys), later the 4th Battalion Royal Regiment of Fusiliers (now disbanded); The 23rd Foot Royal Welch Fusiliers; The 25th Foot, the King's Own Scottish Borderers; The 37th Foot, later the Royal Hampshire Regiment; and The 51st Foot, KOYLI (King's Own Yorkshire Light Infantry, which became the 2nd Battalion the Light Infantry in 1968 (see Yorkshire Day).

Millenary/Millennium
A period of a thousand years.

Millimicrosecond
A thousandth of a millionth of a second; one nanosecond.

Millisecond
A thousandth of a second.

Mindel
The second of the Ice Ages that occurred in Europe during the Pleistocene Epoch; see also Günz, Riss and Würm, and Geological Time Divisions.

Minoan
Pertaining to Minos, the legendary king and law-giver of Crete. At his death, he was made supreme judge of the lower world, before whom all the dead appeared to give an account of their stewardship and to receive the rewards of their deeds. He was the husband of Pasiphae and the owner of the Labyrinth constructed by Daedalus. Minoan denotes pertaining to ancient Crete, and the Minoan period is the Cretan bronze age, about 2500–1200BCE.

Minute
A measure of time, 60 seconds, and one-sixtieth part of an hour; see Units of Time.

Miocene Epoch
A geological Epoch during the Tertiary period of the Cenozoic era, following the Oligocene Epoch and preceding the Pliocene, roughly between 25 million and 5 million years ago. The sea level continued to fall during the Epoch, increasing the amount of land surface and promoting the growth of grasses which, in turn, encouraged the spread of grazing mammals, but the average temperature also continued to fall; see Geological Time Divisions.

Misrule
In mediaeval and Tudor times the practice of licensed tomfoolery at certain times of the year, of the sort where the roles of servant and master are reversed, was overseen by the Abbot, King, or Lord, of Misrule. Such frivolities may have arisen from long-established events such as the Roman Saturnalia, and took place in the seasons of Christmas, Easter and May. A practice at Hocktide (the second week after Easter) was for the men of the community to capture the women and release them for a forfeit; on the following day, the women would capture the men. Not many such customs survive in these PC days.

Model Parliament

That summoned by Edward I in 1295, the first attempt at gathering a proper selection of representatives.

Modern

That which is up to date, as modern art, modern music, modern dance, the modern novel.

Modernism

A movement in the RC Church that sought to interpret ancient church teachings with due regard to the current teachings of science, modern philosophy and history. It arose in late C19 and was formally condemned by Pope Pius X in 1907 in the encyclical *Pascendi*, which stigmatised it as the 'synthesis of all heresies'.

The term 'modernist' is also applied to liberal and radical critics of traditional theology in other churches. The Modern Churchmen's Union was founded in 1898 and was strongly critical of Anglo-Catholic and RC ideals. Dean Inge (1860–1954) and Bishop Barnes (1874–1953) were prominent among its members.

Modranicht

Mother Night, annual festival held on 24 December.

Mohammedan Calendar

See Muslim calendar.

Moment

1   A short unspecified period of time.
2   A millicé = 0.864 seconds; see **Units of Time**.

Mongrel Parliament

That summoned to Oxford by Charles II to thwart attempts to allow an RC succession.

Month of Sundays

A long and unspecified length of time.

Moon

The earth's single satellite, 3,476km in diameter, and with a mass of 5.476×10^{24}kg; its mean distance from earth is 384,400km and its periods of revolution and of rotation are both 27.32 days, so that it always presents the same part of its surface to us. The first man to set foot on the moon was the American astronaut Neil Armstrong, on 21 July 1969, from *Apollo 11*.

Month

1 One of the 12 divisions of a calendar year (calendar month).
2 A period of four weeks (28 days) or 30 days.
3 A period from a given day in one month to the same day in the next month.
4 The period of time taken for the moon to return to the same longitude after one complete revolution round the earth (solar month: 27.32158 days: 27d7h43m5.4s).
5 The period of time taken by the moon to make one complete revolution round the earth measured between two successive conjunctions with a chosen star (sidereal month:27.32166 days: 27d7h43m11s).
6 The time taken for the moon to make one complete revolution round the earth, measured between successive new moons (lunation, or lunar or synodic month: 29.53059 days: 29d12h44m3s).

Mop fair

An English statute or hiring fair taking place in market towns at Martinmas (11 November), when those for hire would line up for inspection, their trade identified by the emblems they bore (such as mops).

Mordad

Fifth month of the Persian year.

Mother's Day

Originally Mothering Sunday, the 4th in Lent, when children gave their mothers small tokens of affection; reinvented as Mother's Day in the USA (2nd Sunday in May), and re-imported into the UK as a marketing opportunity.

Motsuji Madarajin Matsuri

Japanese festival held at Motsuji, Hiraizumi, Iwate Prefecture, on 20 January, when composite song, dance, and drama performances follow Sutra readings in honour of the Buddha Amida, Motsuji's tutelary deity.

Movable feasts

Annual church feasts which do not fall on a fixed date, but are determined by certain rules; Easter is a notable example. Trying to get all those involved to agree to date-fixing to everyone's benefit is as hard as assembling the bishops to open Joanna Southcott's Box.

Easter Day is the first Sunday after the full moon which occurs upon or the next after 21 March; if the full moon appears on a Sunday, Easter Day is the Sunday After.

Other key dates:

Septuagesima §	Nine Weeks before Easter
Sexagesima §	Eight Weeks before Easter
Quinquagesima §	Seven Weeks before Easter
Quadragesima §	Six Weeks before Easter
Rogation §	Five Weeks after Easter
Ascension Day	40 Days after Easter (hence a Thursday)
Whit §	Seven Weeks after Easter
Trinity §	Eight Weeks after Easter

If 21 March is a Full Moon Saturday, Easter Day will be on its earliest possible date: 22 March.

If 21 March is a Full Moon Sunday, Easter day will be on the next Sunday: 28 March.

MPH, mph

Miles per hour.

MST

Mountain Standard Time; see **Time Zones**.

MTBF

Mean Time Between Failures: a statistical measure of reliability.

Muharram

First month of the Muslim calendar, *qv*.

Mumping Day

St. Thomas' Day, 21 December, when in some areas the poor would go about 'mumping', or seeking gifts in preparation for Christmas; in Lincolnshire, mumping was a Boxing Day custom; in Warwickshire it was 'going a-corning', since the gift sought was corn.

Muslim calendar

A calendar used in Islamic countries, which dates from 16 July 622, the day of Hegira. It consists of 12 lunar months of 29 days 12 hours 44 minutes each. As a result the Muslim year consists of only 354 or 355 days; a cycle is 30 years; see **Part 3**.

Musical periods

As with any other discipline, it is impossible to tie down the beginnings and ends of periods as if all compositions in, say, 1749 were Baroque, and all those in 1751 Classical. There will be forward-thinking composers in any period, and in the following period there will be those who are not ready to move on. Given that caveat, musical periods in the Western world are more or less as follows:

Before C–8	Prehistoric
C–8–C4	Primitive (Ancient Greece and Rome)
C4–C6	Ambrosian
C6–C10	Gregorian
1100–1300	Mediaeval
1300–1600	Renaissance
1600–1750	Baroque
1750–1800+	Classical
1800–1850	Early Romantic
1850–1900	High Romantic
1900–Modern	Avant-Garde

It is interesting that the word 'classical' has caught on as the 'opposite' of jazz and pop. The more simplistic one is, the less defined one's terms.

Naga Panchami
Hindu celebration of the birth of serpents, when pots of milk are poured over snakes from the temple of Shiva; in the Gregorian calendar, it falls in July–August.

Nagasaki Suwa Matsuri
Japanese festival held at Suwa Shrine, Nagasaki, Nagasaki Prefecture, on 7–9 October, when there is a parade of floats carrying groups of young men who whirl umbrellas, and a Chinese-style dragon dance.

Nanosecond
Tiny unit of time equal to 1 billionth of a second; 10^{-9}s; see **Units of Time**.

Nantes, Edict of
Whereby Henry IV of France guaranteed in 1598 Huguenots' rights of worship in certain named towns; revoked by Louis XIV in 1685.

Nara Yamamaki

Japanese festival held at Nara, Nara Prefecture, on 15 January when, at twilight, people costumed as warrior monks burn the turf on the hillside at Wakakusayama to commemorate the resolution of a boundary dispute between the temples Todaiji and Kofukuji.

Nativity, Feast of

The Christian festival celebrating the birth of Jesus; Christmas.

Natural Cycles

Because time is related to the motions of heavenly bodies (and *vice versa*), it is natural that astronomy and timekeeping should have developed hand in hand. The problem is that the observed periods of the Sun, the Moon and the Earth are not related to one another. The alternation of night and day is clear enough, but the periods of light and darkness are not generally of equal length from one day to the next. The phases of the Moon are equally obvious, but the relationship between the lunar cycle and the rotation and orbiting of the earth is disconnected. Yet the moon, giving – as it does when full – some nocturnal illumination, must have been of particular importance to those without means of portable artificial light – the expressions 'Hunter's Moon', and 'Harvest Moon' speak for themselves. The year is a less obvious period in time than either the day or the lunar cycle, but is manifested by the procession of seasons, the behaviour of plants and animals, and large events such as tides and floods.

Naughty Nineties, The

The 1890s in England, when the puritanical Victorian code of behaviour gave way in certain wealthy and fashionable circles to growing laxity in sexual morals, a growing cult of hedonism, and a more light-hearted approach to life.

Nautical Timekeeping

See **Bells**.

Nebonassar, Era of

An era that began on Wednesday 26 February 747BCE, the date of the accession of Nebonassar; for centuries, the Chaldean astronomers used it for reckoning; it was followed by the eras of Hipparchus and Ptolemy.

Nebraskan

First period of glaciation within the Ice Ages as experienced in North America, from about 1,200,000 to about 1,136,000 years ago.

Nebuta Matsuri

Japanese festival held at Aomori and Hirosaki, Aomori Prefecture, on 1–7 August; it is one of the many festivals associated with the Bon Festival, when there is a series of night-time parades of enormous paper floats lit from within and depicting popular or legendary figures, accompanied by dancing and singing townspeople.

Neocene

In geological time, a collective name for the second part of the Tertiary Period, including the Miocene and Pliocene Epochs, and lasting from about 25 million years ago to about 3 million years ago; see Geological Time Divisions.

Neogene

In geological time, a collective name for the later part of the Tertiary Period and all the time since (the so-called Quaternary Period) – in other words, the last 25 million years; see Geological Time Divisions.

Neolithic

The New Stone Age, when techniques for producing stone tools were improved; as man began to understand the seasons, settled farming (rather than hunting and gathering) became the norm, and this in turn led to the domestication of animals to provide food and drink throughout the year. Experiments with materials continued, and the development of metallurgy moved civilisation from the Stone to the Bronze Age. Despite White Man knowing what's best, there are still some remaining Neolithic cultures in north-eastern South America, southern Africa, and New Guinea.

New Style

Dates according to the Gregorian calendar; applied particularly at the time of its introduction to reduce confusion with the Old Style (Julian) calendar, and specified by historians as may be necessary for the avoidance of doubt when citing document dates; abbreviations: NS and OS.

Nicholas, St

His day is 6 December; he is one of the most popular saints in Christendom, and appears sonically corrupted as Santa Claus, aka Father Christmas, Father Frost, Joulupukki, Kris Kringle, Père Noël, Sabdiklos, Sancte Claus, Sinter Klaas, and Weihnachtsmann.

Nicka-Nan Night

Cornish term for the night preceding Shrove Tuesday.

Night of Forgiveness

An Islamic Festival held on 15 Shaabân.

New Year

The Romans began their year in March; the Anglo-Saxons celebrated New Year on December 25. This was later changed to March 25 – Annunciation Day – in the early mediaeval period. The Gregorian calendar restored January 1 as the beginning of the year in 1582, although Britain continued to use the Julian calendar until 1752. Different calendars and cultures may celebrate New Year on different dates; in the Islamic calendar, for example, the New Year festival falls on 1–10 Muharram, which precesses through the Gregorian year.

In England, from the 12th century until 1752, Lady Day (25 March) was the legal beginning of the year and 25 March is still the beginning of the ecclesiastical year. Dates from 1 January to 24 March in any year were written *eg* 28 February 1659–60 or 1659/60 indicating the historical year of 1660 but the ecclesiastical, legal and official year of 1659; see also Part 3.

Niino Izu Yuki Matsuri (Niino Snow Festival)

Japanese festival held at the Izu Shrine, Anan, Nagano Prefecture, on 14–15 January, when snow is offered to the shrine gods in the hope of improving the coming harvest.

Nine Days' Wonder

An event on everyone's lips at the time, but then completely forgotten, named for the actor Will(iam) Kempe (c1550–c1603), a member of Shakespeare's Company who in 1600 performed a nine-day Morris dance from London to Norwich, and wrote *Nine Daies Wonder*.

Nine First Fridays

In the RC Church the observance of the first Fridays of nine consecutive months, following the revelation unto St Margaret Mary Alacoque (1647–90) that special grace would be bestowed upon those following the practice.

Nisan

First month of the sacred and seventh month of the civil Jewish calendar. Its name is derived from the Babylonian month of Nisannu; it corresponds roughly to the Gregorian months of March–April; it has 30 days.

Nisannu

See Nisan.

Nivôse
(Snows); fourth month of the French Revolutionary Calendar *qv*.

Nonagenarian
Someone in his or her tenth decade.

Nones
Latin *nonus* = ninth.

1   In the Roman calendar, the ninth day before the Ides, that is to say the 5th of the month when the Ides is the 13th, and the 7th of the month when the Ides is the 15th (March, May, July, October) – see **Roman calendar**.

2   The fifth RC divine office of the seven, originally at 1500hrs, supposedly nine hours after daybreak. The service originally held at 1500hrs was moved back to mid-day, hence the word 'noon'.

Nonidi
Ninth day of the French Revolutionary week; see **French Revolutionary Calendar**.

Noon
Mid-day; halfway between two midnights; the sun directly overhead; from Latin *nona hora* = the ninth hour, as it was originally the ninth hour after sunrise; see **Nones**.

Nooning
(US) mid-day, or a mid-day break.

Noon-time
Noon.

Nos y lolgen
Welsh for Christmas Eve.

November
Eleventh month of the Gregorian year (*qv*); named in the Julian calendar from the Latin *novem* = nine; birthstone: topaz.

NS
New Style, *qv*.

Oak-apple Day or Royal Oak Day
29 May, the birthday of Charles II (1630–85); also the day on which he entered London in 1660; thus was the King restored to his throne – the Restoration. The significance is enhanced by the story of Charles II's hiding in an oak tree at Boscobel (near Shifnal, Shropshire) after his defeat at Worcester (3 September 1651).

Oatmeal Monday
The mid-term Monday at Scottish Universities when the father of a poor student would bring him a sack of oatmeal to provide his staple diet for the rest of the term. In the apocryphal tale, the student fills a drawer with porridge, and cuts off a chunk to eat daily.

Obon
See Ulambana.

Observance Day
See Uposatha.

O'clock
'Of the clock', referring to the hour, as in 'two o'clock', a reminder of the novelty of clocks, especially those that struck the hour. The word 'clock' is derived from 'cloche' (French = bell), so the phrase is rich in meaning. The use in phrases such as 'half past two o'clock' is less common.

Octave
The eighth day of a Church observance. The most devout may keep a feast or fast not just for the specified day but for the following week: 'keeping the octave'.

Octave Day of Christmas
1 January.

Octennial
Once every eight years; lasting for eight years.

Octidi
Eighth day of the French Revolutionary week; see **French Revolutionary Calendar**.

October
Tenth month of the Gregorian year (*qv*); named in the Julian calendar from the Latin *octo* = eight; birthstone: opal or tourmaline.

Octogenarian
Someone in his or her ninth decade.

Okunchi or Okunichi
Japanese = ninth day; it refers to the ninth day of the ninth month according to the lunar calendar, the traditional starting date of autumn festivals.

Old Age
The final period of an average lifespan of that type of organism; hence an old cat or dog might be 20, an old human 90, and an old tortoise 200 years old.

Old Style

Refers to dating by the Julian calendar, as opposed to the Gregorian calendar, which was introduced gradually between 1582 and 1923; see **New Style**.

Oligocene Epoch

A geological Epoch during the Tertiary Period of the Cenozoic era, corresponding roughly to between 38 million years ago and 25 million years ago. During the preceding Eocene Epoch, there was a general warming of the Earth's surface and atmosphere, promoting the widespread growth of tropical and subtropical vegetation in many forms still visible today. The Oligocene reversed many of these trends, as the overall temperature decreased markedly, and the seas retracted. Mammals became the dominant terrestrial life form, and the first primates appeared; see **Geological Time Divisions**.

Olympiad

A period of four years, particularly that between two Olympic games; hence it was an ancient Greek measure of time dating back to 776BCE.

Ombashira Matsuri (Sacred Post Festival)

Japanese festival held at the Suwa Shrine, Suwa, Nagano Prefecture, early in May every sixth year, when the four fir posts at each of the two shrines' sacred enclosures are renewed.

Omizutori (Water-Drawing)

Japanese ceremony held at the hall Nigatsudo of the temple Todaiji, Nara Prefecture, on 12 March, when monks purify the hall and the spectators by means of flaming torches and the ceremonial drawing of water from the nearby well, Wakasai, and then offer it to Kannon, the hall's principal deity.

Omer, the 33rd Day of Counting

See **Lag Ba'Omer**.

One's bum year

*Sun*speak for Annus Horribilis, *qv*.

Opinion, La Fête de l'

Opinion Day; see **French Revolutionary Calendar**.

Orangeman's Day

Kept by Northern Irish Protestants on 12 July to commemorate the Battle of the Boyne (1690) when William III of England fought the former King James II in Ireland. It was fairly insignificant *per se* but for the memorable spectacle of two kings fighting in Ireland for the throne of England. The lesser remembered Battle of Aughrim was fought on 12 July; Boyne itself was on 1 July.

Ordibehesht

Second month of the Persian year.

Ordovician Period

A geological Period during the Palaeozoic or Primary Era, between the Cambrian and Silurian Periods, roughly between 505 and 438 million years ago; terrestrially, it was a period of volcanic activity and mountain-building. In spite of these upheavals, graptolite invertebrates flourished; limpet-, clam-, or lampshell-like brachiopods diversified; gastropods and cephalopods abounded; and the trilobites developed; moreover, vertebrate life-forms appeared for the first time; see **Geological Time Divisions**.

OS

Old Style, *qv*.

pa, p.a.

An abbreviation for Latin *per annum* = per year, or annually; not to be confused with *per anum*, which makes a welcome change from paying through the nose.

Pack and Penny Day

The last day of a fair when traders dispose of their remaining goods by selling them cheaply; it saves having to pack them up and take them home, probably in a soiled state. For modern manifestations, witness the last hours of the London Bookfair and the Chelsea Flower Show.

Pack-Rag-Day

Old May Day, so called in Lincolnshire because servants hired for the year packed up their clothes ('rags') to go home or to seek new employment.

Palaeo-, paleo-

Prefix denoting 'ancient', in fact usually referring not merely to prehistoric times but to geological times.

Pal(a)eocene Epoch

A geological Epoch during the Tertiary Period of the Cenozoic Era, corresponding roughly to between 65 million years ago and 55 million years ago. It began at the apparently cataclysmic end of the Upper Cretaceous Period of the Mesozoic Era (when the dinosaurs and other groups seem rapidly to have become extinct), and ended when the warmer Eocene Epoch started. During the Palaeocene there was a general draining of the shallow inland seas. Animal evolution took most of the Epoch to recover from the loss of life sustained in the cataclysm but it was, nonetheless, during the Palaeocene that the first primates evolved; see **Geological Time Divisions**.

Palaeochronology

Deriving an age for a fossil through a knowledge of its stage of evolution.

Palaeolithic

From prehistoric times, of the very first Stone Age form of human culture – the stage at which the early *Homo sapiens* and other hominid species began to learn how to make and use tools that they could fashion for themselves not only out of wood and bone but also out of the harder varieties of rock around them (particularly flint). During this period even the use of fire may not have been well known.

Palaeolithic Age

The first of the Stone Ages when man was essentially a hunter using somewhat primitive stone or flint implements and weapons.

Palaeozoic Era

The Geological Era that followed the Precambrian, Archaeozoic, or Proterozoic Era and was in turn succeeded by the Mesozoic or Secondary Era, corresponding roughly to between 590 and 248 million years ago. The Era is characterised by those very early forms of organic life now found as fossils within rock strata – ferns and fern-like trees – among which roamed early insects, primitive reptiles, and amphibians still emerging from seas inhabited by primitive fishes. During the Era, the seas rose until much of the land surface was covered and the most numerous species were fishes; by the end of the Era, it was still marine and near-marine animals – the molluscs, anthropods, and brachiopods – that were most numerous, although the waters had by then receded once more; see Geological Time Divisions.

Palio

2 July and 16 August, when jockeys dressed in mediaeval costume honour the Virgin Mary by racing bareback around the main square of Siena, Italy.

Palm Sunday

Any Sunday between 15 March and 18 April; the last Sunday of Lent marks Christ's entry into Jerusalem when His way was lined by palm branches. It is the Sunday before Easter Sunday.

Palmy days

Prosperous or happy days.

Palynology

The study of plant pollens and spores; banks of fossil specimens of known age are continually being developed, enabling further specimens to be dated as they are studied.

Pancake day
Shrove Tuesday, when pancakes are traditionally eaten, a custom arising from the need to finish up food before the Lenten fast; in some places pancake making became, or has become, a tradition and pancake races are held wherein the participants have to run towards the finishing line tossing a pancake in a frying pan as they go.

Parsec
A unit of astronomical distance equal to the distance from earth at which a length of 1 astronomical unit (AU = 1.496×10^{11} metres; 0.000016 light-years) subtends an angle of 1 second of arc:
206,265 AU
3.262 light-years
3.0857×10^{13} km
1.92×10^{13} miles.

Paschal Lamb, Festival of
See Pesach.

Passion Sunday
The Sunday before Palm Sunday.

Passover
See Pesach.

Patrick's Day, St
The national day of Ireland, celebrated on 17 March.

Patriots' Day
In the USA, the anniversary of the battle of Lexington, 19 April 1775, the first battle in the War of Independence.

Paush
Tenth month of the Hindu year.

Pavarana Day
The day marking the end of Vassa, the Rains retreat.

Peiron Boat Race
Japanese festival held in Nagasaki, Nagasaki Prefecture, in mid-June, when races are held between long, narrow boats manned by up to 36 oarsmen; the races are believed to have been introduced from southern China; 'peiron' is derived from the Chinese word for 'dragon'.

Penitence, Days of
In the Jewish calendar, 1–10 Tishri; 1 and 2 Tishri constitute Rosh Hashanah (New Year); 3 Tishri is Tzom Gedaliah, the Fast to commemorate the assassination of the Judean governor Gedaliah in 585BCE; 10 Tishri is Yom Kippur: the Day of Atonement.

Pendulum

A body suspended from a fixed point so as to swing freely periodically under the action of gravity and commonly used to regulate movements, *eg* of clockwork. Galileo (who made exhaustive studies of phenomena due to gravity) observed a lamp swinging in Siena Cathedral in about 1580, and realised that the period of the swing was independent of the amplitude – that if the swing was greater, the suspended object moved faster to complete its swing in the same period of time. And this, he saw, could be a means of regulating a clock.

The period of swing, in seconds, is equal to $2\pi \bullet (l/g)$ (l = length from suspension point to centre of gravity of bob (pendulum weight); g = acceleration due to gravity; use whatever compatible units you prefer).

The Dutch physicist Christiaan Huygens designed a pendulum clock in 1656; he found that in fact swings through greater arcs took longer than those through lesser ones, and that ideally the bob should swing in a cycloidal arc. Huygens achieved this effect by causing the suspension spring to work between cycloidal cheeks, but unfortunately introduced other inaccuracies that mitigated the cycloidal advantages.

Pennsylvanian or Upper Carboniferous Epoch

The second of the two Epochs that make up the Carboniferous Period, known outside North America as the Upper Carboniferous. During this time club-mosses and horsetails formed swampy forests that were later to become the coal and oil deposits of today; see Geological Time Divisions.

Pensioner Parliament

See Cavalier Parliament.

Pentecost (Whit Sunday)

7th Sunday after Easter Sunday; thus any Sunday between 10 May and 13 June. It commemorates the descent of the Holy Spirit upon the apostles; its English name 'Whit' Sunday is said to come from 'White' Sunday in reference to the white robes worn by the newly baptised. Whit Monday is also a public holiday in some Christian countries. In England, Whit Monday has been dumbed down to 'Spring Holiday'.

Pentecost (Jewish Festival)

See Shavuot.

Per annum; – diem

Per annum – Latin = yearly; per year. *Per diem* – Latin = per day; each day.

Per diem

When on the road, a daily sustenance allowance paid to members of the band and the road crew; it is generally not taxable, but on most days there is more free food than you can possibly eat, so the per diem's a useful perk.

Perennial

Throughout the year, lasting at least one a year.

Period

In geology, a subdivision of an Era; Periods themselves are divided into Epochs.

Permian Period

The last Period of the Palaeozoic or Primary Era, immediately following the Upper Carboniferous or Pennsylvanian Epoch, and followed by the Triassic Period of the Mesozoic Era, corresponding roughly to between 286 million years ago and 248 million years ago. It was characterised by severe glaciation of the land-masses of the Southern Hemisphere, and the cold may well also have contributed to the extinction of the previously numerous trilobites. As it was, those animals that left the water and went on to land survived best, especially the reptiles whose later dominance is well known. Similarly, the swamp-loving ferns and club-mosses of the Carboniferous were quickly replaced by forests of dry-land conifers. In Europe, because of the difficulty in distinguishing the effects, it is common to merge the Permian and Triassic Periods into the Permo-Triassic System; see **Geological Time Divisions**.

Perpetual calendar

A minimal table for finding a maximum number of dates; see **Part 3**.

Person-day

Formerly man-day (as if women didn't work); the amount of effort extracted from one person working for a day, constituting a unit for calculating costs and schedules in relation to output. Although building a bridge might take 1,000,000 person-days, the effort is more likely to come from 1,000 people working for 1,000 days (four years (of 250 days)) than one person working 1,000,000 days (4,000 years). So also person-shift, person-hour and person-year.

Pesach

Jewish Feast of Passover; aka the Festival of the Matzot; the Festival of the Paschal Lamb; the Season of our Freedom; Spring Festival; in the

Jewish calendar, a Pilgrim Festival commemorating the deliverance of the Jews from Egyptian bondage, and thus the birth of the Hebrew nation; it is also the Festival of Spring. it is kept for eight days (seven in Israel) from 15 Nisan. The four middle days are semi-holy days known as Weekdays of the Festival.

Pesach Sheni
In the Jewish calendar, Second Passover celebrated by those ritually impure or absent on a journey during Pesach; it is observed on 14 Iyyar.

Phalgun
Twelfth month of the Hindu year.

Phanerozoic
That time-span in the Earth's history incorporated by the Palaeozoic, Mesozoic, and Cenozoic Eras from about 590 million years ago to the present day. It is so called because only in these Eras is there evidence of major geological change and organic evolution; see **Geological Time Divisions**.

Phœnix period or cycle
At the end of its life, the legendary phœnix builds a nest of spices in Arabia, sings a melodious dirge, flaps its wings to set fire to the nest, burns itself to ashes, and comes forth with new life, only to repeat the former one. There are various estimates for the life cycle of the phœnix: Tacitus gives 250 years; R. Stuart Poole 1,460 (Julian years, like the Sothic Cycle); Lipsius 1,500 years. However, the Phœnix is said to have appeared in Egypt five times: (1) in the reign of Sesostris; (2) in the reign of Am-asis; (3) in the reign of Ptolemy Philadelphos; (4) a year or two before the death of Tiberius; and (5) during the reign of Constantine in 334CE. This suggests that the phœnix cycle is 300 years.

Photographic emulsion speed
A measure of the rapidity of response of a photographic emulsion to light; see **Film Speed**.

Phrase
A group of musical notes forming a natural unit of melody that is usually three of four bars in length, and may last between 5 and 10 seconds.

Picnic Day

A day fit for going on a picnic, likely to be a holiday such as 4 July in the US or August Bank Holiday in Britain. In Australia, picnic races are for amateur riders in rural areas.

Picosecond

A millionth of a millionth of a second; 10^{-12} s; see **Units of Time**.

Piece work

That which is paid for by tasks completed, rather than by time taken (time work, *qv*).

Pilate, Pontius

Regarded as a martyr by the Coptic Church, his feast day is 25 June.

Pisces

(Latin = the Fishes); twelfth sign of the zodiac; 19/20 February – 20 March; first southern (austral) sign – first winter sign – ascending sign; see **Zodiac**.

Plaisancian

A Stage in the Pliocene Epoch; see **Geological Time Divisions**.

Plastochron

In biology, a unit of developmental progress; an interval between stages of progressive organic development.

Pleistocene Epoch

The earlier of the two Epochs of the Quaternary Period when, some 2–3 million years ago, hominids appeared on the surface of the Earth (although mammals had been present for many millions of years already). It is characterised by at least four ice ages although, because the present Holocene Epoch is reckoned to have begun only about 10,000 years ago, it may turn out to be one of the ordinary periods of remission between ice ages within an ongoing Pleistocene Epoch. Flatter areas of northern Europe, Asia and Canada still show the marks of the severe glaciation of the Pleistocene ice ages, notably in the multiplicity of lakes and low ridges; see **Geological Time Divisions**.

Pliocene Epoch

The last geological Epoch of the Tertiary Period of the Cenozoic Era, corresponding roughly to between 5 million and 2-3 million years ago. During this Epoch the average temperature at the planetary surface began the long decline towards freezing cold of the ice ages that were to characterise the succeeding Pleistocene Epoch (vs). The result was the lowering of sea-levels around the world, and the migration of animals to warmer climates, some wandering from one continent to another. Mammals excelled at such migration – among them, the anthropoid apes that were the ancestors of humankind. The Miocene and Pliocene Epochs are sometimes together known as the Neocene; the two Epochs together with the Pleistocene and Holocene Epochs of the Quarternary Period are sometimes known as the Neogene; see **Geological Time Divisions**.

Plough Festival

A festival where a plough race is held in the common fields, each contestant being allowed to sow the land he succeeded in ploughing. The modern equivalent is the ploughing match, for both tractor- and horse-drawn ploughs, and a fine sight it is too – especially if there is a plethora of heavy horses and a demonstration of a pair of ploughing engines.

Ploughing Festival (Buddhist)

See **Raek Na**.

Plough Monday

The first Monday after Twelfth Night, when the plough festival was held, especially by the mid-C15. Plough boys would also drag a plough around their neighbourhood to collect money from residents and passers-by.

Pluvôise

(Rainy); fifth month of the French Revolutionary Calendar *qv*.

Plygain

Welsh candlelit assembly before dawn on Christmas Day.

PM; pm

Latin *post meridiem* = after noon.

Poisson d'avril

French = April fish; the Gallic equivalent of April Fool.

Pongal

Hindu Festival marking the harvest in Southern India; in the Gregorian calendar it falls in January.

Poets' Day

Facetious epithet for Friday, especially in the workplace (Piss Off Early, Tomorrow's Saturday).

Post

Prefix denoting 'after'. Example: post-meridian – after midday, *ie* the afternoon (*cf* ante- and pre- = before).

Poya Day

See **Uposatha**.

Prairial

(Meadows); ninth month of the French Revolutionary Calendar *qv*.

Prayer Time

To pray is to speak reverently to God or a god in order to express thanks, make a request or deliver a set text by means of a prayer. In Muslim countries or communities, everything stops five times a day for prayers, as signalled from the Mosque. Prayer times vary according to latitude and longitude, and the times of sunrise and sunset. The sequence is: Dawn Prayer, Noon Prayer, Afternoon Prayer, Sunset Prayer and Night Prayer.

Pre-

1 Earlier than; prior to, as in *prehistoric*.
2 In advance; beforehand, as in *prefabricate*; preparatory to, as in *premedical*.
3 Situated in front of; anterior to, as in *premolar*.

Precambrian or Pre-Cambrian or Archaeozoic or
Proterozoic Era

In the history of the planet Earth, the extended period during which only primitive life forms existed. The Solar System came into existence some 4,600 million years ago; the earliest fossils with hard parts giving evidence of life date from about 590 million years ago, at the beginning of the Cambrian Period of the Palaeozoic or Primary Era. Between stretched the Precambrian Era; evidence of the geological events of that era is visible at sites in Northern Canada, western England, Finland, Scotland, and Sweden, and in many different areas of Africa; see Geological Time Divisions.

Pre-Columbian

In American history, the time before the arrival of Christopher Columbus in 1492.

Predynastic Egypt

In the history of ancient Egypt, before 3100BCE – when dynastic rule became the norm.

Pre-exilic/exilian

In the history of the ancient Israelites, before 586BCE, when the Israelites were deported en masse to (the Exile in) Babylon.

Prehistory

That period of history before written records, known only through artefacts and fossils.

President's Day

An American holiday on 16 February.

Preston Guild, once every

Not very often. Preston Guild meetings have been held every 20 years since 1542 (save that the 1942 meeting was deferred until 1952), on the first Monday after the Feast of the Decollation of St John the Baptist (*ie* the Last Monday in August); the next will be in 2012 'and the inhabitants of Proud Preston, England's newest city, are already looking forward to that day with eager anticipation'.

Primæval/Primeval

Describing the earliest times (particularly the earliest ages in the history of the planet Earth). It is from the 'Primeval Sludge' that some say life developed.

Primary or Palaeozoic Era

One of the four geological Eras; see **Geological Time Divisions**.

Primidi

The first day of the French Revolutionary week; see **French Revolutionary Calendar**.

Primordial

Describing the earliest state or condition (particularly the first stage in the geological history of the planet Earth).

Primrose Day

19 April, the anniversary of the death of Benjamin Disraeli (1804–81), Lord Beaconsfield, to whose funeral HM Queen Victoria sent a wreath of primroses from Osborne: 'His favourite flowers'; not true, but the idea caught on in the name of the Conservative League founded in 1883.

Proclamation Day

The day on which something of public importance is proclaimed.

Proterozoic

See **Precambrian**.

Protolithic

See **Eolithic**.

Prox.

Short for the Latin *proximo* = the next (month); from the mid-1500s to perhaps the 1970s a common method of referring to dates of the next month in formal correspondence, the expression is now rapidly becoming obsolete, and is generally regarded as stylistically questionable (*cf* Ult. and Inst.)

PST

Pacific Standard Time; see **Time Zones**.

Ptolemaic System

Ptolemy's C2 system to account for the apparent motion of the heavenly bodies. He believed in a geocentric universe with 'the heavens' revolving from east to west, in which there were spheres, each with its own period of rotation, bearing the sun, the planets and the fixed stars. The tenth, outer, sphere was the *primum mobile* that carried all the others. The whole thing was somewhat like a geocentric orrery, and made sweet sounds to boot: the 'music of the spheres' (*vi*). The heliocentric Copernican System, was introduced by Nicholas Copernicus (1473–1543), but was prohibited by the RC church in 1616. Galileo (1564–1642) was no mean astronomer, and affirmed the truth of the Copernican System in 1632; this brought him before the Inquisition which caused him to recant (but uttering under his breath, it is said, 'Eppur si muove' = 'and yet it [the earth] moves'). It's this sort of man-delivered short-sightedness that brings God into disrepute.

Ptolemaic
Pertaining to
1. Ptolemy, C2 Egyptian astronomer, mathematician, and geographer.
2. The Ptolemaic system.
3. The Graeco–Egyptian Ptolemies who ruled Egypt from 323BCE to 30BCE.

Public holidays
A day on which all (or most) shops, offices and factories are (or were) closed for a holiday; today, with the rise of home computing, DIY, and gardening, more people shop on public holidays than ever before.

Purim
In the Jewish calendar, the Festival of Lots celebrates the deliverance of the Persian Jews from the evil Haman in C5 BCE. It is named after the lots cast by Haman to decide when to institute the slaughter of the Persian Jews, and falls on 14–15 Adar, or 14–15 Ve-Adar in a leap year.

Quaaltagh
See **First Foot**.

Quadragesima
The forty days of Lent.

Quadrennial
Once every four years; lasting four years.

Quarantine

The period, originally forty days, that a ship suspected of being infected with some contagious disorder is obliged to lie off port. Now applied to any period of segregation to prevent infection, particularly relating to animals.

Quartan

Recurring every fourth day, inclusively – that is, with two days' interval between recurrences, or every 72 hours. Fevers symptomatic of some tropical diseases (notably malaria) recur like this.

Quart d'heure, Un mauvais

A bad quarter of an hour. Used for a short, disagreeable experience. In the film *The Prime of Miss Jean Brodie*, the headmistress of Marcia

---

Quarter Days

Days dividing a year into four 13-week periods, on which rents become due:

1   New Style: Lady Day (25 March)
                     Midsummer Day (24 June)
                     Michaelmas Day (29 September)
                     Christmas Day (25 December).

2   Old Style: Lady Day (6 April)
                     Old Midsummer Day (6 July)
                     Old Michaelmas Day (11 October)
                     Old Christmas Day (6 January).

Half-quarter days fall on:
                     Candlemas (2 February)
                     9 May
                     11 August
                     Martinmas (11 November).

In Scotland, old quarter days were:
                     Candlemas Day (2 February)
                     Whitsunday (15 May)
                     Lammas Day (1 August)
                     Martinmas Day (11 November).

And new quarter days:
                     Candlemas (28 February)
                     Whitsuntide (date varies)
                     Lammas (28 August)
                     Martinmas (28 November).

Blane High School for Girls summons Miss Brodie to a meeting at quarter to eleven; Miss Brodie observes: 'She seeks to intimidate me by the use of quarter hours;' perhaps she had *un mauvais quart d'heure* in mind.

Quarter Hour
1   A period of 15 minutes.
2   Specifically quarter to or quarter past a stated hour; see **Quart d'heure, Un mauvais**.

Quarter Sessions
From mid-C14 Justices of the Peace sat four times a year in Quarter Sessions to deal with appeals from the more-frequent Petty Sessions, criminal charges, and some civil cases, as well as administrative work.

Quarterly
Every three months.

Quartidi
Fourth day of the French Revolutionary week; see **French Revolutionary Calendar**.

Quasimodo Sunday
The first Sunday after Easter, or Low Sunday, when the Introit at Mass begins: *Quasi modo geniti infantes*.

Quasquicentennial/quasquicentenary
Of 125 years; the term is American and is derived by analogy with the regular English word *sesquicentenary/sesquicentennial*, 'of 150 years', which is based on Latin *sesqui–* '(one-)and-a-half' + 'century'. 'Quasqui-' is an attempt at constructing an element to mean 'one-and-a-quarter'.

Quaternary Period
The present geological period which began between 3 and 2 million years ago, so-called because it follows the Tertiary Period. It comprises the glacial Pleistocene Epoch (the ice ages) followed by the post-glacial Holocene Epoch. The Quaternary Period is that during which first humanoids, and now humans, have lived on the earth; thus its beginning is constantly being redefined as evidence accumulates for earlier human ancestry; see **Geological Time Divisions**.

Queen Anne
Daughter of James II and his first wife Anne Hyde. She was born on 6 February 1665, and succeeded William III on 8 March 1702; she died 1 August 1714. She gives her name to a certain style of design and decoration in architecture, furniture, etc.

Queen's Birthday
It is customary for the British sovereign to have an official birthday for ceremonial purposes about the middle of June, apart from his or her actual birthday.

Queen's Day
17 November, the day of the accession of Queen Elizabeth I.

Quinquagenarian
Someone aged between 50 and 59, in his or her fifties.

Quinquagesima
Shrove Sunday, or the Sunday of the week that contains Ash Wednesday. It is so called because in round numbers it is the fiftieth day before Easter.

Quinquennial
Once every five years; lasting for five years.

Quintan
Recurring every fifth day, inclusively – that is, with three days' interval between recurrences, or every 96 hours. Fevers symptomatic of some tropical diseases such as malaria recur like this.

Quintidi
Fifth day of the French Revolutionary week; see French Revolutionary Calendar.

Quotidian
Daily; liable to occur or recur every day. In medical practice, this term describes a fever that may recur irregularly but frequently.

Rabîa I
Third month of the Muslim calendar, qv.

Rabîa II
Fourth month of the Muslim calendar, qv.

Raek Na (The Ploughing Festival)
Held at half full moon in Thailand in May, when two white oxen pull a gold-painted plough, followed by four girls dressed in white scattering rice seeds from gold and silver baskets, to celebrate the Buddha's first moment of enlightenment, when he went to watch the ploughing with his father at the age of seven.

Railway time
As the railways began to spread over the land, they found it necessary to run to a timetable which operated to a standard (railway) time, rather than to the numerous local times then usual. Fortunately, the

developing telegraph made it relatively easy to synchronise time-pieces; see **Standard time**.

Rajab
Seventh month of the Muslim calendar, *qv*.

Raksha Bandhan
Old Hindu Festival when sisters give brothers wristbands to ward off evil spirits; in the Gregorian calendar it falls in July–August.

Ramadan
The ninth month of the Muslim calendar; that of fasting in honour of Muhammad's flight from Mecca in 622CE. During this month, Muslims do not eat, drink, smoke or take part in sexual activity from dawn till dusk until the Imam announces that Ramadan is over and the festival of *Is-al-Fitr* begins; see **Muslim calendar**.

Ramakrishna Utsav
A Hindu Festival for the Hindu Saint Ramakrishna; in the Gregorian calendar it falls in February–March.

Ramanavami
A Hindu Festival celebrating the birth of Shi Rama with sanctity and fasting; in the Gregorian calendar it falls in March–April.

Ratha-yatra
See **Jagannatha**.

Raviwar
(Sunday); First day of the Hindu week.

Real Time (n), Real-time (adj)
Denoting that something is happening now, rather than being replayed after storage; hence real-time (as opposed to time-shift (*qv*)) TV viewing, or a computer processing data as presented, rather than from storage.

Récompenses, La Fête des
Rewards Day; see **French Revolutionary Calendar**.

Red Letter Day
A lucky day; a day to be recalled with delight. In ecclesiastical calendars important feast days and saints' days were illuminated (now printed) in red (rubrication), other days in black.

Regency Period
Period in Great Britain between 1811 and 1820, during which George, Prince of Wales (later King George IV), acted as regent for his father King George III, who was unable to reign due to mental imbalance (now thought to be) caused by the disease porphyria. George IV

acceded to the throne on 29 January 1820 and died (of alcoholic cirrhosis) on 26 June 1830.

Regency style

1 In Britain, the style relating to the Regency Period, *vs.*
2 In France, that relating to the period from 1715 to 1723, during which Philippe, Duke of Orléans (nephew of the 'Sun King' Louis XIV), acted as regent for the child Louis XV until he came of age.

Regilius

In Ancient Rome, the Battle of Lake Regilius was commemorated by a fête held on 15 July.

Regular year

See Jewish calendar.

Rejoicing, The Season of our

See Sukkot.

Release Group

A British National Service indication of when one would be discharged after 18 months' or two years' service. There were two intakes every month, on Thursdays, so 5304 would indicate someone serving from Thursday 19 February 1953 to Thursday 17 February 1955. 'Gripping' was the name given to the practice of gloating: 'My release date's earlier than yours', shortened to 'I can grip you'.

Remembrance Day (Jewish)

See Yom H'zikharon.

Remembrance Sunday

After World War I, Armistice day, or Remembrance Day, commemorating the fallen, was observed on 11 November. From 1945 to 1956 Remembrance Sunday was observed instead on the first or second Sunday of November, commemorating the fallen of World Wars I and II. In 1956 it was fixed as the second Sunday of November; it may therefore fall on any date between 8 and 14 November. The Armistice was signed at the eleventh hour of the eleventh day of the eleventh month (1918), and there is a widely-observed two-minute silence marked in London by ceremonial gunfire on Big Ben's first stroke of eleven, and another firing two minutes after.

Renaissance

Describing the style and culture in Europe during the 1400s and 1500s – a period when there was a great rebirth (French *renaissance*) of interest in the sciences and a flowering of art and architecture.

Regnal year

A year beginning with the date of a monarch's accession, used until fairly recently (1962) for dating statutes and for other legal purposes. In earlier times, the use of the regnal year was the normal way of expressing a given year – hence Domesday Book was ordered in the 23rd year of the reign of King William, rather than 1089. The following table shows the start and finish of the regnal years for most monarchs since William I; there is more detail as needed for the less straightforward entries.

Year of reign	Monarch	Beginning	Ending	Note
1	William I	25 December 1066	24 December 1067	A
21	William I	25 December 1086	9 September 1087	
1	William II	26 September 1087	25 September 1088	A
13	William II	26 September 1099	2 August 1100	
1	Henry I	5 August 1100	4 August 1101	A
36	Henry I	5 August 1135	1 December 1135	
1	Stephen	22 December 1135	21 December 1136	B
19	Stephen	22 December 1153	25 October 1154	
1	Henry II	19 December 1154	18 December 1155	A
35	Henry II	19 December 1188	6 July 1189	
1	Richard I	3 September 1189	2 September 1190	A
10	Richard I	3 September 1198	6 April 1199	
1	John	27 May 1199	17 May 1200	C
2	John	18 May 1200	2 May 1201	
3	John	3 May 1201	22 May 1202	
4	John	23 May 1202	14 May 1203	
5	John	15 May 1203	2 June 1204	
6	John	3 June 1204	18 May 1205	
7	John	19 May 1205	10 May 1206	
8	John	11 May 1206	30 May 1207	
9	John	31 May 1207	14 May 1208	
10	John	15 May 1208	6 May 1209	
11	John	7 May 1209	26 May 1210	
12	John	27 May 1210	11 May 1211	
13	John	12 May 1211	2 May 1212	
14	John	3 May 1212	22 May 1213	
15	John	23 May 1213	7 May 1214	
16	John	8 May 1214	27 May 1215	
17	John	28 May 1215	18 May 1216	
18	John	19 May 1216	19 October 1216	
1	Henry III	28 October 1216	27 October 1217	A

Year of reign	Monarch	Beginning	Ending	Note
57	Henry III	28 October 1272	16 November 1272	
1	Edward I	20 November 1272	19 November 1273	A
35	Edward I	20 November 1306	7 July 1307	
1	Edward II	8 July 1307	7 July 1308	
20	Edward II	8 July 1326	20 January 1327	D
1	Edward III	25 January 1327	24 January 1328	A
13	Edward III	25 January 1339	24 January 1340	
14/1	Edward III	25 January 1340	24 January 1341	E
34/21	Edward III	25 January 1360	8 May 1360	E
34	Edward III	9 May 1360	24 January 1361	
43	Edward III	25 January 1369	10 June 1369	E
43/30	Edward III	11 June 1369	24 January 1370	
51/38	Edward III	25 January 1377	21 June 1377	
1	Richard II	22 June 1377	21 June 1378	
23	Richard II	22 June 1399	29 September 1399	
1	Henry IV	30 September 1399	29 September 1400	
14	Henry IV	30 September 1412	20 March 1413	
1	Henry V	21 March 1413	20 March 1414	
10	Henry V	21 March 1422	31 August 1423	
1	Henry VI	1 September 1422	31 August 1423	
39	Henry VI	1 September 1460	4 March 1461	F
1	Edward IV	4 March 1461	3 March 1462	
10	Edward IV	4 March 1470	3 March 1471	
49/1	Henry VI	9 October 1470	14 April 1471	G
11	Edward IV	4 March 1471	3 March 1472	
23	Edward IV	4 March 1483	9 April 1483	
1	Edward V	9 April 1483	25 June 1483	
1	Richard III	26 June 1483	25 June 1484	
3	Richard III	26 June 1485	22 August 1485	
1	Henry VII	22 August 1485	21 August 1486	
24	Henry VII	22 August 1508	21 April 1509	
1	Henry VIII	22 April 1509	21 April 1510	
38	Henry VIII	22 April 1546	28 January 1547	
1	Edward VI	28 January 1547	27 Jan 1548	
7	Edward VI	28 January 1553	6 July 1553	
1	Jane	6 July 1553	19 July 1553	
1	Mary	19 July 1553	5 July 1554	H

Year of reign	Monarch	Beginning	Ending	Note
2	Mary	6 July 1554	24 July 1554	
1/2	Philip & Mary	25 July 1554	5 July 1555	I
1/3	Philip & Mary	6 July 1555	24 July 1555	
2/3	Philip & Mary	25 July 1555	5 July 1556	
2/4	Philip & Mary	6 July 1556	24 July 1556	
3/4	Philip & Mary	25 July 1556	5 July 1557	
3/5	Philip & Mary	6 July 1557	24 July 1557	
4/5	Philip & Mary	25 July 1557	5 July 1558	
4/6	Philip & Mary	6 July 1558	24 July 1558	
5/6	Philip & Mary	25 July 1558	17 November 1558	
1	Elizabeth I	17 November 1558	16 November 1559	
45	Elizabeth I	17 November 1602	23 March 1603	
1/36	James I	24 March 1603	23 July 1603	J
1/37	James I	24 July 1603	23 March 1604	
23/58	James I	24 March 1625	27 March 1625	
1	Charles I	27 March 1625	26 March 1626	
24	Charles I	27 March 1648	30 January 1649	K
1	Charles II	30 January 1649	29 January 1650	
Commonwealth		30 January 1649	29 May 1660	L
37	Charles II	30 January 1685	6 February 1685	
1	James II	6 February 1685	4 February 1686	
4	James II	6 February 1688	11 December 1688	
Interregnum		12 December 1688	12 February 1689	
1	William & Mary	13 February 1689	12 February 1690	
6	William & Mary	13 February 1694	27 December 1694	M
6	William III	28 December 1694	12 February 1695	
14	William III	13 February 1702	8 March 1702	
1	Anne	8 March 1702	7 March 1703	
13	Anne	8 March 1714	1 August 1714	
1	George I	1 August 1714	31 July 1715	
13	George I	1 August 1726	11 June 1727	
1	George II	11 June 1727	10 June 1728	
25	George II	11 June 1751	10 June 1752	
26	George II	11 June 1752	21 June 1753	N
34	George II	22 June 1760	25 October 1760	
1	George III	25 October 1760	24 October 1761	
60	George III	25 October 1819	29 January 1820	

Year of reign	Monarch	Beginning	Ending	Note
1	George IV	29 January 1820	28 January 1821	
11	George IV	29 January 1830	26 June 1830	
1	William IV	26 June 1830	25 June 1831	
7	William IV	26 June 1836	20 June 1837	
1	Victoria	20 June 1837	19 June 1838	
64	Victoria	20 June 1900	22 January 1901	
1	Edward VII	22 January 1901	21 January 1902	
10	Edward VII	22 January 1910	6 May 1910	
1	George V	6 May 1910	5 May 1911	
26	George V	6 May 1935	20 January 1936	
1	Edward VIII	20 January 1936	11 December 1936	O
1	George VI	11 December 1936	10 December 1937	
16	George VI	11 December 1951	16 February 1952	
1	Elizabeth II	6 February 1952	5 February 1953	
10	Elizabeth II	6 February 1961	5 February 1962	P

A Date of coronation.
B Date of coronation according to William of Malmesbury.
C John was crowned on Ascension Day, and his regnal years follow that movable date.
D Edward II deposed.
E In 1340, Edward III asserted his claim to the crown of France, and added his French regnal years to his English ones. He renounced his claim to the crown of France in 1360, and re-asserted it in 1369.
F Henry VI deposed; Edward IV accepted.
G Short-lived restoration of Henry VI.
H Mary ignored Jane and backdated the start of her reign to 6 July.
I Mary married Philip of Naples and Jerusalem, and later Spain; he was never crowned king of England.
J James (1st and 6th) acceded to the Scottish throne on 24 July 1567.
K Charles I was beheaded on 30 January 1649; it was assumed that Charles II succeeded on that date.
L Oliver Cromwell took over until his death on 3 September 1658; his heir Richard Cromwell abdicated on 24 May 1659; Parliament and the Army then governed until Charles II was restored to the throne on 29 May 1660.
M Queen Mary died during the night of 27–28 December 1694.
N The year in which the 11 days were omitted.
O Edward VIII abdicated on 11 December 1936.
P Since 1962, Acts of Parliament have been dated by calendar years. However, the anniversary of the accession of a monarch is still clearly of interest during that monarch's reign.

Restoration period
1   In Britain, the relaxed period after the Commonwealth collapsed and Charles II took the throne; it was marked by a general flowering of science and the arts (particularly Restoration Comedy).
2   In France, the attempt to restore the royal house of Bourbon after the fall of Napoleon (1815).

Revolutionary Calendar
See French Revolutionary Calendar.

Revolution, La Fête de la
Revolution Day; Leap Year Day; see French Revolutionary Calendar.

Rhaetian
A Stage in the Triassic Period; see Geological Time Divisions.

Rhythm
1   The pattern of recurrent alternation of strong and weak or long and short elements in the flow of sound, especially in music and speech; rhythm is superimposed on the tempo, or beat.
2   The pace of the interaction of the elements in a play, novel, film, painting, etc.

Riss
The third of the Ice Ages that occurred in Europe during the Pleistocene Epoch; see also Günz, Mindel, and Würm, and Geological Time Divisions.

Rock Day
7 January, also called St Distaff's Day; the day after twelfth day when the women returned to their distaffs (also called rocks).

Rococo
A European decorative style of architecture, furniture, etc that emerged in France in early C18, characterised by heavy ornamentation that can become overpowering.

Rogation ceremonies
Ceremonies carried out in May to bless orchards, mainly carried out in Kent; another custom was (and is) to beat the bounds of the parish.

Rogation Days
Rogation Sunday is the Sunday before Ascension Day, the Rogation Days are the Monday, Tuesday and Wednesday following Rogation Sunday.

Rolling period
1   In planning events, a rolling period looks ahead for, say, five years, and the plans are updated every so often so that they are always looking (about) five years ahead.

2   The time a ship takes to roll (from an upright position, to one side, then over to the other side, and back upright).

Roman Empire

The Empire was established by the Emperor Augustus in 27BCE, and lasted until 475CE.

Romantic Movement

A literary movement that began in Germany at the end of C18, and spread through revolutionary France, and England; it sought to put an end to literary formalism, and move towards romanticism.

Roman Year

From 153BCE, the Roman year officially began on 1 January.

Rose Sunday

The fourth Sunday in Lent.

Rosh Hashanah

New Year; The Day of Judgement; The Day of Memorial; The Day of Sounding the Shofar (ram's horn); in the Jewish calendar, a High Festival marking the Jewish New Year on 1–2 Tishri.

Rosh Hodesh

In the Jewish calendar, a monthly Festival celebrating the new moon.

Royal houses

In England/Great Britain:

927–1066	Cedric and Denmark
1066–1135	Normandy
1135–1154	Blois
1154–1485	Anjou or Plantagenet
1495–1603	Tudor
1603–1689	Stuart
1689–1702	Stuart and Orange
1702–1714	Stuart
1714–1901	Hanover and Brunswick-Lüneburg
1901–1917	Saxe-Coburg and Gotha
1917–	Windsor

Royal Oak Day

See Oak Apple Day.

Rump Parliament
In Cromwell's time, the remnant of the Long Parliament, that abolished the monarchy and the House of Lords.

Running Thursday
13 December 1688, two days after the flight of James II, when many people ran into the country in fear of French and Irish papists.

Running Time
The length of time a stage performance takes, not including intervals (intermissions). It may vary from one performance to another, depending on the pace of the actors and the response of the audience.

Rush-bearing Sunday
A Sunday generally near the festival of the Saint to whom a church is dedicated, when the rushes on the floor might be renewed. At St Anne's Ambleside a rush-bearing procession is held on the Saturday nearest St Anne's Day (26 July).

S; s
Sabbath, Saturday, September, Sunday; second. Note that 'sec' is not the preferred abbreviation for 'second' (*ie* one-sixtieth of a minute).

Sabbath

(Heb *shabath* = to cease from work)
1   Having made and equipped the Earth, God rested on the seventh day; the Jewish Sabbath is sunset Friday to sunset Saturday, a day for refreshing the spirit and taking part in religious activity. No work is to be done, but an exception is made if life is in danger. There are four Special Sabbaths: *The S of the Shekels* (S before 1 Adar, or on 1 Adar if it's a S), *The S of Remembrance* (S before Purim), *The S of the Red Heifer* (S after Purim), *The S of the Month* (S before 1 Nisan, or on 1 Nisan if it's a S). Note also *The Great S* (immediately before the Festival of Pesach), *The S of the Vision* (Preceding the Fast of Av), *The S of Comfort* (the S following 9 Av), *The S of Repentance* (between Rosh Hashanah (New Year) and Yom Kippur (the Day of Atonement)), and the S following the Feast of Tabernacles.
2   Gentiles may speak of 'the Sabbath' meaning 'Sunday' especially in the Rotarian patois known as 'Home Counties banter'.
3   Witches' Sabbath: a midnight-to-dawn meeting of witches, demons and hangers-on led by the coven (12 witches and a devil) held on All Hallows' Eve, Candlemas, Lammas, and Roodmas.

Sabbatical Year

1 One year in seven, when all the land, according to Mosaic law, was to lie fallow (Exod 23).
2 In education, especially in universities, a sabbatical year gives a member of staff time off to study or travel. The term has gained wider currency in industry, and has been reduced to 'taking a sabbatical' (*cf* 'an en-suite').

Sad Palm Sunday

The battle of Towton, the bloodiest of the Wars of the Roses, was fought on Sunday 29 March 1461; more than 30,000 men fell that day.

Safar

Second month of the Muslim calendar, *qv*.

Sagittarius

(Latin = the Archer); ninth sign of the zodiac; 22/23 November – 21/22 December; third southern (austral) sign – third autumn sign – sixth descending sign; see Zodiac.

Saikusa no Matsuri (Lily Festival)

Japanese ceremony dating from at least C8 held at Isakawa Shrine, Sakurai, Nara Prefecture, on 17 June, when shrine maidens, holding lilies and dressed in white kimonos with red skirts, dance in honour of the Shrine's deity; there is also a procession of priests and parishioners holding bunches of lilies.

Saining

A C18 Shetland Islanders' ritual intended to safeguard people and property against the powers loose in that time of darkness, and during the coming year.

Saint's or Saints' Day

In the Christian Church, a day for commemorating a particular saint or saints.

Salad Days

The days of one's youth, 'cos one is 'green'. Through association with the Julian Slade musical of that title, the term also seems to recall the carefree living of those endless summers of the 1950s.

Samhain

31 October – One of ancient Celtic quarter days.

Sand glass, hour glass or egg-timer

A device for measuring an exact period of time, involving two glass bulbs connected by a narrow waist through which sand (or other fine granular material) runs from the upper to the lower. In an hourglass, the sand takes precisely one hour to empty completely from the upper bulb into the lower. A sandglass may be timed to last for a longer or shorter duration, and an egg-timer generally has a maximum period of six minutes; usually less. The ancient Greeks used sand glasses as we do today – for measuring cooking times, particularly when boiling eggs. The art of blowing glass was revived at the end of C8 by the monk Luitrand of Chartres, and the sand glass took on a new lease of life. In C14, the practice of paying workmen by the hour was introduced, and hour glasses were again in demand.

The particles in the glass must be perfectly dry (powdered eggshell, marble dust or sand) and carefully sieved so that they are all about the same size. The hole through which they flow should be about ten times the diameter of the particles. The rate of flow is irrespective of the amount waiting to pass through, and the air displaced from the lower to the upper chamber finds its way through the particles so that there is no back pressure. The aesthetic properties of the sand glass have also been remarked: its silent running, and the shape of the conical pile below echoing that of the conical depression above.

Sangamon

Describing the period of time regarded as the third interglacial stage of the Pleistocene Epoch in North America. The term derives from the names of a river in Illinois; see Geological Time Divisions.

Sangha Day

See Magha Puja Day.

Sanja Matsuri

Japanese festival held at Sanja Asakusa Shrine, Tokyo, on the Saturday or Sunday nearest 17–18 May when there is a parade of about 100 portable shrines, and geisha dance.

Sanno Matsuri

Japanese festival held in odd-numbered years to honour the deities of Sanno Hie Shrine, Tokyo, on 10–16 June, when portable shrines (two from the Sanno Hie and others from round about) are paraded through the streets of Chuo and Chiyoda wards.

Sansculottides or Sans-Culottides, Les

See French Revolutionary Calendar.

Saphar

See Muslim calendar.

Sapporo Yuki Matsuri (Sapporo Snow Festival)

Japanese non-religious festival held at Sapporo, Hokkaido, on the first Friday to Sunday in February, when there is a competition for large snow and ice sculptures in Odori Park, Sapporo.

SAT
South Australian Time; see Time Zones.

Saturday
See Week.

Saturnalia
The feast of Saturn in the Roman calendar, in the days after 17 December.

Saxonian
A Stage in the Permian Period; see Geological Time Divisions.

SC
Solar Cycle.

Scheiner system
See Film speed.

Scorpio
(Latin = the Scorpion); eighth sign of the zodiac; 23/24 October – 21/22 November; second southern (austral) sign – second autumn sign – fifth descending sign; see Zodiac.

Season of our Freedom
See Pesach.

Season, The London
The part of the year when the Court and fashionable society generally is (or was) in town – May, June, July.

Seasonal beginning
The seasons traditionally begin on Candlemas (Spring), May Day (Summer), Lammas (Autumn) and All Saints' Day (Winter).

Sec, sec
Non-preferred abbreviation for second (period of time), but usable colloquially: 'Half a sec ...!'

Second
The fundamental unit of time. The 13th CGPM (Conférence Générale des Poids et Mesures 1968) defined the SI second as the duration of 9,192,631,770 periods of the radiation corresponding to the transition between two hyperfine levels of the ground state of the caesium–133 atom. Before that, it was the unit of time identical to the astronomical second of ephemeris time (now called the ephemeris second): 1/31 556 925.9747 of the tropical year 1900. See Units of Time.

Secondary or Mesozoic Era
One of the four geological eras; see Geological Time Divisions.

Seasons

The four seasons in the northern hemisphere are astronomically speaking:

Spring
From the vernal equinox (20 March) to the summer solstice (21 June in 1982).

Summer
From the summer solstice (21 June) to the autumnal equinox (23 September in 1982).

Autumn
(or Fall in USA) from the autumnal equinox (23 September) to the winter solstice (22 December in 1982).

Winter
From the winter solstice (22 December) to the vernal equinox (20 March in 1982).

In the southern hemisphere, of course, autumn corresponds to spring, winter to summer, spring to autumn, and summer to winter.

The solstices (from Latin *sol*, sun; *stitium*, standing) are the two times in the year when the sun is farthest from the equator and appears to be still. The equinoxes (from Latin *aequus* = equal; *nox* = night) are the two times in the year when day and night are of equal length when the sun crosses the equator.

Segue
(Pron seg-way) a musical production term for the seamless transition from one tune to another.

Sell-by date
A mixed blessing; the date by which a perishable item, such as a food product, must (at least notionally) be sold if it is to be consumed in a fresh or fit state. It is not the same as a use-by or best-before date, which is usually a day or two later, at which time the goods may be reduced in price, or disposed of. The expression has gained a facetious general sense to refer to a person who is 'getting on', so that if one is past one's sell-by date, one is past one's prime.

Semester
(Latin *sex* = six, *mensis* = month) Originally half a year, but now, especially in the US, a term of attendance at school, college, or university.

Different countries have developed educational terms of differing duration; some have two, some three (as in the UK) and some four. In Germany a semester is a half-year of a school or university course, including any holidays (vacations) within that half-year.

Semesterisation
Somewhat clumsy word used to describe playing about with the dates and durations of school or college terms to provide four or even six terms in a year.

Semiannual
1 Once every six months (half-year).
2 Lasting six months.

Semicentenary/semicentennial
A fiftieth anniversary (and its celebration).

Semidiurnal
1 Once every twelve hours (half a day).
2 Lasting for twelve hours.

Senior citizen
A pseudo-polite or euphemistic term for the even less attractively described 'old-age pensioner'.

Sennight
A week: seven nights; *cf* fortnight: fourteen nights.

Senonian
A Stage in the Upper Cretaceous Epoch; see Geological Time Divisions.

September
Ninth month of the Gregorian year (*qv*); named in the Julian calendar from the Latin *septem* (= seven); birthstone: chrysolite or sapphire.

September Massacres
An indiscriminate slaughter during the French Revolution lasting from 2 to 7 September 1792.

Septenary/septennial/septennate
Of the number 7; having 7 as the base; comprising 7 elements; occurring or lasting for 7 years; seventh anniversary (and its celebration).

Septennium
A period of seven years: a synonym for *septennate*.

Septentrional Signs
The first six signs of the zodiac.

Septidi

Seventh day of the French Revolutionary week; see French Revolutionary Calendar.

Septuagenarian

A person who has passed the seventieth birthday, but has not yet reached the eightieth.

Septuagesima

The third Sunday before Lent.

Services midnight

2359hrs, for the avoidance of doubt the time given on a pass at which a leave ends.

Sesquicentenary/sesquicentennial

Of 150 years, (celebrating) a 150th anniversary. The term derives from Latin elements meaning 'one-and-a-half centuries'.

Setsubun

(Bean throwing Night) Japanese families throw beans around their home every 3 February.

Settlers' clock

The Laughing Jackass or Kookaburra, the Australian Great Kingfisher; so called because it tends to utter its cry more especially at sunrise and sunset.

Seven Ages of Man

According to Jaques in Shakespeare's *As You Like It*, II, vii (1599) the seven ages of man are: (1) the infant, (2) the schoolboy, (3) the lover, (4) the soldier, (5) the justice, (6) the pantaloon and (7) second childhood.

Seventh-day Adventists

A sect of Adventists who observe Saturday (seventh day) as their Sabbath; they emerged in 1844 when the expected Second Coming failed; they believe it may happen any time now.

Seventh-day Baptists

A group of German Baptists in the USA who observe Saturday (seventh day) as their Sabbath.

Seven Weeks War

The war between Austria and Prussia, 14 June – 26 July 1866.

Seven Year Itch

1   An informal term for scabies.

2 A term implying that people seek a change of lifestyle every seven years, promoted by the 1955 Billy Wilder film of that name starring Tom Ewell and Marilyn Monroe.

Seven Years War

1756–1763 fought over colonial and commercial rivalries by France, Austria, Russia, Poland, and Sweden against Prussia, Great Britain, and Hanover.

Sexagenarian

A person who has passed his or her sixtieth birthday, but has not yet reached the seventieth.

Sexagesima Sunday

The second Sunday before Lent.

Sexcentenary

Of 600 (elements or constituents); once every 600 years; lasting for 600 years, (celebrating) a 600th anniversary.

Sexennial

Once every six years, lasting for six years; (as a noun, also a *sexennium*) a period of six years, a sixth anniversary.

Sextan

Recurring every sixth day inclusively – that is, with four days between recurrences, or every 120 hours. Fevers symptomatic of various tropical diseases (notably some forms of malaria) recur like this.

Sextidi

Sixth day of the French Revolutionary week; see French Revolutionary Calendar.

Sextilis

See Roman calendar.

Shaabân

Eighth month of the Muslim calendar, *qv*.

Shabâtu

Beating; the Babylonian month from which the Jewish month of Shebat takes its name.

Shadowboard; Shadowstick

Shadowboards (provided with a post to cast a shadow) are still used in Upper Egypt for measuring the time taken to perform tasks, or for timing the distribution of water for irrigation. A water clock is used to calibrate the movement of the shadow.

Shahrivar

Sixth month of the Persian year.

Shaniwar
(Saturday); Seventh day of the Hindu week.

Sharp Thursday
See Maundy Thursday.

Sharvan
Fifth month of the Hindu year.

Shavuot
Pentecost; The Feast of Weeks; The Season of the Giving of the Torah; The Festival of the First Fruits; The Feast of the Harvest; the Concluding Festival: in the Jewish calendar, commemorates the Children of Israel receiving the Law on Mount Sinai; it also marked the beginning of the summer harvest in ancient Palestine. It is held on 6–7 Sivan; in Israel, this Festival occupies only one day.

Shawwâl
Tenth month of the Muslim calendar, *qv*.

Shebat
Eleventh month of the sacred and fifth month of the civil Jewish year. Its name is derived from the Babylonian month Shabâtu; it corresponds roughly to the Gregorian months of January–February; it has 30 days. Tu B'Tebet (the New Year of the Trees) falls on 15 Shebat.

Sheer Thursday
See Maundy Thursday.

Shemini Atzeret
See Sukkot.

Shere Thursday
See Maundy Thursday.

Ship's time
See Bells.

Shiva, Great Night of
See Mahashivrati.

Shivrati
The main Hindu Festival in honour of the god Shiva, characterised by meditation; in the Gregorian calendar it falls in February–March.

Shofar, Day of Sounding the
See Rosh Hashanah.

Shortest day, night
See Day.

Short Parliament

That summoned by Charles I on 13 April 1640; it lasted but 22 days.

Short-swing

In commercial transactions (especially in the United States), describing a period for the completion of a transaction of six months or less.

Shrift Thursday

See Maundy Thursday.

Shrovetide

The three days before Lent.

Shrove Tuesday

Any Tuesday between 3 February and 9 March – Pancake day, the day before Ash Wednesday. This last day before the start of Lent was originally set aside for the confession of sins ('shrove' is the past tense of 'shrive', meaning 'to hear confession'); later, it came to be marked by festivities before the rigours of Lent and is celebrated by carnivals in such countries as Portugal and Brazil and in parts of Germany.

Shroving

Tradition of confessing sins before the beginning of Lent.

Shukla

The 'light fortnight' of a Hindu month (see also Krishna).

Shukrawar

(Friday); Sixth day of the Hindu week.

Shushan Purim

In the Jewish calendar, the day on which Purim (*qv*) was celebrated in the capital Shushan.

Shutter speed

The amount of time that a camera shutter is open; the length of the exposure.

Sidereal time, year

Time counted in terms of the rotation of the Earth relative to distant stars, rather than with respect to the Sun, as in solar time.

Silurian Period

A geological Period during the Palaeozoic or Primary Era. The third Period of the era, immediately following the Ordovician Period, it corresponds roughly to between 438 and 408 million years ago; it was followed by the Devonian period. Life forms of the Silurian period were almost entirely marine – trilobites, primitive slugs and snails, and brachiopods were common, and the first jawed fishes evolved. Plants first appeared on land, and the mountains of Scotland and Scandinavia were formed. The Period is named after the ancient Celtic tribe known to the Romans as Silures, who lived mainly in the area that is now represented by the Welsh counties of Gwent and Glamorgan. Rocks – especially limestones – characteristic of the period are, however, more common in the area that surrounds the southern half of the Wales–England border; see Geological Time Divisions.

Simânu
Babylonian month from whose name the Jewish month of Sivan is derived.

Simhat Torah
In the Jewish calendar, the day for rejoicing in the Torah; it falls on 23 Tishri.

Sinemurian
A Stage in the Lower Jurassic Epoch; see Geological Time Divisions.

Sivan
Third month of the sacred and ninth month of the civil Jewish calendar. Derived from the Babylonian month of Simânu, it corresponds roughly to the Gregorian May–June; it has 30 days. Shavuot (the Feast of Weeks) is held on 6–7 Sivan.

Sleepyhead Day
In the town of Naantali, Finland, the harvest festival begins with Sleepyhead Day, when anyone who has provided a particular service to the town is honoured by being thrown into the Baltic Sea. It must be a great incentive to doing good.

Small Hours (of the morning)
One, two and three after midnight; cliché: wee small hours. Time when bodily strength may be at a low ebb, and death may visit silently.

Snow Hut Festival
See Kamakura Matsuri.

Sol
One Martian day; the length of the day on Mars, specifically 24 hours 37 minutes 22 seconds, corresponding to one rotation of the planet on its axis. There are 669.774 Martian days to 1 Martian year (the equivalent of 686.98 Earth days in time).

Solar cycle; day

The 11.1-year cycle of activity on the Sun's surface, during which sunspots appear and fade, the frequency of solar flares and solar prominences waxes and wanes, and at the end of which the polarity of the Sun's magnetic field reverses. The frequency of an aurora, as sighted on Earth, is similarly linked to the solar cycle.

Solstice

Either of the two times of year when the Sun reaches its most north-westerly (mid-winter) or most south-westerly (mid-summer) position away from the equator, corresponding in the first case to the 'shortest day' of the year (in the Northern Hemisphere, 21 December), and in the second case to the 'longest day' (in the Northern Hemisphere, 21 June). Also, either of a pair of points on the ecliptic that are midway between the equinoxes; see Seasons.

Soma Nomaoi Matsuri (Soma Wild Horse Chase Festival)

Japanese festival, believed to have originated in C10, held at Ota, Nakamura and Kotaka Shrines, Haramachi, Fukushima Prefecture, on 23–25 July, when participants dress as feudal warriors and there are horse races, a parade of horses, a competition among several hundred horsemen for shrine flags, and a wild horse chase.

Somawar

(Monday); Second day of the Hindu week.

Songkran

A Thai Buddhist festival during several hot days in the middle of April, when people clean their houses, wash their clothes and enjoy sprinkling perfumed water on everybody – including monks and novices. People gather on the river bank, carrying fishes rescued from dried-out ponds in jars to put into the water. People splash one another with jars or buckets of water, and when everyone is happily wet there are boat races on the river.

Sothic year/cycle

The Sothic year was the ancient Greek term for the ancient Egyptian year of 365 days, as based on careful measurement of the exact return of the Dog Star, Sirius (Greek *Sothis*), to its position in the night sky at the end of that period. By this measurement, the ancient Egyptians were well aware that the actual year was near enough 365¼ days, but they reckoned that the loss of one day every four years made little or no difference during an individual lifetime (at a time when the average lifespan was less than forty years), and in any case they knew that in 1,460 years – the Sothic cycle (or Sothic period: 4 × 365 years) – the year would have revolved completely back to its original calendar position.

Souling, Soul-caking
Cheshire begging custom, at the beginning of November, similar to Hallowe'en Trick or Treat.

South Australian Time
See Time Zones.

Space Age
The era in which the exploration of space and space travel have become possible.

Space flight, first
4 October 1957; the launch of the Russian spacecraft *Sputnik 1*.

Space traveller, first
Soviet Cosmonaut Yuri Gagarin (1934–68), on 12 April 1961.

Sparrers
Very early in the morning (from sparrow's fart).

Speech Day
A School's annual prize-giving day, often marked by the guest speaker asking the Head to grant the pupils a half-holiday amid cheers.

Sporting seasons
The periods during which hunting a given species is allowed; see Close season.

Spring
The season of the year between Winter and Summer; from the September equinox to the December solstice in the Southern hemisphere, and from the March equinox to the Summer solstice in the Northern hemisphere.

Spring Equinox
21 March; see Equinox.

Spring Festival
See Pesach.

Spy Wednesday
A name given in Ireland to the Wednesday before Good Friday, when Judas bargained to become the spy of the Jewish Sanhedrin.

ST
See Sidereal Time.

Standard Time

Until 1880, 'the time' was a local affair or, in the smaller countries, based on the time kept in the capital city. But the spread of the railways gave rise to great time-keeping confusion. and it was clear that time was no longer a local preserve. In 1880, Greenwich Mean Time (GMT) became the legal time in the British Isles (which are half-an-hour wide) and international time zones were instituted in 1884; see Time Zones.

The equator is divided into 360°, which gives 24 time zones each 15° (= 1 hour) wide. The 0° meridian passes through Greenwich, and the 12 zones to the east are fast on Greenwich time, and the 12 to the west are slow on Greenwich time (occasioned by the direction of rotation of the Earth).

Each zone extends 7½° on either side of its central meridian, although local convenience has resulted in some displacements of the ideal line. The International Date Line – with some variations due to the convenience of political geography – runs down the 180° meridian. If you cross this line from east to west, Sunday becomes Saturday – and vice versa.

A very few countries or areas do not adhere to the Greenwich system; others, even though they be more than 15° wide, keep the same time throughout. Yet others, such as the Middle East, India and the central area of Australia adopt half-hour differences.

Stade

In describing a period of glaciation, a division of time less than a glacial stage but which has some feature or event to distinguish it. The word is the French for 'stage', but ultimately derives through Latin from the ancient Greek word represented in English by *stadium*.

Stampian

A Stage in the Oligocene Epoch; see Geological Time Divisions.

St Andrew's Day

30 November.

Statute Fairs

A mop fair *qv*.

St Distaff's Day

See Rock Day.

Stephanian

A Stage in the Upper Carboniferous Epoch; see Geological Time Divisions.

St George's Day
23 April; also Shakespeare's deathday and thus traditionally his (unknown) birthday as well.

Stilo Novo
Newfangled notions.

Stir-up Sunday
The last Sunday after Trinity; it originally took its name from the opening of the collect: 'Stir up, we beseech thee O Lord, the wills of they faithful people' but by a happy coincidence it was a convenient day, falling somewhere between 24 May and 27 June, for making Christmas puddings.

Stone Age
The earliest form of human culture, in which the mode of subsistence was largely hunting and gathering, although, by the end of the Stone Age, the rudiments of agriculture were being learned and there was some domestication of animals. But what particularly distinguishes such a culture is that the tools and implements were of wood or stone: the use of metals came later in first the Bronze Age and then the Iron Age. The Stone Age itself is customarily divided into the Palaeolithic, Mesolithic, and Neolithic Periods spanning 2,500,000 – 5,000 BCE.

Stop
There are many phrases exhorting someone to cease from some (annoying) activity, for example: call it a day, cut it out, give over, jack

Stonehenge
Britain's most famous prehistoric monument has stood on Salisbury Plain for 5,000 years or more. Why its builders should have gone to such lengths to bring such huge stones such long distances is not clear; neither is its purpose. Whatever drove them to the achievement must have been very powerful indeed. There are many theories of its alignment as a huge astronomical clock, presumably driven by the fact that the so-called Heel or Hele stone is aligned with the Midsummer Day sunrise. The remarkable thing is that such 'primitive' people as its builders could have decided *what* measurements to take from the heavens, and *how* to take and record them, and *how* to pass the information on from one generation to the next, and *how* to translate the results into the design of a structure susceptible to micro-adjustments only with extreme difficulty.

it in, knock it off, lay off, leave it out, pack it in, pack it up, pull the plug, put a sock in it, stuff it, toss it in, turn it up, wrap it up ...

Stopwatch

A watch whose two hands describe minutes and seconds (rather than hours and minutes) in great detail, that can be started and stopped at a precise moment (on some watches, to the nearest hundredth of a second) depending on the skill of the user. Such a device is used for accurate timing in many fields – sporting, entertainment, experimental science and the like. Modern stopwatches give (electronic) digital displays of times, and are usually triggered by the beginning and end of the event itself. The possibility of such timing has itself had an effect on the way events to be measured are conducted – for example, faith in the equipment is such that the losing competitor seldom complains if the performances are separated by 1×10^{-4} seconds.

Stratum, geological

A horizontal layer of any homogenous material.

St Stephen's Day

26 December, a public holiday in some countries. The day following Christmas Day is traditionally when Christmas 'boxes' or presents are exchanged – hence the alternative name Boxing Day. Nowadays, family presents are usually exchanged on Christmas Day, and Christmas Boxes keep the dustmen, and the postman, and the paper boy (who has probably sent you a Christmas card) sweet. The day is referred to in the Christmas Carol *Good King Wenceslas*: 'Good King Wenceslas looked out, on the feast of Stephen ...'

Stuart

Relating or belonging to the royal house that ruled Scotland from 1371 to 1603 and Britain from 1603 to 1649 and from 1660 to 1714.

James I	24 March 1603 to 27 March 1625
Charles I	27 March 1625 to 30 January 1649
[Commonwealth	30 January 1649 to 29 May 1660]
Charles II	(30 January 1649) to 6 February 1685
James II	6 February 1685 to 11 December 1688
Interregnum	11 December 1688 to 12 February 1689
William and Mary	13 February 1689 to 27 December 1694
William III	27 December 1694 to 8 March 1702
Anne	8 March 1702 to 1 August 1714

On this day also, groups of 'wren-boys' went from house to house seeking money, carrying a holly bush, and singing a song which had slight local variations. This was rather more innocuous than their original mission – see **Wrenning**.

St Swithin's Day

15 July; it is said that if it rains on that day it will continue to rain for forty days.

Sturm und Drang

German (= storm and stress) artistic movement of the late C18, founded in literature, but influencing other arts as well; it soon gave way to romanticism.

Sukkot

The Feast of Tabernacles or Booths; the Festival of Ingathering, The Season of our Rejoicing; or simply The Feast; in the Jewish calendar, a Festival lasting nine days (eight in Israel) commemorating the wanderings of the Children of Israel in the Wilderness, when they dwelt in huts (or booths).

The first two days are called Sukkot, the seventh day is The Great Hoshana, the eighth day is the Feast of the Eighth Day, or of the Eighth Day of Solemn Assembly, and the ninth day is the Rejoicing of the Law. The Feast is held on 15 or 16 – 22 or 23 Tishri.

Summer

The hottest season of the year, between spring and autumn; astronomically speaking from the June solstice to the Autumnal equinox in the Northern hemisphere, and at the opposite time of the year in the Southern hemisphere.

Summer Solstice

In the Northern hemisphere about 21 June, the time at which the sun is at its northernmost point in the sky (in the Southern hemisphere about 22 December, the southernmost point); the point on the celestial sphere (opposite the winter solstice) at which the ecliptic is furthest north from the celestial equator; right ascension 6 hours; declination 23.5°.

Sunday

See **Week**.

Sunday Letters

(Dominical letters) A to G, according to the day on which the first Sunday of a year falls; see Part 3.

Sundial

A means of measuring the passage of time whereby the shadow of a rod or pointer (gnomon), as cast by the Sun, falls on a dial calibrated with the hours of the day. The main disadvantages of this timepiece are that it is unusable except during sunlit periods, and that as the day lengthens and shortens according to the season of the year, so do the

Summer Time

Advancing the clock one hour on GMT in order to make fuller use of the hours of daylight without having to change one's lifestyle. In the UK, Summer Time was introduced by a 1916 Act of Parliament, and then by the Summer Time Acts 1922–25 which laid down that Summer Time begins when the clocks are moved forward by one hour at 0200 (GMT) on the day after the third Saturday in April, but if that Sunday happens to be Easter Day (as in 1965, 1976, 1981, 1990 and 1992) Summer Time will start a week earlier. Statutorily, Summer Time should end by putting the clocks back by one hour at 0200 (BST) on the day after the first Saturday in October. Notwithstanding this, either start or finish date may be varied by the Home Secretary by means of an Order in Council. The earliest onset was on 18 February in 1968. Double Summer Time (GMT + 2hours) was introduced from 1941 to 1945, and again in 1947.

Year	BST began	BST ended	DST began	DST ended
1935	14 April	6 October	•	•
1936	19 April	4 October	•	•
1937	18 April	3 October	•	•
1938	10 April	2 October	•	•
1939	16 April	19 November	•	•
1940	25 February	31 December	•	•
1941	1 January	31 December	4 May	10 August
1942	1 January	31 December	5 April	9 August
1943	1 January	31 December	4 April	15 August
1944	1 January	31 December	2 April	17 September
1945	1 January	7 October	2 April	15 July
1946	14 April	6 October	•	•
1947	16 March	2 November	13 April	10 August
1948	14 March	31 October	•	•
1949	3 April	30 October	•	•

From 1948 until 1952, and since 1961, the period of BST was extended, while the Act operated normally between 1953 and 1960.

hours as measured. The earliest sundials known date from Egypt in the eighth century BCE. The latest may be the analemmatic sundial, as set up in the market square at Ely, Cambridgeshire, where the on-stander acts as the gnomon; the analemma is a graduated scale shaped in a figure of eight that indicates the daily declination of the sun.

Sung dynasty

In China, the time period between 960 and 1279CE. Now regarded as one of China's golden ages, it was a period notable for its artistic works on ceramics and in painting, and for the philosophical dominance of Confucianism.

Sunrise/sunset

The Nautical Almanac gives the GMT of sunrise and sunset for each two degrees of latitude for every third day in the year. The sunrise is the instant when the rim of the sun appears above the horizon, and the sunset when the last segment disappears below the horizon. But because of the Earth's atmosphere, the transition from day to night and *vice versa* is a gradual process, the length of which varies according to the declination of the sun and the latitude of the observer. The intermediate stages are called twilight, *qv*.

Swinging Sixties

The decade beginning with 1960, when (in Britain) the austerity of WW2 had at last been shaken off, and pop music, fashion, modelling, psychedelia and the like all changed 'for ever'.

Swithin's Day, St

15 July, and it is said that if it rains on that day it will rain for forty days more.

Taanit Behorim

In the Jewish calendar, the day before Pesach (*qv*), 14 Nisan, on which is held the minor Fast of the Firstborn (in thanksgiving for the deliverance of the Israelites' firstborn, before the Jews left Egypt) when firstborn sons fast during the day; on the eve of Pesach unleavened bread hidden about the house is sought out for burning the following day; Chametz (leavened commodities) are symbolically sold to Gentiles so as not to be in Jewish possession during Pesach.

Taanit Esther

In the Jewish calendar, the Fast of Esther, a minor fast instituted in memory of Queen Esther's fast before she pleaded with the king to save her people under Persian rule from the plotting of the evil Haman; held on 13 Adar.

Tabernacles, Feast of

See Sukkot.

Tabêtu
Babylonian month of flooding from which the Jewish month of Tebet (Tevet) takes its name.

Ta Ch'ing
Another name for the Manchu Dynasty in China.

TAI
Temps Atomique International; see Time.

Takayama Matsuri
Japanese festival held at Hie Shrine, Takayama, Gifu Prefecture, on 14–15 April, when 12 high-wheeled floats, roofed and decorated, parade through the streets of Takayama to the accompaniment of music and song.

Tammuz
Fourth month of the sacred, and tenth month of the civil Jewish calendar. See Jewish calendar. Derived from the Babylonian Du'ûzu (a god), it corresponds roughly to the Gregorian June–July; it has 29 days. A fast is held on 17 Tammuz to mark the breaching of the Walls of Jerusalem by Nebuchadnezzar and Titus.

Tang/T'ang dynasty
Period in China between AD 618 and 907. A time of literary, especially poetic, flowering, during which Buddhism reached the country and took on its localised forms, it was also an era in which rules expanded the national territory towards central Asia.

Tango-No-Sekku
5 May, giant kites depicting red and black carp are flown by Japanese families in honour of their young sons.

Tap-up Sunday
A local name in Guildford for the Sunday preceding 2 October, when a fair was held on St Catherine's Hill.

Taurus
(Latin = the Bull); second sign of the zodiac; 20/21 April – 20/21 May; second northern (septentrional) sign – second spring sign – fifth ascending sign; see Zodiac.

Tax Year
In the UK, the tax year starts on 6 April and ends on 5 April. In the twelfth century, the Church decided that the year should begin on Lady Day, March 25. When the Gregorian calendar came into effect in Britain in 1752, the end of that tax year was pushed forward by 11 days to 5 April 1753 to appease those objected to paying (as they saw it) 365 days' worth of tax on 354 days' worth of income.

TARDIS, The

Time And Relative Dimension(s) In Space; the TV perennial Doctor Who's method of travel (in both time and space); from outside, it looks like an old-fashioned British Police Box 'because the chameleon circuit that allows the TARDIS to appear in any form got jammed on earth in 1963'. Its exterior appearance belied the extensive appointments inside, which are said to include libraries, gardens, swimming pools, and a cricket pavilion, as well as two control rooms, a boot cupboard, a very large costume wardrobe and a pink Zero Room.

Tebet

Tenth month of the sacred and fourth month of the civil Jewish year. Its name is derived from the Babylonian month of flooding (Tabêtu); it corresponds roughly to the Gregorian months of December– January; it has 29 days. Hanukkah ends on 2/3 Tebet, and the Fast commemorating the start of the siege of Jerusalem by Nebuchadnezzar is observed on 10 Tebet.

Teenage

Relating to, denoting, or suitable for a teenager or people in their teens. A teenager comes into being on a thirteenth birthday, and ends as the nineteenth year gives way to the twentieth. As for the word, teenagers appeared in the 1940s, teeners having emerged in the 1890s.

Temma Tenjin Matsuri

Japanese festival held on the river Yodogawa in honour of the deity of the shrine Temmangu, Osaka, on 24 July, when there is a parade of portable shrines accompanied by a flotilla of ornately decorated boats, carrying large dolls or filled with musicians.

Tempo

The speed of a musical piece or passage indicated by any of a series of directions and often by an exact metronome marking. The speed or rate of motion or activity. Tempo is the steady beat upon which rhythm is based.

Tempon

See Units of Time.

Tempora mutantur, nos et mutamur in illis

(Latin =) The times change, and we change with them.

Temps Atomique International; TAI

(French =) International Atomic Time; see Time.

Tempus fugit
(Latin =) Time flies.

Tenebrae
The Service of the Shadows; Matins and Lauds of the following day sung on the Wednesday, Thursday and Friday of Holy Week; 15 candles are extinguished one by one after each psalm, the last after the Benedictus, and the Miserere is sung in darkness.

Tercentenary/tercentennial
Of 300 years, describing a 300th anniversary.

Term day
A less common expression for any of the four Quarter Days.

Tertian
Recurring every third day, inclusively – that is, with one day's interval between recurrences, or every forty-eight hours. Fevers symptomatic of some tropical diseases (notably specific forms of malaria) follow this pattern.

Tertiary Period
The geological period immediately before the present (quaternary) period, corresponding to between roughly 65 million years ago and 3 million years ago. Within the Tertiary period were the Palaeocene, Eocene, and Oligocene Epochs – sometimes together known as the Eogene – and the Miocene and Pliocene and the beginning of the icy Pleistocene Epoch of the Quaternary Period are difficult to distinguish, but in any case the Tertiary and Quaternary Periods together are all part of the Cenozoic Era. The period is called the Tertiary because it follows the Mesozoic era, known also as the Secondary era; see Geological Time Divisions.

Teshuvah
In the Jewish calendar, repentance observed during the 29 days of the month of Elul.

Th
Thursday; see Week.

Thanetian
A Stage in the Palaeocene Epoch; see Geological Time Divisions.

Thanksgiving
An annual holiday in the USA usually held on the last Thursday in November.

Thermidor
(Heat) eleventh month of the French Revolutionary Calendar *qv*.

Therblig

A modified reversal of the surname of the American engineer Frank Bunker Gilbreth (1868–1924) who invented the term (which it must be said has a somewhat Swiftean appearance) in about 1919 to describe any of the types of action involved in carrying out a task, as a means of task analysis – time-and-motion study. Therbligs include:

Assemble
Disassemble
Find
Grasp
Inspect
Load/unload transport
Position
Release load
Rest (take a break)
Search
Select
Use
Wait (avoidable delay)
Wait (unavoidable delay)

Thirty Years War

The wars in Germany that began in Bohemia in 1618 and were ended by the peace of Westphalia in 1648.

Thoth

(alt spellings Djehuti, Zehuti) complex ancient Egyptian god; represented as human with the head of an ibis or an ape with the head of a dog; the god of wisdom who gambled with the moon to win intercalary days, and thus became master of time.

Three Kings' Day

Epiphany of Twelfth night, designed to commemorate the visit of the 'three kings', Magi, or Wise Men of the East to the infant Jesus.

Thuringian

A Stage in the Permian Period; see Geological Time Divisions.

Thursday

See Week.

Time

The fundamental unit of time in all current systems of measurement is the second (see Second). In astronomy, there are various forms of time (see *Mean Solar Time*; Sidereal Time), as there are in everyday life (see Greenwich Mean Time; Standard Time); see also Day; Minute; Month; Hour; Year.

Time

In East Anglian parlance, we append the word 'time' to reinforce our meaning: 'I'll come round yours about quarter past five time'.

Time and a half, quarter, etc

For those paid by the hour, a rate of pay for overtime, unsocial working and so on.

Time-and-motion study

Scientific (or pseudo-scientific) analysis of tasks and the time it takes to complete them as a means of costing, and increasing efficiency; see Therblig.

Time ball

Knowing the 'exact' time at sea is necessary for fixing one's position. Armed with a sextant and a chronometer set to the time at the home port, the navigator can work out the position of the vessel. Chronometers of the necessary accuracy were developed from the end of the 18th century, but how to fix the time at one's home port?

To avoid ships' timekeepers having to go ashore, a visible time signal was needed, and the first was the 'time ball' which, set on high, drops at a known time each day. This device was proposed by Captain Robert Wauchope of the British Royal Navy in 1824. A manually operated device was first set up at the Royal Observatory, Greenwich, in 1833. In due course, time balls were erected in London and in many ports and, in 1862, time balls in The Strand and Cornhill in London, and at the ports of Deal and Liverpool, were dropped by telegraph signals from Greenwich to inaugurate Greenwich Mean Time.

In the United States, the Naval Observatory was set up at Washington in 1845; one of its tasks was to provide a national time service, and it first sent out automatic time signals in 1880.

Time bomb

1 An explosive device containing a pre-set timer which causes it to detonate.
2 Figuratively, anything that will come to pass with an adverse effect – for example 'a pensions time bomb' or 'the millennium time bomb' (which was more like a damp squib).

Time capsule

A sealed container filled with objects chosen to typify the time at which it was buried or walled up for the earnestly expected benefit of those who disinter it in time to come.

Time clock and time card

A means whereby workers can 'clock in and out' of their works so that the wages department can calculate how much they are to be paid for a given period. Some time clocks have a drum carrying a record sheet on which the clocking action impresses the time against one's clock number; others have a card for each worker on which the times are stamped, with the machine clipping out a marginal piece so that the card drops lower each time.

Time constant

The time taken for a current or voltage in a circuit to rise or fall exponentially to 63% of its maximum or minimum.

Time delay

A device which holds something up on purpose for a specific period of time, for example that which enables a photographer to take a picture of him or herself by delaying the action of the shutter, or prevents anyone from opening a safe until a predetermined time.

Time deposit

In banking, a deposit which may be withdrawn only on giving a certain period of notice (or perhaps earlier with a penalty).

Time exposure

A photograph taken with a relatively long exposure time, or the technique whereby this is done.

Time immemorial, from

Not just an expression – sometimes used facetiously – to mean 'a jolly long time', but one with a definite legal meaning 'before the reign of Richard I' – *ie* 1189.

Time keeper, Timekeeper

A person or device that sets, measures and records time.

Time lag

The pause between a cause and its effect; it has its importance in visual humour.

Time-lapse photography

A means of showing and analysing a normally slow event by taking photographic exposures at suitable intervals and then showing them at a higher speed.

Time lock

A type of lock fitted to a safe or strongroom which prevents its being opened before a predetermined time.

Time machine

A (hypothetical) device enabling its user to travel forwards or backwards in time. Means have to be incorporated to ensure that, when arriving at some time other than 'real time', the presence of the device does not affect what, at that point, has or has not already happened. This is why time travel often takes place in a different dimension.

Time out, time-out

Time taken away from some activity such as a sporting event; the act of something (such as a computer) turning itself off through inactivity for a set period.

Timepiece

Something that tells the time, but does not give audible signals of its passing.

Time server

Someone whose purpose is to keep a clean nose and move quietly towards a pension with no hassle.

Time sheet

A paper or card upon which a worker records time spent on various tasks.

Time-shift viewing

Recording a television programme and watching it later; see Real Time.

● ● ● ● ● ●

Time signal

The 'Six Pips' from Greenwich were first broadcast by the BBC on 5 February 1924, so that 'listeners-in' could use the wireless to adjust their clocks. In 1972 the sequence changed from six short pips to five short pips and one longer pip. The last Greenwich pips were broadcast on 4 June 1990, and the BBC began receiving its signal from atomic clocks, GPS satellite systems, and the 60kHz radio transmitter at Rugby.

There is a story concerning the Paris time signal regularly broadcast from the Eiffel Tower; it appears that the Director of the Paris Observatory was making an official visit to the Tower and enquired about the time-signal transmission: 'Tell me, how do you set your clocks?' 'Why, M le Directeur, we telephone your Observatory twice a day and check our clocks against yours. But I've often wondered ... how do you maintain *your* time standards?' After some reddening discussion, it emerged that the Observatory set its clocks by listening to the time signals transmitted from the Eiffel Tower.

Time zones

The earth takes 24 hours to rotate on its axis. Thus in 24 hours the sun is overhead at noon over every meridian in turn. Rather than every point on earth having its local time, there are by convention 24 time zones, or meridians, each 360/24 = 15° wide, the first centred on Greenwich so that GMT (or UTC) extends from 7.5° east of Greenwich to 7.5° west of Greenwich. The imaginary hour-wide zones embrace the earth, save that in places it is convenient to modify the lines for local convenience.

The International Date Line is on the meridian 180° from Greenwich; the date to its east is one day earlier than the date to its west. In the first table below, the world's time zones are arranged from UTC −12 hours to UTC +12 hours.

Abbr	Full name	Location	Time zone UTC±
Y	Yankee Time Zone	Military	− 12 hours
X	X-ray Time Zone	Military	− 11 hours
HAST	Hawaii-Aleutian Standard Time	North America	− 10 hours
W	Whiskey Time Zone	Military	− 10 hours
AKST	Alaska Standard Time	North America	− 09 hours
HADT	Hawaii-Aleutian Daylight Time	North America	− 09 hours
HNY	Heure Normale du Yukon	North America	− 09 hours
V	Victor Time Zone	Military	− 09 hours
AKDT	Alaska Daylight Time	North America	− 08 hours
HAY	Heure Avancée du Yukon	North America	− 08 hours
HNP	Heure Normale du Pacifique	North America	− 08 hours
PST	Pacific Standard Time	North America	− 08 hours
U	Uniform Time Zone	Military	− 08 hours
HAP	Heure Avancée du Pacifique	North America	− 07 hours
HNR	Heure Normale des Rocheuses	North America	− 07 hours
MST	Mountain Standard Time	North America	− 07 hours
PDT	Pacific Daylight Time	North America	− 07 hours
T	Tango Time Zone	Military	− 07 hours
CST	Central Standard Time	North America	− 06 hours

Abbr	Full name	Location	Time zone UTC±
HAR	Heure Avancée des Rocheuses	North America	− 06 hours
HNC	Heure Normale du Centre	North America	− 06 hours
MDT	Mountain Daylight Time	North America	− 06 hours
S	Sierra Time Zone	Military	− 06 hours
CDT	Central Daylight Time	North America	− 05 hours
EST	Eastern Standard Time	North America	− 05 hours
HAC	Heure Avancée du Centre	North America	− 05 hours
HNE	Heure Normale de l'Est	North America	− 05 hours
R	Romeo Time Zone	Military	− 05 hours
AST	Atlantic Standard Time	North America	− 04 hours
EDT	Eastern Daylight Time	North America	− 04 hours
HAE	Heure Avancée de l'Est	North America	− 04 hours
HNA	Heure Normale de l'Atlantique	North America	− 04 hours
Q	Quebec Time Zone	Military	− 04 hours
HNT	Heure Normale de Terre-Neuve	North America	− 03:30 hours
NST	Newfoundland Standard Time	North America	− 03:30 hours
ADT	Atlantic Daylight Time	North America	− 03 hours
HAA	Heure Avancée de l'Atlantique	North America	− 03 hours
P	Papa Time Zone	Military	− 03 hours
HAT	Heure Avancée de Terre-Neuve	North America	− 02:30 hours
NDT	Newfoundland Daylight Time	North America	− 02:30 hours
O	Oscar Time Zone	Military	− 02 hours
N	November Time Zone	Military	− 01 hour
GMT	Greenwich Mean Time	UK	00 UTC
UTC	Coordinated Universal Time	Europe	00 UTC
WET	Western European Time	Western Europe	00 UTC
Z	Zulu Time Zone	Military	00 UTC
A	Alpha Time Zone	Military	+ 01 hour
BST	British Summer Time	UK	+ 01 hour

Abbr	Full name	Location	Time zone UTC±
CET	Central European Time	Central Europe	+ 01 hour
IST	Irish Summer Time	Irish Republic	+ 01 hour
MEZ	Mitteleuropäische Zeit	Europe	+ 01 hour
MEZ	Central European Time	Western Europe	+ 01 hour
WEST	Western European Summer Time	Western Europe	+ 01 hour
B	Bravo Time Zone	Military	+ 02 hours
CEST	Central European Summer Time	Central Europe	+ 02 hours
EET	Eastern European Time	Eastern Europe	+ 02 hours
MESZ	Mitteleuropäische Sommerzeit	Europe	+ 02 hours
EEST	Eastern European Summer Time	Eastern Europe	+ 03 hours
C	Charlie Time Zone	Military	+ 03 hours
D	Delta Time Zone	Military	+ 04 hours
E	Echo Time Zone	Military	+ 05 hours
F	Foxtrot Time Zone	Military	+ 06 hours
CXT	Christmas Island Time	Australia	+ 07 hours
G	Golf Time Zone	Military	+ 07 hours
AWST	Australian Western Standard Time	Australia	+ 08 hours
H	Hotel Time Zone	Military	+ 08 hours
WST	Western Standard Time	Australia	+ 08 hours
I	India Time Zone	Military	+ 09 hours
ACST	Australian Central Standard Time	Australia	+ 09:30 hours
AEST	Australian Eastern Standard Time	Australia	+ 10 hours
EST	Eastern Standard Time	Australia	+ 10 hours
K	Kilo Time Zone	Military	+ 10 hours
ACDT	Australian Central Daylight Time	Australia	+ 10:30 hours
AEDT	Australian Eastern Daylight Time	Australia	+ 11 hours
EDT	Eastern Daylight Time	Australia	+ 11 hours

Abbr	Full name	Location	Time zone UTC±
L	Lima Time Zone	Military	+ 11 hours
NFT	Norfolk (Island) Time	Australia	+ 11:30 hours
M	Mike Time Zone	Military	+ 12 hours

World time zones arranged alphabetically

Abbr	Full name	Location	Time zone UTC±
A	Alpha Time Zone	Military	+ 01 hour
ACDT	Australian Central Daylight Time	Australia	+ 10:30 hours
ACST	Australian Central Standard Time	Australia	+ 09:30 hours
ADT	Atlantic Daylight Time	North America	− 03 hours
AEDT	Australian Eastern Daylight Time	Australia	+ 11 hours
AEST	Australian Eastern Standard Time	Australia	+ 10 hours
AKDT	Alaska Daylight Time	North America	− 08 hours
AKST	Alaska Standard Time	North America	− 09 hours
AST	Atlantic Standard Time	North America	− 04 hours
AWST	Australian Western Standard Time	Australia	+ 08 hours
B	Bravo Time Zone	Military	+ 02 hours
BST	British Summer Time	UK	+ 01 hour
C	Charlie Time Zone	Military	+ 03 hours
CDT	Central Daylight Time	North America	− 05 hours
CEST	Central European Summer Time	Central Europe	+ 02 hours
CET	Central European Time	Western Europe	+ 01 hour
CST	Central Standard Time	North America	− 06 hours
CST	Central Standard Time	Australia	+ 09:30 hours
CXT	Christmas Island Time	Australia	+ 07 hours
D	Delta Time Zone	Military	+ 04 hours
E	Echo Time Zone	Military	+ 05 hours
EDT	Eastern Daylight Time	North America	− 04 hours
EDT	Eastern Daylight Time	Australia	+ 11 hours

Abbr	Full name	Location	Time zone UTC±
EEST	Eastern European Summer Time	Eastern Europe	+ 03 hours
EET	Eastern European Time	Eastern Europe	+ 02 hours
EST	Eastern Standard Time	North America	– 05 hours
EST	Eastern Standard Time	Australia	+ 10 hours
F	Foxtrot Time Zone	Military	+ 06 hours
G	Golf Time Zone	Military	+ 07 hours
GMT	Greenwich Mean Time	UK	00 UTC
H	Hotel Time Zone	Military	+ 08 hours
HAA	Heure Avancée de l'Atlantique	North America	– 03 hours
HAC	Heure Avancée du Centre	North America	– 05 hours
HADT	Hawaii-Aleutian Daylight Time	North America	– 09 hours
HAE	Heure Avancée de l'Est	North America	– 04 hours
HAP	Heure Avancée du Pacifique	North America	– 07 hours
HAR	Heure Avancée des Rocheuses	North America	– 06 hours
HAST	Hawaii-Aleutian Standard Time	North America	– 10 hours
HAT	Heure Avancée de Terre-Neuve	North America	– 02:30 hours
HAY	Heure Avancée du Yukon	North America	– 08 hours
HNA	Heure Normale de l'Atlantique	North America	– 04 hours
HNC	Heure Normale du Centre	North America	– 06 hours
HNE	Heure Normale de l'Est	North America	– 05 hours
HNP	Heure Normale du Pacifique	North America	– 08 hours
HNR	Heure Normale des Rocheuses	North America	– 07 hours
HNT	Heure Normale de Terre-Neuve	North America	– 03:30 hours
HNY	Heure Normale du Yukon	North America	– 09 hours
I	India Time Zone	Military	+ 09 hours
IST	Irish Summer Time	Irish Republic	+ 01 hour

Abbr	Full name	Location	Time zone UTC±
K	Kilo Time Zone	Military	+ 10 hours
L	Lima Time Zone	Military	+ 11 hours
M	Mike Time Zone	Military	+ 12 hours
MDT	Mountain Daylight Time	North America	– 06 hours
MESZ	Mitteleuropäische Sommerzeit	Europe	+ 02 hours
MEZ	Mitteleuropäische Zeit	Europe	+ 01 hour
MEZ	Central European Time	Western Europe	+ 01 hour
MST	Mountain Standard Time	North America	– 07 hours
N	November Time Zone	Military	– 01 hour
NDT	Newfoundland Daylight Time	North America	– 02:30 hours
NFT	Norfolk (Island) Time	Australia	+ 11:30 hours
NST	Newfoundland Standard Time	North America	– 03:30 hours
O	Oscar Time Zone	Military	– 02 hours
P	Papa Time Zone	Military	– 03 hours
PDT	Pacific Daylight Time	North America	– 07 hours
PST	Pacific Standard Time	North America	– 08 hours
Q	Quebec Time Zone	Military	– 04 hours
R	Romeo Time Zone	Military	– 05 hours
S	Sierra Time Zone	Military	– 06 hours
T	Tango Time Zone	Military	– 07 hours
U	Uniform Time Zone	Military	– 08 hours
UTC	Coordinated Universal Time	Europe	00 UTC
V	Victor Time Zone	Military	– 09 hours
W	Whiskey Time Zone	Military	– 10 hours
WEST	Western European Summer Time	Western Europe	+ 01 hour
WET	Western European Time	Western Europe	00 UTC
WST	Western Standard Time	Australia	+ 08 hours
X	X-ray Time Zone	Military	– 11 hours
Y	Yankee Time Zone	Military	– 12 hours
Z	Zulu Time Zone	Military	00 UTC

Time signature

Described as duple, triple, quadruple, quintuple or septuple depending on the number of beats in a bar (2, 3, 4, 5 or 7). The first three are by far the most usual. The time signature is shown as a fraction on the stave: the numerator shows how many beats in the bar, and the denominator shows what sort of beats they are. So $\frac{2}{4}$ indicated two crotchets in a bar, $\frac{3}{4}$ three crotchets (normal waltz time), $\frac{4}{4}$ four crotchets (march time), and so on. ($\frac{4}{4}$ is so usual that it is known as 'common time', and has a special symbol like a capital C.) For the relative time values of notes, see Time value below. Note that, although the time signature tells you about the construction of the music, it doesn't give away how fast it is to be played. That will usually be indicated by an entry such as '60 crotchets per minute'.

Times table

An abhorrent expression meaning 'multiplication table'.

Timetable

1   For travellers, a list of destinations on a route showing at what times services are supposed to arrive and depart.

2   For those attending an event, a programme showing at what time various activities are expected to take place.

3   For those involved in completing a project, a schedule of tasks each taking so long to complete, often presented graphically and subject to periodic review and reassessment.

Time trial

An event wherein participants (especially cyclists) compete against the clock.

Time value

In music, the relative lengths of notes. Convention provides a series where each type of note lasts half as long as the one before it; the breve (rarely used nowadays; it is the sign whereby an organist triturates the audience with a 64-foot stop); the semibreve (US: whole note); the minim (US: half note); the crotchet (US: quarter note); the quaver (US: eighth note); the semiquaver (US: sixteenth note); the demisemiquaver (US: thirtysecond note); and so on. As an indication of the length of each note, a 'normal' piece of music might be marked at 70–80 crotchets per minute.

Time work

Work paid for by the time it takes (as opposed to piece work, paid for by the amount achieved).

Timing

The art of optimising the effect of a number of actions; the secret of ... er ... comedy.

Tir

Fourth month of the Persian year.

Tisha B'Av

In the Jewish calendar, the Fast of 9 Ab commemorates the destruction of both the First and the Second Temples (586BCE and 70CE), the fall of Bethar in the Bar-Kochba rebellion (135CE), and other sad or tragic occurrences particularly the Expulsion of the Jews from Spain in 1492.

Tishri

Seventh month of the sacred and first of the civil Jewish calendar. Its name is derived from the Babylonian month Tashrêtu (beginning); it corresponds roughly to the Gregorian September–October; it has 30 days. It is rich in observances: Rosh Hashanah (New Year) on 1&2; Tsom Gedaliah on 3; Yom Kippur (Day of Atonement) on 10; Days of Penitence 1–10; Sukkot (Festival of Booths or Tabernacles) 15–21; Shemeni Atzeret (Eighth Day of the Solemn Assembly) 22; Simhat Torah (Rejoicing of the Law) 23.

Toarcian

A Stage in the Lower Jurassic Epoch; see Geological Time Divisions.

Toka Ebisu (10th Day Ebisu)

Japanese festival held at Imamiya Ebisu Shrine, Osaka, on 10 January when prayers are offered to Ebisu, one of the Osaka Seven Deities of Good Fortune, for a prosperous business year. Bamboo branches hung with replicas of coins or other valuable articles are on sale to shrine visitors, who take them home to display on family altars as good luck charms for business matters.

Tokonoma

Girls' Festival; in Japanese homes dolls are arranged and offered fruit and vegetables by young girls to encourage the development of feminine qualities.

Tontine

A form of annuity shared by several subscribers, in which the shares of those who die are added to the holdings of the survivors till the last survivor inherits all; the name is derived from its progenitor, the C18 Neapolitan banker Lorenzo Tonti.

Tooth, The Festival of the

Kandy is a beautiful city in Sri Lanka where, on a small hill, stands a great temple built to house a tooth, a relic of the Buddha. The tooth is kept inside many caskets and can never be seen but, once a year, on the night of the August full moon, a special procession is held for it.

Torah, Rejoicing in
See Simhat Torah.

Torah, Season of Giving the
See Shavuot.

Tortonian
A Stage in the Miocene Epoch; see Geological Time Divisions.

Trafalgar Day
21 October 1805, when the British Fleet under Admiral Lord Nelson on HMS *Victory* defeated the French off Cape Trafalgar (between Cape Cádiz and Gibraltar), using the daring tactic of attacking the French longitudinally rather than broadside, thus establishing British naval supremacy for over a century. Nelson (*b* 1758) was mortally wounded in the battle.

Traffic unit
See Erlang.

Travail, La Fête du
Labour Day; see French Revolutionary Calendar.

Trees, Festival for New
See Tu B'shevat.

Tremadocian
A Stage in the Ordovician Period; see Geological Time Divisions.

Triassic period
The first geological Period during the Mesozoic, or Secondary, Era, following the Permian Period of the Palaeozoic Era and preceding the Jurassic Period; roughly between 248 and 213 millions years ago. The actual geological boundary between Permian and the Triassic is often difficult to distinguish because the great natural disaster that rendered so many marine creatures – particularly corals, foraminifera, and brachiopods – extinct at the end of the Palaeozoic Era did not affect the deposition of rock strata. However, the final stage of the Triassic Period is marked by marine sedimentation deposited in previous continental strata, indicating yet another comparatively sudden and sizable rise in sea-levels. During the drier stages, in which there was considerable volcanic activity, reptiles flourished and the period saw the emergence of the early dinosaurs. As the waters rose, molluscs and echinoderms became more profuse. The German geologist Friedrich von Albertini named the period in 1834 from a triple-layered stratum of rocks (*Trias*) of the period found in Germany; see Geological Time Divisions.

Tricentenary/tercentenary
Of 300 years, describing a 300th anniversary.

Tridi
Third day of the French Revolutionary week; see French Revolutionary Calendar.

Triennial
Once every three years; lasting for three years; a third anniversary.

Triennium
A period of three years.

Trimester
A period of three months, especially as a division of a school or university year or of pregnancy. The word derives through French from Latin *tri-mestris* = of three months.

Trinity Sunday
Any Sunday between 17 May and 20 June. The first Sunday after Whit Sunday, celebrating the Holy Trinity.

Tropical year
Solar year – the time taken by the earth to move once around the sun, about 365¼ days.

Tsom (Tzom) Gedaliah
In the Jewish calendar, the minor Fast of Gedaliah commemorates the murder (585BCE) of Gedaliah, of the royal house of Judah, whom Nebuchadnezzar appointed governor of Judea, and whose assassination led to trouble for the Jews living under Babylonian rule; it is observed on 3 Tishri.

Tsurugaoka Hachimangu
Japanese festival held at Tsurugaoka Hachiman, Hachiman Shrine, Kamakura, Kanagawa Prefecture, on 16 September, when horsemen dressed in the hunting costume of feudal warriors compete in a contest of traditional mounted archery (yabusame).

Tu
Tuesday; see Week.

Tu B'Av
In the Jewish calendar, the festival of 15 Ab commemorates the vanquishing of the Almohads, a fanatic anti-Jewish Spanish sect, in 1212.

Tu B'shevat
In the Jewish calendar, this modern Festival for New Trees commemorates the planting of trees in Israel; it is held on 15 Shebat.

Tudor times

The period in English history between 1485 and 1603, when members of the Tudor (*Tudwr* = a Welsh version of the name Theodore) family were on the throne. The monarchs were:

Henry VII   22 August 1485 to 21 April 1509 (24 years)
Henry VIII   22 April 1509 to 28 January 1547 (38)
Edward VI   29 January 1547 to 6 July 1553 (6)
Jane   6 July 1553 to 19 July 1553
Mary   19 July 1553 to 17 November 1558 (5)
Elizabeth I   17 November 1558 to 23 March 1603 (45)

Tuesday
See Week.

Tulipomania
The mania for the purchase of tulip-bulbs that spread from Holland in C17 and was at its greatest height in the mid-1630s.

Twilight

That time of day when the sun has just sunk below the horizon; there are three sorts of twilight:

Civil Twilight, when the centre of the sun is 6° below the horizon. Before this moment in the morning and after in the evening ordinary outdoor activities are impossible without artificial light.

Nautical twilight, when the sun is 12° below the horizon. Before this time in the morning and after it in the evening the sea horizon is invisible.

Astronomical twilight, when the centre of the sun is 18° below the horizon. Before this time in the morning or after it in the evening there is a complete absence of sunlight.

Section 17 of the Road Transport Lighting Act, 1957 deems that lighting-up time for vehicles is half an hour after sunset.
In England, lighting-up time is later in the west (*eg* at Land's End) than in the east (*eg* at Lowestoft), for England is half-an-hour wide. Similarly, lighting-up time in the north (*eg* at Aberdeen) is also later than at London in summer but earlier in winter.

Turn of the century

1 Loosely, somewhere between the end of one century and the beginning of the next, *eg* The Wright Brothers first flew at the turn of the last century.

2 The point at which one century ends and the next begins. For those who start counting at year 1, the century turns at midnight at the end of year 100. Less logical individuals mark the turn at the end of year 99.

Turonian

A Stage in the Upper Cretaceous Epoch; see Geological Time Divisions.

Twelfth Day; Night

The twelfth day after Christmas is 6 January, the feast of the Epiphany; twelfth night is either the eve of the twelfth day (*ie* 5 January), or the evening of the 12th day itself (*ie* 6 January).

Twirly

Bus Drivers' facetious name for old people with bus passes who, hoping it's time for their concessionary fares, step forward waving their wallets saying: 'Am I twirly?'

Tynwald Day

5 July, Old Midsummer Day, when the proclamation of laws takes place on the Isle of Man, the only place where this old Icelandic custom survives; officials are sworn in and the laws are proclaimed in English and Manx. All present are charged not to 'quarrel, brawl, or make any disturbance on pain of death'.

Ulambana (Ancestor Day)

Is celebrated throughout the Mahayana tradition from the first to the fifteenth days of the eighth lunar month; some Theravadins from Cambodia, Laos and Thailand also observe this festival. It is believed that the gates of Hell are opened on the first day and the ghosts may visit the world for fifteen days. On the fifteenth day, people visit cemeteries to make offerings to the departed ancestors. Ulambana is also a Japanese Buddhist festival known as Obon, beginning on 13 July and lasting for three days, to celebrate the reunion of family ancestors with the living.

Ult.

Abbreviation of the Latin word *ultimo* = 'of last month'. From the mid-1500s to perhaps the 1970s a common method of referring to dates of the previous month in formal correspondence, the expression is now rapidly becoming obsolete, and is generally regarded as stylistically questionable (*cf* Inst. and Prox.)

Units of time

The familiar units are:

60 second = 1 minute	12 months; 365 or 366 days = 1 year
60 minutes = 1 hour	10 years = 1 decade
24 hours = 1 day	10 decades; 100 years = 1 century
7 days = 1 week	10 centuries; 1,000 years = 1 millennium
28, 29, 30 or 31 days = 1 month	
3 months = 1 quarter	

	Second	Minute	Hour	Day	Week	Year	Decade	Century
Second	1							
Minute	60	1						
Hour	3,600	60	1					
Day	86,400	1,440	24	1				
Week	604,800	10,080	168	7	1			
Year	31,536,000	525,600	8,760	365	52½	1		
Leap year	31,622,400	527,040	8,784	366	52²⁄₇	•		
Decade (0L)	315,360,000	5,256,000	87,600	3,650	521³⁄₇	10	1	
Decade (2L)	315,552,800	5,258,880	87,648	3,652	521⁵⁄₇	•	•	
Decade (3L)	315,639,200	5,260,320	87,672	3,653	521⁶⁄₇	•	•	
Century (0L)	3,153,600,000	52,560,000	876,000	36,500	5,214²⁄₇	100	10	1
Century (24L)	3,155,873,600	52,594,560	876,576	36,524	5,217³⁄₇	•	•	•
Century (25L)	3,155,760,000	52,596,000	876,600	36,525	5,217⁵⁄₇	•	•	•
Millennium (0L)	31,536,000,000	525,600,000	8,760,000	365,000	52,142⁶⁄₇	1,000	100	10
Millennium (242L)	31,556,908,000	525,948,480	8,765,808	365,242	52,177³⁄₇	•	•	•
Millennium (243L)	31,556,995,000	525,949,920	8,765,832	365,243	52,177⁵⁄₇	•	•	•

This table shows the number of units of time within other units of time. For the sake of completeness, we show decades, centuries and millennia containing no leap years (for basic calculations), and those containing possible numbers of leap years depending on the starting year. For example, the decade starting with 1961 contained 2 leap years, and the decade starting with 1971 contained 3 leap years. The century starting 1801 contained 24 leap years, and the century starting 1901 contained 25 leap years. And so on.

As time measurement for scientific or sporting purposes becomes more and more accurate, the second is divided in the standard metric way: millisecond = 10^{-3} s, microsecond = 10^{-6} s, nanosecond = 10^{-9} s, picosecond = 10^{-12} s and so on.

The Congrès International de Chronometer (1900) sought to introduce a metric system where none was feasible. The unit to be divided was the (24-hour) day, of which one hundredth was to be called the cé or degré. The proposals are shown in the table below; note that the pronunciation is French.

Name	Popular name	Alternative	Part of a day	Seconds
degré		cé	0.01	864.0
decigrade	minute première	dedicé	0.001	86.4
centigrade	minute seconde		0.0001	8.64
milligrade	moment, blink	millicé	0.00001	0.864
decimilligrade	instant, wink		0.000001	0.0864

It takes but a decimilligrade to see why the proposal didn't catch on, and an equal period of time to imagine the confusion – through the nomenclature alone – that would have ensued had the scheme been put to the test.

The eon, or æon, is defined as 10^9 years.

The chron was proposed by JS Huxley (1957): 1 Chron = 10^6 years; 1 millichron = 1 millennium.

Somewhat confusingly in the light of the above, the michron is proposed as the time of vibration of a wave of wavelength 1 micron (one-millionth of a metre). The term derives from the first syllables of the ancient Greek words *mikros* = small and *chronos* = time, and is clearly a scientific pun on micron.

The darwin was proposed by JBS Haldane (1948): when the population of a species increases or decreases by an exponential factor e in 106 years, its rate of change is 1 darwin = a rate of change of 10^{-3} in 1,000 years. In nature, the rate of change rarely exceeds 1 darwin, whereas in domestic animals rates may reach 1 kilodarwin.

The chronon or tempon has been proposed as the shortest unit of time; that taken for electromagnetic radiation to cover a distance equal to the radius of an atom – about 10^{-23}s.

The ephemeris second is defined as 1/31 556 925.9747 of the tropical year that began on 1 January 1900. Compare this with the straightforward multiplication $365 \times 24 \times 3,600 = 31\,536\,000$; the difference is 11.25 minutes short of six hours. The six hours are caught up every four years when the leap-year day is inserted; the 11.25 minutes are caught up by the rule relating to leap years ending in 00.

Ultradian

Recurring in a cyclic pattern completed in more than twenty-four hours. The word is used especially in relation to body rhythms such as regular digestive processes and other neurologically-organised periodic functions. The term is as crassly derived as the related Circadian, in this case supposedly coming from Latin elements *ultra* 'outside' and *dies* 'day'.

Ulûlu

Babylonian month of purification, from which the Jewish month of Elul takes its name.

United Nations' Day

October 24

Universal Time

An alternative name for Greenwich Mean Time, *qv*.

Unlucky days

According to a record from the time of King Henry VI ...

'These underwritten be the perilous days, for to take any sickness in, or to be hurt in, or to be wedded in, or to take any journey upon, or to begin any work on, that he would well speed. The number of these days be in the year 32; they be these:

January: 1, 2, 4, 5, 7, 10, 15.
February: 6, 7, 18.
March: 1, 6, 8.
April: 6, 11.
May: 5, 6, 7.
June: 7, 15.
July: 5, 19.
August: 15, 19.
September: 6, 7.
October: 6.
November: 15, 16.
December: 15, 16, 17.'

The days seem to have lost their influences after the Reformation, and survived only in a general superstition that fishermen do not set sail, and (especially in the north) that couples are not wed, on a Friday. Analysis of the above list shows that, for a year starting on a Tuesday, there are nine unlucky Fridays, and only four of every other day except Wednesday, of which there are three. Readers may draw their own conclusions.

Uphaliday
Scottish name for Twelfth Night, the end of the Christmas holidays.

Up-Helly; Up-helly-aa
A procession at Lerwick, capital of Shetland, held at the end of January.

Uposatha (Observance Days)
Theravada countries continue to observe four monthly holy days (in Sri Lanka Poya Days): the new moon, the full moon, and the two quarter moon days.

Upper Carboniferous or Pennsylvanian Epoch
The more recent Epoch of the Carboniferous Period; see Geological Time Divisions.

Upper Cretaceous
The most recent Epoch in the Cretaceous Period; see Geological Time Divisions.

Upper Jurassic or Malm Epoch
The most recent in the Jurassic Period; see Geological Time Divisions.

Useless Parliament
That summoned by Charles I on 8 June 1625; it spent all its time quarrelling with the king, and was dissolved on 12 August.

UT; UTC
Universal Time; — Co-ordinated.

Vaishakh
Second month of the Hindu year.

Valentine's Day
St Valentine's Day is on 14 February; the C14 writers Chaucer and Gower both cite the day as that upon which birds (of whom Valentine was patron saint) choose their mates; later, it became the day upon which, with much merrymaking, tokens of affection are sent by members of both sexes to those of the other. Valentine was a Roman who was martyred for becoming a Christian and a priest to boot, on 14 February 269. Some say he left a note for the jailer's daughter, who had befriended him, signed 'From your Valentine'; others add that 14 February was a holiday for the love-goddess Juno, and the day before the beginning of the love-feast of Lupercal (*qv*).

Vasanta Panchami
Hindu Festival in honour of the goddess Saraswati; in the Gregorian calendar it falls in January–February.

Vassa
Buddhist monks' three months' retreat during the rainy season.

Ve-Adar
See Adar.

Vendémiaire
(Vintage); first month of the French Revolutionary Calendar *qv*.

Ventôse
(Windy); sixth month of the French Revolutionary Calendar *qv*.

Verge escapement
By the middle of C14 – perhaps earlier – there were several weight-driven striking clocks in Europe (at Milan and Rouen for example). Their escapement was a *crown wheel*, controlled by *pallets* on a vertical shaft, or *verge*. The verge oscillates about its vertical axis, and the pallets alternately engage with and release the teeth on the crown wheel, allowing it to turn half a tooth at a time. The oscillation of the verge is governed by a *foliot*: an arm with adjustable weights rotating this way and that. If the arbor (axle) of the escape wheel is vertical, the verge may be governed by a (short) pendulum, though the resemblance to the later pendulum whose length regulates the clock with some accuracy is purely coincidental, since the mechanism can be made to go faster by increasing the driving force, or decreasing the weight of the pendulum 'bob'.

Vernal
Pertaining to the spring.

Vernal Equinox
1   The notional beginning of spring, and the end of winter, when the Sun crosses the plane of the equator toward the relevant hemisphere, and day and night are of equal length. In the Northern hemisphere it occurs about 21 March, and 23 September in the Southern hemisphere.

2   In astronomy, the point on the celestial sphere in Pisces at which the ecliptic intersects the celestial equator.

Vertu, La Fête de la
Virtue Day; see French Revolutionary Calendar.

Vesak or Visakah Puja (Buddha's Birthday Celebrations)
Traditionally, Buddha's Birthday is the major Buddhist festival of the year, celebrating the birth, enlightenment and death of the Buddha on the one day: the first full moon day in May (except in a leap year, when the festival is held in June). Vesak is the name of the month in the Indian calendar.

Vespers, Fatal
26 October 1623, when 100 members of a Jesuit congregation were killed when the floor of the room gave way.

Veterans' Day
The US equivalent of Armistice Day, later Remembrance Sunday.

Vicennial
Occurring once every twenty years; lasting for twenty years.

Victoria Day
The Monday preceding 24 May, observed in Canada as a legal holiday. Originally commemorating Queen Victoria's birthday (24 May 1819).

Victorian age/era
Queen Victoria (1819–1901) occupied the British throne from 20 June 1837 to 22 January 1901; this is strictly the Victorian era, but in reality there was some inertia before the era began, and its end is fuzzy as it ran into the Edwardian era (qv) that seems from our view to end as the First World War broke out.

Vinalia
Roman wine festivals in honour of Jupiter and also associated with Venus as a goddess of vineyards. The first such festival was held on 23 April, when the wine of the previous season was broached and the second on the 19 August when the vintage began.

Virgo
(Latin = the Virgin); sixth sign of the zodiac; 23/24 August – 22/23 September; sixth northern (septentrional) sign – third summer sign – third descending sign; see Zodiac.

Vula
i balolo lailai, – i balolo levu, – i cukicuki, – i doi, – i gasau, – i kelikeli, – i liliwa, – i nuqa levu, – i sevu, – i vavakada, – ni nuqa lailai, – ni werewere; see Fijian calendar.

W; Wed
Wednesday; see Week.

Waitangi Day
Waitangi Day – 6 February: New Zealand's national day, celebrated (from 1960) to commemorate the signing of the Treaty of Waitangi in 1840 between the Governor William Hobson and the Maori chiefs.

Wake
A watch or vigil.

Walking the Wheat
A Monmouthshire custom, called 'corn showing' in adjacent Herefordshire, when farmers and bailiffs walked their fields on the afternoon of Easter Day, carrying plum-cakes and cider to eat and drink to the success of their crops. The practice seems to have died out at the end of C19.

Walpurgis Night

(Ger *Walpurgisnacht*) The eve of the feast day of the C8 abbess St Walpurga (1 May) when, according to German folklore, witches hold a Sabbath on high ground, particularly the Brocken in the Harz Mountains. Hence the significance of Spectre of the Brocken, seen when one's image is projected on to a screen of fog by the sun at one's back.

War

A state or period of usually open and declared armed hostile conflict between states or nations. A struggle between opposing forces or for a particular end. To engage in warfare. To be in active or vigorous conflict. To be opposed or inconsistent.

Watch

On board ship the 24-hour day is divided into seven watches, five of them are 4 hours long and the remaining two are 2 hours long. The latter two 'dog watches' are from 16.00 (4pm) to 18.00 (6pm) and 18.00 (6pm) to 20.00 (8pm), with the purpose that those who regularly alternate duty on watch automatically get a daily change of hours and at a time when an evening meal is available. The word dog is here a corruption of 'dodge'. The object of these is to prevent the same men always being on duty during the same hours each day.

On British naval ships, the bells (*qv*) that sound the time every half-hour – culminating in eight bells rung in paired chimes at 4 o'clock, 8 o'clock, and 12 o'clock, am and pm – follow the watch system, thus beginning at one bell (rather than five) at 18.30 (6.30pm). This practice derives from the time of the naval mutiny at the Nore (1797) when the signal for the mutiny was the five bells at the beginning of the last (second) dogwatch. Five bells at that time of day has since then never been sounded on a British naval ship.

By derivation, however, a watch was a period of duty during the night, when a person had to stay awake (Old English *waeccan* = both 'watch' and '(stay) awake'). The ancient Hebrews had three watches during the night; the ancient Greeks and Romans four, or in some cities five.

In England, the night Watch (an early form of nocturnal police force) was introduced in C13, under the control of local Watch Committees, that the streets might be safer at night. 'Period drama' may suggest that the Watch went round crying: 'Three [or whatever] in the morning, and all's well' but it seems unlikely that those sleeping easy in their beds would have put up with such behaviour for long.

Washington, George

(22 February 1732–14 December 99); first President of the United States 1789–97; his birthday is a US holiday.

Wassail

1   A toast or salutation, especially over the spiced ale cup at the New Year.
2   The whole occasion of such toasts.
3   The drink itself, usually mulled wine or the like.
4   House-to-house carolling at Christmastide.

Watch Night

31 December, to see the Old Year out and the New Year in, perhaps by a religious service.

Water Drench Monday

Easter Monday, when Hungarian men splash their girlfriends with water until they are rewarded with coloured Easter eggs.

Waterloo Day

Commemorating 18 June 1815, when British and Prussian forces under Wellington and Blücher routed the French under Napoleon near the Belgian town of Waterloo in Brabant province south of Brussels; by cruel fate, the London terminus of the Channel Tunnel Rail Link is at Waterloo; on this day, a small flag is presented to the British Monarch as rent for the Strathfield Saye Estate.

Waucobian

A Stage in the Cambrian Period; see Geological Time Divisions.

We-Adar

See Jewish calendar.

W; Wed

Wednesday; see Week.

Weekdays of the Festival

See Pesach.

Week of Sundays

A long time, an indefinite period.

Weeks, Feast of

See Shavuot.

Well Dressing

The custom of decorating village wells with intricate designs or scenes made with flowers is an annual tradition unique to Derbyshire, England. The custom was originally known as Well Flowering, and it consists of decorating wells, or springs – at one time the only source of

Week

A period normally of seven days, chosen for its relevance to the rhythm of life. 'Once a week' seems about right for religious observance, meeting friends and going to market. One supposes that the seven-day week is of great antiquity, as it has become woven into the creation legend, but the Ancient Egyptians had a 10-day week, as did the French Revolutionaries (qv), though theirs lasted but 13 years. The Soviet Union introduced a 5-day week in 1930, increased to a 6-day week the following year, but the USSR had adopted the Gregorian calendar in 1917, and the strain of running a different week, especially with the onset of WW2 and the need to co-operate with allies, saw a return to the 7-day week on 26 June 1940.

Now that communications can be immediate, and international travel swift, those wishing to take their place in the modern world must live by the Gregorian calendar, even if they use a different model for their religious life. The next step must be the universal calendar (see Part 3), though it may never be possible to persuade everyone concerned of its value.

The names of the English days of the week are of Anglo-Saxon origin.

English	Latin	Saxon	French	German	Welsh
Sunday	Dies Solis	Sun's Day	Dimanche	Sonntag	Dydd Sul
Monday	Dies Lunae	Moon's Day	Lundi	Montag	Dydd Llun
Tuesday	Dies Martis	Tiu's Day	Mardi	Dienstag	Dydd Mawrth
Wednesday	Dies Mercurii	Woden's Day	Mercredi	Mittwoch	Dydd Mercher
Thursday	Dies Jovis	Thor's Day	Jeudi	Donnerstag	Dydd Iau
Friday	Dies Veneris	Frigg's Day	Vendredi	Freitag	Dydd Gwener
Saturday	Dies Saturni	Saeternes' Day	Samedi	Samstag	Dydd Sadwm

Tiu was the Anglo-Saxon counterpart of the Nordic Tyr, son of Odin, God of War, who came closet to Mars (Greek, Ares) son of the Roman God Jupiter (Greek, Zeus). Woden was the Anglo-Saxon counterpart of Odin, Nordic dispenser of victory, who came closest to Mercury (Greek, Hermes), the Roman messenger of victory. Thor was the Nordic God of Thunder, eldest son of Odin and nearest to the Roman Jupiter (Greek, Zeus), who was armed with thunder and lightning. Frigg (or Freyja), wife of Odin, was the Nordic Goddess of Love, and equivalent to Venus (Greek, Aphrodite), Goddess of Love in Roman mythology. Thus four of the middle days of the week are named after a mythological husband and wife and their two sons. Similar influences may be seen in the French, German and Welsh days in the table.

local water – with botanical material in order to give thanks for their beneficence (though there is a possibility that animal sacrifice once played a part in the custom when it was wholly serious). Nowadays, well dressing plays its part as a fund-raising attraction during the tourist season, lasting as it does from May to September. The decorations are carried on a wooden frame supporting a clay background into which moss, berries, flowers, petals and other botanical materials are pressed. Many themes are religious, though local scenes and commemorations are often chosen.

Wenlockian
A Stage in the Silurian Period; see Geological Time Divisions.

Wesak (Vesak) Day
A Buddhist festival commemorating the birth, enlightenment, and death of the Buddha, celebrated in May.

Western Standard Time
See Time Zones.

Westphalian
A Stage in the Upper Carboniferous Epoch; see Geological Time Divisions.

Whip-dog Day
18 October, St Luke's Day.

Whit Sunday
The seventh Sunday after Easter; see Pentecost.

Whitsun Farthing
Offerings made to the Parish Priest at Whitsuntide.

Wink
To shut one eye briefly as a signal or to indicate that one is teasing; half a blink; a very short time; see Units of Time.

Wessex

Royal House of England 802–1066.

802– 839	Egbert
839– 855	Æthelwulf
855– 860	Æthelbald
860– 866	Æthelbert
866– 871	Æthelred
871– 899	Alfred the Great
899– 925	Edward the Elder
925– 940	Athelstan
940– 946	Edward the Magnificent
946– 955	Eadred
955– 959	Eadwig (Edwy) All-Fair
959– 975	Edgar the Peaceable
975– 978	Edward the Martyr
978–1016	Æthelred the Unready
1016	Edward Ironside

Danish line
1014	Svein Forkbeard
1016–1035	Canute the Great
1035–1040	Harald Harefoot
1040–1042	Hardicanute

Wessex restored
1042–1066	Edward the Confessor
1066	Harold II

Wild Horse Chase Festival
See Soma Nomaoi Matsuri.

Winter
The coldest season of the year, between autumn and spring; astronomically speaking from the December solstice to the March equinox in the Northern hemisphere, and at the opposite time of the year in the Southern hemisphere.

Winter Nights
A pagan feast in October, which opened the winter season.

Winter Solstice
In the Northern hemisphere about 21 December, the time at which the sun is at its southernmost point in the sky (in the Southern hemisphere about 21 June, the northernmost point); the point on the celestial sphere (opposite the summer solstice) at which the ecliptic is furthest south from the celestial equator; right ascension 18 hours; declination −23.5°.

Wk; wk
Week.

Wonderful Parliament
See Merciless Parliament.

Wren hunting/Wrenning Day
St Stephen's Day, 26 December, used to be so called, because it was a local custom among villagers to stone a wren to death on that day in commemoration of the stoning of St Stephen.

WST
Western Standard Time; see Time Zones.

Würm
The fourth of the Ice Ages that occurred in Europe during the Pleistocene Epoch; see also Günz, Mindel, and Riss, and Geological Time Divisions.

Year and a day
In law the period of time which in certain matters determines a right or liability.

Yearbook
The name given to an annual publication summarizing the events, changes, etc., in the preceding year.

Year of Confusion
46BCE, a year of 445 days when the Julian calendar was introduced.

Year of Grace
The year of our Lord; a year of the Christian era.

Yellow River
'When the Yellow River runs clear' is a Chinese saying for 'never'.

Yom ha-Shoah
In the Jewish calendar, 27 Nisan remembers the victims of the Holocaust, but is not a public holiday.

Year

The time taken for the earth to complete one orbit round the sun. It is approximately 365.25 days, a period known to the Egyptians and Babylonians over 4,000 years ago, and sometimes called the Julian year. There are a number of different years. A terrestrial observer sees the sun moving in a geocentric circle (the ecliptic) on a geocentric sphere (the celestial sphere), so the lengths of a year are defined with respect to the Sun's apparent motion.

A solar, or tropical, year is the average time for the Sun to return to the First Point of Aries at the vernal equinox; it is $365.242\ 199 - 0.000\ 006\ T$ days, where T is the time in centuries since 1 January 1900.

An astronomical year (Besselian year or *annus fictus*) is the time during which the right ascension of the mean Sun (*ie* the angle between the meridians of the Sun and the vernal equinox) increases by 360°; it is $365.253\ 189\ 7$ days. The civil year begins when the angle is 280° – *ie* 1 January.

A sidereal year is the average time for the Earth to complete one revolution round the Earth with reference to the fixed stars; it is $365.256.360 + 0.000\ 000\ 1\ T$ days. It is longer than the tropical year by 20.4 minutes.

An anomalistic year is the time between two successive passages of the Sun through the perigee; it is $365.256\ 641 + 0.000\ 003\ T$ days. It is longer than a tropical year by 20.8 minutes.

A Gaussian year is the theoretical time (by calculation) for the Earth to orbit the sun once; it is $365.258\ 898$ days.

An eclipse year is the time between two successive passages of the Sun through the same node on the orbit of the Moon; it is $365.620\ 03$ days.

To remind us that a year is a man-decreed length of time, remember that an Islamic year is lunar, and some 10 or 11 days shorter than the years defined above.

Yom Ha'Atzmaut

Israel Independence Day, 5 Iyyar. See Jewish calendar.

Yom H'zikharon
Remembrance Day; in the Jewish calendar, a modern commemoration day observed on 4 Iyyar, but is not a public holiday.

Yom Kippur
In the Jewish calendar, the Day of Atonement: a High Festival dedicated to repentance, and marked by total abstinence from all food and drink from the eve of 10 Tishri to nightfall on 11 Tishri.

Yom Yerushalayim
In the Jewish calendar, Jerusalem Day, a Festival on 28 Iyyar remembering Jerusalem.

Yonks
A long period of time, commonly believed to be derived from components of Years, mONths, and weeKS.

York, House of
See Plantagenet.

Yorkshire Day
1 August, marking the Battle of Minden (*qv*) in 1759 when British and Prussian forces defeated the French. Soldiers including those of the 51st Foot, the King's Own Yorkshire Light Infantry (which became the 2nd Batallion the Light Infantry in 1968) picked white roses from the battlefield in memory of the fallen. Celebrations include the Yorkshire 'Declaration of Integrity' being read throughout the three Ridings.

Ypresian
A Stage in the Eocene Epoch; see Geological Time Divisions.

Yuga
In Hindu cosmology, an age: any of the four ages of the duration of the world, each comprising 4.32 million years.

Yule
Scandinavian term for Christmas.

Zeitgeist
German = The spirit of the age.

Zero hour
A military term for the exact time at which an attack, etc., is to begin.

Zone Time
A system of timekeeping based on 24 meridians each 15° apart; see Time Zones.

Zodiac

The zodiac (Greek *zōdiakos kyklos* = circle of animals) relates to a system for describing the apparent motions of heavenly bodies with respect to the constellations devised in Mesopotamia some 5,000 years ago.

The imagination of those who named the constellations is equalled in the present day by that of those who interpret ultrasound scans. The zodiac is an imaginary belt of pictorial constellations whose (arbitrary) width is 8° on either side of the annual path or ecliptic of the sun. The belt is divided into twelve sectors, each of 30°, and each bearing the name of the constellation which at one time occupied that sector. The present lack of correlation between the zodiacal sectors and the constellations from which they are named is the same as that which dogged the Julian calendar. The original order is nonetheless adhered to; otherwise, the work of the astrologer (*qv*) would be even more difficult than it is.

Here are details of the 'star signs'; note that there may be some variation in start and finish dates:

The signs   **Elemental guide**

Northern (Septentrional) signs – Spring – Ascending signs

1 Aries – the Ram	21 March–19/20 April	Fire	Cardinal
2 Taurus – the Bull	20/21 April–20/21 May	Earth	Fixed
3 Gemini – the Twins	21/22 May–21/22 June	Air	Mutable

Northern (Septentrional) signs – Summer – Descending signs

4 Cancer – the Crab	22/23 June–22/23 July	Water	Cardinal
5 Leo – the Lion	23/24 July–22/23 August	Fire	Fixed
6 Virgo – the Virgin	23/24 August– 22/23 September	Earth	Mutable

Southern (Austral) signs – Autumn – Descending signs

7 Libra – the Balance	23/24 September–22/23 October	Air	Cardinal
8 Scorpio – the Scorpion	23/24 October–21/22 November	Water	Fixed
9 Sagittarius – the Archer	22/23 November–21/22 December	Fire	Mutable

Southern (Austral) signs – Winter – Ascending signs

10 Capricorn – the Goat	22/23 December–18/19 January	Earth	Cardinal
11 Aquarius – the Water Carrier	19/20 January–18/19 February	Air	Fixed
12 Pisces – the Fishes	19/20 February–20 March	Water	Mutable

Mnemonic

The Ram, the Bull, the Heavenly Twins,
And next the Crab the Lion shines,
The Virgin and the Scales;
The Scorpion, Archer and the Goat,
The Man that bears the water-pot,
The Fish with silvery tails.

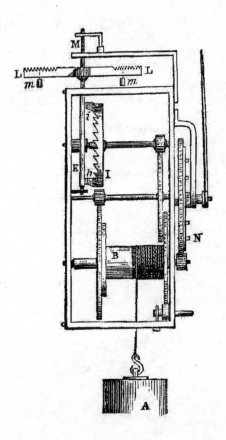

Part 2
The 366-day calendar

This section looks at the 366 days of a Gregorian leap year, starting on a Monday. Unfortunately, there is no such thing as an idealised year, because of the difficulties of showing movable feasts and the dates that depend on them, and cross references to other calendars. We have therefore taken our year as 1996, the most recent leap year starting on a Monday (the next will be 2024).

The holidays we have shown are those that fell in 1996, and of course some may shift from year to year so that they avoid clashes with weekends, for example. And those related to other calendars may move steadily in relation to the Gregorian calendar from one year to the next. Easter Day in 1996 was 7 April, so we have taken that date as an example, but we have also showed the earliest and the latest dates upon which it, and the various movable days related to it, may fall.

What does it all mean?
Each month begins with its name, the derivation of its name, and its birthstone.

Each day begins with the International Standard Week Number; then the place of that day in the year (how many have elapsed; how many to go, with the leap-year equivalent in parentheses); and then the name of the day itself.

Below that are listed saints associated with that day, but note that there is some lack of agreement between authorities on who should be remembered when.

Lastly, Holidays etc gives a variety of information about each day; we have used the word 'observance' to cover a whole range of events between joyous festivals and solemn rites.

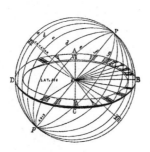

January

Takes its name from Janus, the two-faced god of doorways and of beginnings.
Birthstone   Garnet.

Week number 1   Day number 1–364 (1–365)   **Monday 1 January**

Saints' days   St Fugentius, Bp and con • St Odilo or Olou, 6th ab of Cluny – Institutor of the feast of All Souls – invoked for souls in Purgatory and against jaundice • St Almachius M • St Eugendus, ab • St Faine or Fanchea, V of Ireland • St Mochua or Moncain, aka Claunus, ab in Ireland • St Mochua, aka Cronan of Balla, ab in Ireland.

Holidays etc   Gregorian New Year's Day • Japanese year Heisei 8 begins • The Birthday of Guru Gobind Singh Ji falls in January (Sikh) • PH in UK (since 1974), Scotland (by Statute; if 0101 is ⑤, the next two days are PHs), USA, Canada, HK, Australia, and New Zealand • Cuba   Day of Liberation • Haiti National Day • Slovakia   Establishment of Slovak Republic • Sudan Independence Day • PH also in Austria, Bahrain, Belgium. Bolivia, Brazil, Bulgaria, Chile, China, Colombia. Denmark, Estonia, Finland, France, Germany, Ghana, Greece, Hungary, Iceland, Indonesia, Republic of Ireland, Italy, Japan, Kenya, Republic of Korea, Latvia, Lithuania, Mexico, Netherlands, Nigeria, Norway, PNG, Paraguay, Peru, Philippines, Poland, Portugal, Romania, Russian Federation, Singapore, South Africa, Spain, Sweden, Switzerland, Taiwan, Thailand, Turkey, UAE, USA, Venezuela.

Week number 1   Day number 2–363 (2–364)   **Tuesday 2 January**

Saints' days   St Marcarius, anchoret, patron saint of confectioners • St Concordius, M • St Adelard, ab • St Basil the Great – Patriarch of Eastern Monks – patron saint of Russia • St Gregory of Nazianzus – champion of Nicene orthodoxy • St Caspar del Bufalo • St Seraphim of Sarov.

Holidays etc   Jewish observance   10 Tebet – Fast to commemorate Nebuchadnezzar's siege of Jerusalem • PH   Scotland, NZ, Romania, Russian Federation, Taiwan.

Week number 1   Day number 3–362 (3–363)   **Wednesday 3 January**

Saints' days   Ste Geneviève V – Defender of Paris – patron saint of Paris, disasters and fever • St Peter Balsam, M • St Anterus, Pope 235 • St Gordius, M.

Week number 1   Day number 4–361 (4–362)   Thursday 4 January

Saints' days   St Titus, disciple of Paul • St Gregory, Bp 541 • St Rumon, Bp • St Rigobert or Robert c750.

Holidays etc   Myanmar [Burma]   National Day.

Week number 1   Day number 5–360 (5–361)   Friday 5 January

Saints' days   St Simeon Stylites – first of the 'pillar saints' 459 • St Telesphorus 7th Bp of Rome 128 • St Syncletica V.

Holidays etc   Lailat Bara'ah (Islamic day, AH 1416) • First Full Moon of the Gregorian year; eleventh month of the Theravadan Buddhist year • Theravadan Buddhist Uposatha (Observance Day) = Sri Lankan Poya Day • Buddhist observance   Mahayana   Buddhist New Year.

Week number 1   Day number 6–359 (6–360)   Saturday 6 January

Saints' days   St Melanius Bp 490 • St Peter ab of St Austin's Canterbury 608

Holidays etc   Epiphany; Twelfth Day (after Christmas); DO Ireland • Buddhist observance   Vesak or Visakah Puja (Buddha Day) • PH Austria, Finland, Greece, Italy, Spain, Sweden.

Week number 1   Day number 7–358 (7–359)   Sunday 7 January

Saints' days   St Lucian of Antioch – priest and M • St Cedd Bp of London C7 • St Thillo 702 • St Kentgerna widow 708 • St Aldric Bp of Mans 856 • St Charles of Sezze • St Canut or Canute Lavard 1171.

Holidays etc   1st ⑊ after Epiphany DO England and Wales • Christmas in Christian-Eastern Orthodox calendar (but not Greek Orthodox) • PH Russian Federation • Japanese observance   Dazaifu Usokae (Dazaifu Bullfinch Exchange).

Week number 2   Day number 8–357 (8–358)   Monday 8 January

Saints' days   St Appolinaris – the apologist, bishop, 175 • St Abo • St Gudula • St Pega • St Lucian of Beauvais M 290 • St Nathalan Bp confessor 452 • St Severinus ab of Noricum 482 • St Gudula V c719 • St Vulsin Bp and con 973 • St Thorfinn.

Holidays etc   Plough Monday   first M after Twelfth Day • PH   Colombia.

Week number 2   Day number 9–356 (9–357)   Tuesday 9 January

Saints' days   SS Julian and Basilissa Ms 313 • St Peter of Sabaste Bp and con c387 • St Marchiana V and M c305 • St Vaneng con c688 • St Fillan ab and hermit C7 • St Adrian ab of Canterbury – the schoolmaster of Canterbury 710 • St Brithwald Abp Canterbury 731 • St Philip of Moscow.

Week number 2   Day number 10–355 (10–356)   Wednesday 10 January

Saints' days   St Marcian – priest C5 • St Agatho pope 682 • St William Abp Bourges con 1209 • St Peter Orseolo.

Holidays etc   Falkland Islands   Maggie Thatcher Day • Japanese observance   Toka Ebisu (10th Day Ebisu).

Week number 2   Day number 11–354 (11–355)   Thursday 11 January

Saints' days   St Hygeinus Pope and M 142 • St Theodosius the Cœnobiarch 529 • St Salvius or Sauve Bp of Amiens C7 • St Egwin Bp con 717 • St Tatiana.

Holidays etc   Hilary Law Term begins (ends 0403).

Week number 2   Day number 12–353 (12–354)   Friday 12 January

Saints' days   St Arcadius M • St Ælred – the Bernard of the North 1166 • St Benedict or Bennet Biscop – founder of Wearmouth and Jarrow – patron saint of painters and musicians 690 • St Tygrius priest.

Week number 2   Day number 13–352 (13–353)   Saturday 13 January

Saints' days   St Kentigern aka St Mungo of Glasgow 691 • St Veronica of Milan 1497 • St Hilary of Poitiers – The Athenasius of the West – patron saint of backward children, invoked against snakes.

Holidays etc   New Year's day, Old Style • Moon's last quarter • Theravadan Buddhist Uposatha (Observance Day) = Sri Lankan Poya Day.

Week number 2   Day number 14–351 (14–352)   Sunday 14 January

Saints' days   [St Kentigern – The apostle of Cumbria – patron saint of Glasgow] • SS Isaias and Sabas 273 • St Barba'shmin or Barbasceminus 346 • St Felix of Nola • St Hilary of Poitiers • St Macrina the Elder • St Sava.

Holidays etc   2nd ✟ after Epiphany • Mallard Day   All Souls College, Oxford, in commemoration of an overgrown mallard being found in a drain during foundation digging • Japanese observance (two days) Niino Izu Yuki Matsuri (Niino Snow Festival).

Week number 3   Day number 15–350 (15–351)   Monday 15 January

Saints' days St Isidore priest and hermit patron saint of labourers c390 • St Isidore priest and hospitaller of Alexandria 403 • St John Calybite recluse 450 • St Maurua ab 584 • St Main ab 569 • St Ita or Mida V abs 569 • St Bonitus Bp of Auvergne 710 • St Macarius the Elder • St Paul the first Hermit 342.

Holidays etc USA   Martin Luther King Day (Federal Public Holiday, 3rd M in January) • Hindu observance   Makara Sankranti • Japanese observance   Adults' Day • Japanese observance   Nara Yamamaki (Nara Hill-Burning); also called Wakakusayama no Yamayaki.

Week number 3   Day number 16–349 (16–350)   Tuesday 16 January

Saints' days   St Marcellus pope M 310 • St Macarius the elder of Egypt 390 • St Honoratus Abp of Arles 429 • St Fursey, son of Fintan, K of part of Ireland 650 • St Henry hermit 1127 • St Berard and his companions M.

Week number 3   Day number 17–348 (17–349)   Wednesday 17 January

Saints' days   Antony of Egypt, the patron saint of pigs, basket-makers, and monks, invoked against ergotism; his name gives us the word 'tantony', a diminutive applied to pigs, meaning the smallest of the litter 356 • SS Speusippus, Eleusippus and Meleusippus Ms • St Sulpice (Sulpicius) the Pious Abp 591 • St Sulpicius the second Abp 644 • St Milgithe V C7.

Week number 3   Day number 18–347 (18–348)   Thursday 18 January

Saints' days   Celebration of St Peter's Chair at Rome • St Paul and 36 companions in Egypt • St Prisca V&M c275 • St Deicolus ab C7 • St Ulfrid Bp&M 1028.

Week number 3   Day number 19–346 (19–347)   Friday 19 January

Saints' days   St Knut (Canutus) – King of Denmark, M 1036 • SS Abachum, Audifax, Maris and Martha Ms 270 • St Lomer 593 • St Blaithmaic ab in Scotland 793 • St Wulstan bp of Worcester 1095 • St Henry of England, M in Finland 1151.

Holidays etc   Zodiac   last day of Capricorn – The Goat (from 1222).

Week number 3   Day number 20–345 (20–346)   Saturday 20 January

Saints' days   St Sebastian – The soldier-martyr – patron saint of archers, athletes, soldiers and police, invoked against plague and by the dying 288 • St Euthymius the Great 473 • St Fabian pope 250 • St Fechin ab in Ireland 664.

Holidays etc   Zodiac   first day of Aquarius – the Water Carrier (to 0218) • St Agnes Eve – On this day, legend has it that a woman can divine her future husband. 'They told her how, upon St Agnes Eve/Young virgins might have vision of delight' (Keats) • Japanese observance   Motsuji Madarajin Matsuri; also called Motsuji Ennen • First New Moon of the Gregorian year; thirteenth month of the Chinese year of the Pig • Theravadan Buddhist Uposatha (Observance Day) = Sri Lankan Poya Day.

Week number 3   Day number 21–344 (21–345)   Sunday 21 January

Saints' days   St Agnes – The victorious virgin – patron saint of betrothed couples, gardeners and virgins, invoked for chastity M 304 (or 305) • St Fructuosus of Tarragona 259 • St Epiphanius 497 • St Vimin or Vivian 615 • St Publius • St Meinrad.

Holidays etc   3rd S after Epiphany • 1st Ramadan (Islamic year AH1416) the month of fasting, when between dawn and dusk there should be no food ingested, drink imbibed or sexual pleasure experienced • PH   UAE

Week number 4   Day number 22–343 (22–344)   Monday 22 January

Saints' days   Anastasius – patron saint of goldsmiths, wine growers and drunkards M at Valencia 304 • St Anastasius M in Assyria 628.

Holidays etc   Jewish calendar   Shebat 1 AM5756 • Muslim calendar 1 Ramadan 1416 AH.

Week number 4   Day number 23–342 (23–343)   Tuesday 23 January

Saints' days   St Emerantia V&M c304 • St Clement of Ancyra M 304 • St Agathangelus 304 • St Eusebius ab in Assyria C4 • Ildefonsus Abp of Toledo 667 • St John the Almoner, patriarch of Alexandria cC7 • St Raymond of Peñafort 1275.

Week number 4   Day number 24–341 (24–342)   Wednesday 24 January

Saints' days   St Francis of Sales – Jesuit and bishop – patron saint of writers, editors and journalists – author of several popular books on theology • St Timothy disciple of St Paul M Ephesus 97 • St Babylas Bp Antioch c250 • St Macedonius of Syria C5 • St Cadocus or Cadoc ab of Wales C6 • St Sauranus ab in Umbria M C7.

Holidays etc   Hindu observance   Vasant Panchami or Sarasvati-puja.

Week number 4   Day number 25–340 (25–341)   Thursday 25 January

Saints' days   St Paul's Day • St Juventinus and Maximinus Ms Antioch 363 • St Apollo ab in Thebais c393 • St Publius Ab in Syria C4 • St Projectus or St Prix Bp Clermont M 674 • St Poppo ab of Stavello 1048.

Holidays etc   Burns Night, especially in Scotland, when the Noble Haggis is addressed and the skirl of the pipes is heard throughout the land.

Week number 4   Day number 26–339 (26–340)   Friday 26 January

Saints' days   St Timothy – the young disciple of Paul – invoked against weakness of the stomach • St Paula patron saint of widows 404 • St Alberic • St Eystein • St Polycarp Bp Smyrna 166 • St Conon Bp of Man c648.

Holidays etc   Australia Day – marking the founding of Sydney in 1788 by Governor Arthur Phillip as a penal colony comprising 1,030 people, of whom 736 were convicts. Transportation of convicts, often for the pettiest crime, ended in 1865 • S Tasmania   Hobart Cup Day • PH India – Republic Day.

Week number 4   Day number 27–338 (27–339)   Saturday 27 January

Saints' days   St John Chrysostom Abp 407 • St Julian Bp C3 • St Marius ab 555.

Holidays etc   Moon's first quarter • Theravadan Buddhist Uposatha (Observance Day) = Sri Lankan Poya Day.

Week number 4   Day number 28–337 (28–338)   Sunday 28 January

Saints' days   St Agnes V&M • St Cyril patriarch of Alexandria 444 • SS Callinicus, Leucius and Thyrsus Ms • St John of Reomay ab C6 • St Paulinus patriarch of Aquileia 804 • St Glastian of Scotland 850 • St Margaret princess of Hungary 1271 • St Thomas Aquinas – Doctor Angelicus – patron saint of philosophers, theologians, booksellers, universities, colleges, students and scholars, invoked for chastity and learning • St Peter Nolasco • St Valerius of Saragossa.

Holidays etc   4th ☉ after Epiphany.

Week number 5	Day number 29–336 (29–337)	Monday 29 January

Saints' days   St Sulpicius Severus c407 • St Gildas the Wise or Badonicus ab 570? • St Gildas the Albanian or Scot 512 • St Francis de Sales 1622.

Week number 5	Day number 30–335 (30–336)	Tuesday 30 January

Saints' days   St Barsimæus Bp and M C2 • St Bathild(es) – Slave-girl, queen of France and the humblest of nuns – patron saint of children 680 • St Martina V&M C3 • St Aldegondes B and abs 660.

Week number 5	Day number 31–334 (31–335)	Wednesday 31 January

Saints' days   St John Bosco – popular preacher who became patron saint of editors • St Maidoc or Aidan Bp of Ferns in Ireland 632 • St Serapion M 1240 • Ss Cyrus and John Ms • St Peter Nolasco 1258 • St Marcella widow 410.

Holidays etc   Nauru – Independence Day.

February

Takes its name from Februa, the Roman festival of purification.
Birthstone   Amethyst.

Week number 5	Day number 32–333 (32–334)	Thursday 1 February

Saints' days   St Brigid (or Bride) – The Mary of the Gael – patron saint of Ireland (after St Patrick), poets, blacksmiths, healers, cattle, dairymaids, midwives, newborn babies and fugitives 523 • St Ignatius Bp of Antioch M • St Rionius, P&M 250 • St Kinnoa, V of Ireland C5 • St Sigebert II, K of Austria 656.

Week number 5	Day number 33–332 (33–333)	Friday 2 February

Saint's Day   St Joan de Lestonnac.

Holidays etc   Candlemas, a half-quarter day; old Scottish quarter day (now 0228) • Feast of Purification of the Blessed Virgin Mary, ritually cleansed in the Temple after the birth of Jesus • Japanese observance (first Friday to Sunday): Sapporo Yuki Festival (Sapporo Snow Festival).

Week number 5 Day number 34–331 (34–332) Saturday 3 February

Saints' days St Anskar – The apostle of the North – patron saint of Denmark • St Blaise – The patron saint of sore throats – patron saint of wool-combers, invoked against throat diseases Bp of Sebaste 316 • St Margaret – The patron saint of pregnant women – according to legend, having been swallowed whole by a dragon, she was able to burst out of its belly C12 • St Lawrence Abp of Canterbury 619 • St Auscharius Abp Hamburg and Bremen 865 • St Wereburghe patroness of Chester 699 • St Ia.

Holidays etc The earliest possible date for Shrove Tuesday (latest is 0309) • PH: Thailand.

Week number 5 Day number 35–330 (35–331) Sunday 4 February

Saints' days St Jane or Joan Q France 1505 • St Andrew Corsini Bp 137 • St Gilbert ab of Sempringham 1190 • St Joannicius • St John de Britto • St Philea and Philoromus M in Egypt c309 • St Isidore of Pelusium 449 • St Modan ab in Scotland C7 • St Rembert Abp Bremen 888.

Holidays etc 9th 𝔖 before Easter; Septuagesima • The earliest possible date for Ash Wednesday (latest is 0310) • Second Full Moon of the Gregorian year • Twelfth month of the Theravadan Buddhist year • Buddhist observance: Loy Kathrong (Festival of the Floating Bowls) • Theravadan Buddhist Uposatha (Observance Day) = Sri Lankan Poya Day • Independence Day: Sri Lanka.

Week number 6 Day number 36–329 (36–330) Monday 5 February

Saints' days St Agatha – chaste and immovable – patron saint of Catania, bell-founders and wet-nurses, invoked against eruptions of Etna, diseases of the breast, earthquakes, fire and sterility 251 • The Ms of Pontus 304 • St Abraamius Bp Arbela M 348 • St Abitus Abp Vienne 525 • St Alice (Adelaide) abs Cologne 1015 • The 26 M of Japan 1697.

Holidays etc Jewish observance: 15 Shebat – New Year for Trees • PH: Mexico.

Week number 6 Day number 37–328 (37–329) Tuesday 6 February

Saints' days St Amandus – the itinerant bishop – patron saint of brewers, wine-makers, hotel keepers and bar staff 675 • St Dorothy or Dorothea – one of the patron saints of gardeners VM 304 • St Photius • St

Titus • St Mel Bp Ardagh 488 • St Vedast Bp Arras 539 • St Barsanuphius of Palestine C6.

Holidays etc 45th Regnal year of Queen Elizabeth II begins • PH: New Zealand Day – Waitangi Day; 1840: The Treaty of Waitangi made between Britain and the Maori chiefs gave the Maori full rights and confirmed their possession of land.

Week number 6   Day number 38–327 (38–328)   **Wednesday 7 February**

Saints' days St Romualdo founder of the Order of Camaldoli 1027 • St Theodore (Stratilates) the General M Heraclea 319 • St Augulus Bp London M C4 • St Tresain of Ireland C6 • St Richard K of W Saxons c722.

Holidays etc Independence Day: Grenada.

Week number 6   Day number 39–326 (39–327)   **Thursday 8 February**

Saints' days St Cuthman • St John of Matha founder of the Order of Trinitarians 1213 • St Paul Bp Verdun 631 • St Cuthman of England C8 • St Stephen of Grandmont 1124.

Week number 6   Day number 40–325 (40–326)   **Friday 9 February**

Saints' days St Apollonia – 'That marvellous aged virgin' – patron saint of dentists, invoked against toothache M at Alexandria 249 • St Cyril of Alexandria • St Nicephorus M of Antioch 260 • St Teilo or Theliau Bp Llandaff c580 • St Attracta V in Ireland C5 • St Ausbert Abp Rouen 695 • St Erhard of Scotland C8.

Week number 6   Day number 41–324 (41–325)   **Saturday 10 February**

Saints' days St Scholastica – patron saint of convulsive children V 543 • St Soteris VM C4 • St Erluph of Scotland, Bp M at Verdun 830 • St William of Maleval 1157.

Week number 6   Day number 42–323 (42–324)   **Sunday 11 February**

Saints' days St Benedict of Aniane – the second Benedict • St Caedmon – The father of English sacred poetry c680 • St Severinus 507 • St Theodora Empress 867 • SS Saturninus, Dativus et al M Africa 304.

Holidays etc 8th ☙ before Easter; Sexagesima • National Day: Iran • National Foundation Day: Japan – commemorates the Imperial House Law of 1889 which regulates the descent from the throne.

Week number 7   Day number 43–322 (43–323)   Monday 12 February

Saints' days   St Julian the Hospitaller – Saved by hospitality – patron saint of ferrymen, innkeepers, travellers, wandering musicians and circus people • St Marina • The seven Founders • St Eulalia VM Barcelona c305 • St Meletius patriarch of Antioch 381 • St Benedict of Anian ab 821 • St Anthony Cauleus patriarch of Constantinople 896.

Holidays etc   Moon's last quarter • Theravadan Buddhist Uposatha (Observance Day) = Sri Lankan Poya Day • PH: Japan.

Week number 7   Day number 44–321 (44–322)   Tuesday 13 February

Saints' days   St Katherine de Ricci V 1589 • St Polyeuctus M Melitine 250 • St Martinianus hermit of Athens C4 • St Medomnoc (or Dominic) Bp of Ossory C6 • St Stephen ab in Italy C6 • St Licinius Bp Angers 618 • St Gregory II Pope 631 • Roger ab of Elan in Champagne c1175.

Holidays etc   S Tasmania: Hobart Regatta Day.

Week number 7   Day number 45–320 (45–321) Wednesday 14 February

Saints' days   St Cyril and Methodius – The apostles of the Slavs – patron saints of Europe • St Valentine – The patron saint of lovers – patron saint of beekeepers, affianced couples, travellers, and the young, invoked against epilepsy, fainting and plague and for a happy marriage M c270 • St Abrames Bp in Carres 422 • St Maro ab in Syria 433 • St Auxentius hermit of Bithynia c 470 • St Conran Bp Orkney C7.

Holidays etc   St Valentine's Day.

Week number 7   Day number 46–319 (46–320)   Thursday 15 February

Saints' days   SS Faustinus and Jovita M Brescia c121 • St Sigfride of York, apostle in Sweden 1002.

Holidays etc   Buddhist observance: Paravarana Day, marking the end of Vassa, the Rains Retreat • The Kthina (robe-offering) Ceremony must take place within one month of this day • Japanese observance: Kamakura Matsuri (Snow Hut Festival); also called Yokote Kamakura.

Week number 7   Day number 47–318 (47–319)   Friday 16 February

Saints' days   St Onesimus disciple of St Paul M 95 • SS Elias, Jeremy, Isaias, Samuel and Daniel Egyptian Ms 309 • St Juliana, VM Nicomedia c309 • St Tanco (or Tatto) of Scotland Bp M at Verdun c815 • St Gregory X Pope 1276.

Holidays etc USA: President's Day • PH: Lithuania, Pakistan • Democratic People's Republic of Korea: Kim Jong-Il's birthday.

Week number 7	Day number 48–317 (48–318)	Saturday 17 February

Saints' days SS Theodolus and Julian M Palestine 309 • St Flavian Abp Constantinople M in Lydia 449 • St Loman or Luman 1st Bp Trim C5 • St Fintan of Cloneenagh ab in Leinster C6 • St Silvin of Auchy Bp 718.

Holidays etc Japanese observance (17–20): Hachinohe Emburi (Hachinohe Rice-Planting Dances) • Mahashivrati.

Week number 7	Day number 49–316 (49–317)	Sunday 18 February

Saints' days St Simeon or Simon Bp of Jerusalem M 116 • SS Leo & Paragorius Ms C3 • St Colman of Lindisfarne • St Flavian of Constantinople.

Holidays etc 7th ☗ before Easter; Quinquagesima • Second New Moon of the Gregorian year; first month of the Chinese year • Theravadan Buddhist Uposatha (Observance Day) = Sri Lankan Poya Day • PH: Egypt, Republic of Korea, Taiwan • Independence Day: The Gambia • National Democracy Day: Nepal • Zodiac: Aquarius – The Water Carrier – ends (from 0120).

Week number 8	Day number 50–315 (50–316)	Monday 19 February

Saints' days St Mesrop • St Barbatus Bp Benevento 684.

Holidays etc Duke of York's birthday • Islamic observance: Eid-Al-Fittr (AH1416) • Chinese New Year Festival (for the living; 0219–21); Year of the Rat • PH: Bahrain, Brazil, Egypt, HK, Indonesia, Kenya, Republic of Korea, Malaysia, Nigeria, Pakistan, Saudi-Arabia, Singapore, Taiwan, Turkey, UAE, Venezuela • Zodiac: Pisces – The Fish – begins (to 0320).

Week number 8	Day number 51–314 (51–315)	Tuesday 20 February

Saints' days SS Tyrannio, Zenobius *et al* M Phoenicia *c*310 • St Sadoth Bp Seleucia and Ctesiphon + 128 Ms 342 • St Eleutherius Bp Tourney M 529 • St Mildred V abs in Thanet C7 • St Eucherius Bp Orleans 743 • St Ulrick of Haselbury 1154.

Holidays etc Shrove Tuesday – confessing sins, being *shrived/shrove* = obtaining absolution on this day; the day before Lent • PH: Bahrain, Brazil, China, Egypt, HK, Indonesia, Republic of Korea, Malaysia, Nigeria, Pakistan, Portugal, Saudi Arabia, Turkey, UAE.

Week number 8   Day number 52–313 (52–314) Wednesday 21 February

Saints' days   SS Daniel priest and Verda V Ms 344 • St Severianus Bp Scythopolis M c 452 • Blessed Pepin of Landed, mayor of the palace 640 • SS German ab and Randant Ms c666.

Holidays etc   Ash Wednesday begins Lent; fasting for forty days • Jewish calendar: Adar 1 AM5756 • Muslim calendar: 1 Shawwâl 1416AH • PH: Bahrain, HK, Malaysia, Saudi Arabia, Singapore, Taiwan, Turkey, UAE, USA, Venezuela.

Week number 8   Day number 53–312 (53–313)   Thursday 22 February

Saints' days   St Margaret of Cortona – Patroness of penitent women – patron saint of female penitents 1297 • SS Thalasius and Limneus C5 • St Baradat C5 • St Peter's Day.

Holidays etc   Independence Day: St Lucia • PH: Saudi Arabia • George Washington's birthday.

Week number 8   Day number 54–311 (54–312)   Friday 23 February

Saints' days   St Serenus, gardener M 307 • St Boisil prior of Melross 664 • St Milburge V abs in Shropshire C7 • St Peter Damian cardinal 1072 • St Willigis.

Holidays etc   National Day: Brunei Republic Day: Guyana (see also 0526) • PH: Saudi Arabia.

Week number 8   Day number 55–310 (55–311)   Saturday 24 February

Saints' days   St Matthias' Day (apostle) • SS Montanus, Lucius, Flavian, Julian, Victoricus, Primulus, Rhenus and Donatian Ms Carthage 259 • St Pretextatus Abp Rouen M c585 • St Lethard Bp of Senlis 596 • St Ethelbert 1st Christian K of England 616.

Holidays etc   Independence Day: Estonia.

Week number 8   Day number 56–309 (56–310)   Sunday 25 February

Saints' days   St Victorinus and 6 Ms 284 • St Caesarius physician of Constantinople 369 • St Walburge V of England 779 • St Tarasius patriarch of Constantinople 806.

Holidays etc   1st ⛪ in Lent • National Day: Kuwait • PH: Philippines.

Week number 9	Day number 57–308 (57–309)	Monday 26 February

Saints' days St Alexander, patriarch of Alexandria 326 • St Porphyry (Parphyrius) Bp of Gaza 420 • St Victor of Champagne C7.

Holidays etc Lent Monday (Christian–Eastern Orthodox observance) • Moon's first quarter • Theravadan Buddhist Uposatha (Observance Day) = Sri Lankan Poya Day.

Week number 9	Day number 58–307 (58–308)	Tuesday 27 February

Saints' days St Nestor Bp in Pamphylia M 250 • SS Julian, Chronion and Besas Ms C3 • St Thalilius C5 • St Gabriel Possenti • St Leander Bp Sevile 596 • St Galmier of Lyons c650 • St Alnoth of England M C7.

Holidays etc Independence Day: Dominican Republic (1844).

Week number 9	Day number 59–306 (59–307)	Wednesday 28 February

Saints' days St Oswald of Worcester – Bp, Abp and ab • St Romanus' Day c460 and St Lupicinus abs 479 • The Martyrs of The Plague at Alexandria • St Proterius patriarch of Alexandria M 557.

Holidays etc Candlemas – Scottish quarter-day • S Tasmania: Launceston Cup Day.

Week number 9	Day number (60–306)	Thursday 29 February

Holidays etc Leap Year Day, inserted every four years so that the 365-day calendar year 'catches up' with the 365.242199-day solar year.

March

Named after Mars, the Roman god of war.
Birthstone Aquamarine or Bloodstone.

Week number 9	Day number 60–305 (61–305)	Friday 1 March

Saints' days St David Abp of Caerleon, patron of Wales 544 • St Albinus of Angers 549 • St Swidbert or Swibert of Northumberland Bp 713 • St Monan of Scotland M 374.

Holidays etc St David's Day • The Old Roman New Year's Day • Last day (from 16 February) for holding the Buddhist Kathina Ceremony • Independence Day: Bosnia-Hercegovina (1992) • PH: Republic of Korea, Paraguay.

Week number 9   Day number:61–304 (62–304)   Saturday 2 March

Saints' days   St Simplicius Pope 483 • Ms under the Lombards C6 • St Joavan or Joevin Bp in Armorica C6 • St Marnan of Scotland 620 • St Ceadda or Chad – First Bp of Lichfield Mercia – patron saint of medical springs 673 • St Charles the Good Earl of Flanders M 1124.

Week number 9   Day number 62–303 (63–303)   Sunday 3 March

Saints' days   SS Marinus and Asterius M of Caesarea in Palestine c272 • SS Emeterius and Cheliddonius Ms in Spain; St Winwaloe ab in Armorica c529 • St Lamalisse of Scotland C7 • St Aelred • St Cunegundes empress 1040.

Holidays etc   2nd ☙ in Lent • Earliest date for Passion ☙ (that before Palm ☙) • National Day: Bulgaria • Summertime ends: ACT, NSW, QLD, SA, VIC.

Week number 10 Day number 63–302 (64–302)   Monday 4 March

Saints' days   St Lucius pope and M 253 • St Adrian Bp of St Andrew's, M in Scotland 874 • St Casimir prince of Poland 1482.

Holidays etc   PH: China • Hindu observance: Holi • Jewish observance: 13 Adar – Fast of Esther • Labour Day: WA • Eight Hour Day: Tasmania.

Week number 10 Day number 64–301 (65–301)   Tuesday 5 March

Saints' days   SS Adrian and Eubulus of Palestine Ms 309 • St Kiaran of Saighir Ireland C4 • St Gerasimus • St Phocas of Antioch • St Piran • St Roger a Franciscan 1236.

Holidays etc   Buddhist observance: Birthday of Avalokitesvara (Kuan Yin) • Buddhist observance: Magha Puja Day (Fourfold Assembly or Sangha Day) • Third Full Moon of the Gregorian year; thirteenth month of the Theravadan Buddhist year • Theravadan Buddhist Uposatha (Observance Day) = Sri Lankan Poya Day • Hindu observance: Holi • Jewish observance: 14–15 Adar – Purim (Feast of Lots).

Week number 10 Day number 65–300 (66–300)   Wednesday 6 March

Saints' days   St Fridolin ab 538 • St Baldred of Scotland c608 • SS Kyneburge, Kyneswide and Tibba C7 • St Chrodegang Bp Metz 766 • St Cadroe c975 • St Colette V and abs 1447.

Saints' days Ss Perpetua and Felicity Ms Carthage 203 • St Paul the Simple anchoret c330 • St Thomas Aquinas Dr of the Church and Confessor 1274.

Saints' days SS Apollonius, Philemon *et al* Ms of Egypt c311 • St Senan Bp in Ireland c544 • St Psalmoid, or Saumay, of Ireland c589 • St Felix Bp of Dunwich 646 • St Julian Abp of Toledo 690 • St Rosa V of Viterbo buried 1252 • St Duthak Bp of Ross 1253 • St John of God – founder of the Order of Charity, patron saint of hospitals and the sick, as well as booksellers and pictures, eventually opening a shop in Granada in 1538.

Holidays etc PH: Russian Federation.

Saints' days St Pacian Bp of Barcelona C4 • St Gregory of Nyssa Bp 400 • St Frances widow of Rome – the pious matron – patron saint of motorists, foundress of the Collatines 1440 • St Katherine or Catherine of Bologna V 1463.

Saints' days The Forty Martyrs of St Sebaste 520 • St Mackessog or Kessog Bp in Scotland 560 • St Droctovaeus ab c580.

Holidays etc 3rd ⛪ in Lent • Prince Edward's birthday.

Saints' days St Constantine of Scotland M C6 • St Sophronius Patriarch of Jerusalem 639 • St Aengus the Culdee Bp in Ireland 824 • St Eulogius of Córdoba 859.

Holidays etc Commonwealth Day (2nd M in March) • Labour Day: VIC.

Saints' days St Maximilian of Numidia M 296 • St Paul of Cornwall Bp of Léon c573 • St Gregory the Great – the apostle of the English from Rome – patron saint of masons, singers, musicians, students and teachers, invoked against gout and plague 604.

Holidays etc National Day: Mauritius • Moon's last quarter • Theravadan Buddhist Uposatha (Observance Day) = Sri Lankan Poya Day • Japanese observance: Omizutori (Water-Drawing).

Week number 11 Day number 72–293 (73–293)   Wednesday 13 March

Saints' days St Euphrasia V 410 • St Mochoemoc ab in Ireland 655 • St Gerald Bp in Ireland 732 • St Theophanes ab 818 • St Nicephorus patriarch of Constantinople 828 • St Kennocha V in Scotland 1007.

Holidays etc Japanese observance: Kasuga Matsuri.

Week number 11 Day number 73–292 (74–292)   Thursday 14 March

Saints' days St Acepsimas Bp in Assyria, Jseph and Aithilahas Ms 380 • St Boniface Bp of Roass in Scotland 630 • St Maud Q of Germany 968 • St Matilda.

Week number 11 Day number 74–291 (75–291)   Friday 15 March

Saints' days St Abraham hermit of Mesopotamia and his niece St Mary C4 • St Zachary Pope 752 • St Leocritia of Cordova V M 859 • St Clement Hofbauer • St Louise de Marillac.

Holidays etc National Day: Hungary • Earliest date for Palm S; latest is 18 April. 44BC – 'Beware the Ides of March' – Gaius Julius Caesar was assassinated by conspirators, including Brutus and Cassius in the Senate House in Rome.

Week number 11 Day number 75–290 (76–290)   Saturday 16 March

Saints' days St Herbert of Cologne • St Julian of Cilicia Antioch M c303 • The Martyrs of North America • St Paul the Simple • St Finian Lohbar (or the Leper) of Ireland C8.

Week number 11 Day number 76–289 (77–289)   Sunday 17 March

Saints' days Many Ms of Alexandria c392 • St Gertrude V M of Nivelles in Brabant – the hospitable abbess – patron saint of gardeners, travellers and the recently dead, invoked against vermin 659 • St Patrick – the apostle of Ireland – patron saint of Ireland 464 or 493 • St Joseph of Arimathaea patron of Glastonbury.

Holidays etc 4th S in Lent • Mothering S • St Patrick's Day: National Day: DO Ireland • In the Middle Ages, this was reckoned to be the day Noah entered the Ark as the great Flood began.

Week number 12 Day number 77–288 (78–288)   Monday 18 March

Saints' days St Alexander Bp of Jerusalem M 251 • St Cyril Abp of Jerusalem 336 • St Edward the Martyr • St Frigidian Bp of Lucca 578 • St Edward K of England M 978 • St Anselm Bp of Lucca 1086 • St Salvator of Horta.

Holidays etc Canberra Day: ACT.

Week number 12 Day number 78–287 (79–287)   Tuesday 19 March

Saints' days St Joseph – the foster-father of Jesus – patron saint of carpenters, fathers, workers, social justice and travellers, invoked in doubt and when house-hunting C1 • St Alemund of England M c819.

Holidays etc Earliest date for Maundy Th; latest is 22 April • Third New Moon of the Gregorian year; second month of the Chinese year • Theravadan Buddhist Uposatha (Observance Day) = Sri Lankan Poya Day.

Week number 12 Day number 79–286 (80–286)   Wednesday 20 March

Saints' days St Cuthbert – 'The wonder-worker of Britain' Bp of Lindisfarne 687 • St Wulfran Abp of Sens and apostolic missionary in Friesland 720 • St Herbert • St Martin of Braga.

Holidays etc Earliest date for Good Friday; latest is 23 April • Vernal Equinox; Spring begins; ends at Summer Solstice • Hindu new year begins • National Day: Tunisia • PH: Japan • Zodiac: last day of Pisces – The Fish (19 February – 20 March).

Week number 12 Day number 80–285 (81–285)   Thursday 21 March

Saints' days St Serapion of Thmuis the Sindonite c388 • St Serapion the scholastic Bp in Egypt C4 • St Serapion ab • St Benedict's (or Bennet's) Day ab of Monte Cassino patriarch of the Western monks 543 • St Enna ab in Ireland C6 • St Nicolas von Flue.

Holidays etc Earliest date for last day of Lent, Easter Eve or Holy Saturday (*not* Easter Saturday); latest is 24 April • Jewish calendar: Nisan 1 AM5756 • Muslim calendar: 1 Dhû'l-Qa'da 1416AH • Independence Day: Namibia • PH: Mexico, South Africa • Zodiac: first day of Aries – The Ram (21 March – 24 April)

Week number 12 Day number 81–284 (82–284)   Friday 22 March

Saints' days St Paul Bp of Narbonne C3 • St Basil of Ancyra M 362 • St Lea widow of Rome 384 • St Deogratias Bp of Carthage 457 • St Catharine of Sweden abs 1381 • St Zachary.

Holidays etc Earliest date for Easter ⑤, Easter Day; the first ⑤ after the full moon following the Vernal Equinox; latest is 25 April • Indian (Saka) year begins.

Week number 12 Day number 82–283 (83–283)   Saturday 23 March

Saints' days St Victorian proconsul of Carthage *et al* Ms 484 • St Edelwald of England 699 • St Alphonsus Turibius of Mogroveio – the reluctant, reforming Abp of Lima – patron saint of Peru and the bishops of Latin America 1606 • St Gwinear.

Holidays etc Earliest date for Easter Monday; latest is 26 April • National Day: Pakistan (declared an Islamic Republic 1956).

Week number 12 Day number 83–282 (84–282)   Sunday 24 March

Saints' days St Iranaeus Bp of Sirmium M 304 • St William M at Norwich *aet* 11 1137 • St Simon, an infant M at Trent 1472 • St Gabriel • St Katherine of Vadstena.

Holidays etc 5th ⑤ in Lent – Passion ⑤.

Week number 13 Day number 84–281 (85–281)   Monday 25 March

Saints' days St Mary's Day • St Cammin of Ireland ab.

Holidays etc The Annunciation • Lady Day (Quarter Day in England, Wales and Northern Ireland.) • New Year's Day until 1753 • National Day: Greece (became a republic in 1924 when King George of Greece was deposed).

Week number 13 Day number 85–280 (86–280)   Tuesday 26 March

Saints' days St Braulio Bp of Saragossa 646 • St Ludger Bp of Münster apostle of Saxony 809 • St William of Norwich.

Holidays etc Independence Day: Bangladesh.

Week number 13 Day number 86–279 (87–279)   Wednesday 27 March

Saints' days St John the Egyptian hermit 394 • St John of Damascus • St Rupert or Robert Bp of Salzburg 718.

Holidays etc Moon's first quarter • Theravadan Buddhist Uposatha (Observance Day) = Sri Lankan Poya Day.

Week number 13 Day number 87–278 (88–278)   Thursday 28 March

Saints' days SS Priscus, Malchus and Alexander of Caesarea in Palestine 280 • St Sixtus III Pope 400 • St Gontran K of Burgundy 593 • St John of Capestrano.

Holidays etc Ramanavami.

Week number 13 Day number 88–277 (89–277)   Friday 29 March

Saints' days SS Jonas, Barachisius *et al* Ms 327 • St Mark Bp of Arethusa in Syria C4 • SS Armagastes, Archinimus and Satur Ms 457 • St Gundleus a Welsh K C5 • St Eustasius or Eustachius ab of Luxeu 625 • St Berthold.

Holidays etc Earliest date for Low $ (1st after Easter); latest is 2 May • An old folk belief claimed this to be a 'borrowed day', since it was believed that the last three days of March had been taken from April • PH: Taiwan.

Week number 13 Day number 89–276 (90–276)   Saturday 30 March

Saints' days St John Clamacus the scholastic ab of Mt Sinai 605 • St Zozimus Bp of Syracuse 660 • St Regulus or Rieul Bp of Senlis • St Osburga.

Week number 13 Day number 90–275 (91–275)   Sunday 31 March

Saints' days St Acacius or Achates Bp of Antioch C3 • St Benjamin Deacon M 424 • St Guy (or Wyten) ab at Ferrara 1046.

Holidays etc Palm $ • British Summer Time begins.

April

Named after (1) Aphrodite, Greek goddess of love or (2) the Latin *aperire* = opening (of spring).
Birthstone Diamond.

Week number 14 Day number 91–274 (92–274)   Monday 1 April

Saints' days St Hugh Bp of Grenoble.1132 • St Melito, Bp of Sardis in Lydia C2 • St Gilbert, Bp of Caithness in Scotland 1240.

Holidays etc   All Fools' Day (April Fool's Day) – in France called *poissons d'avril*

Saints' days   St Apian of Lycia M 306 • St Theodosia of Caesarea M 308 • St Nicetius Abp of Lyons 577 • St Ebba or Abba abs M 874 • B Constantine K of Scotland 874 • St Bronacha of Ireland • St Francis of Paola – Founder of the Minim Friars – patron saint of sailors, invoked against plague and sterility 1508 • St Mary the Egyptian.

Saints' days   SS Agape, Chionia and Irene Ms 304 • St Ulpian of Tyre M • St Nicetias ab 824 • St Richard of Chichester – Bishop of Chichester – patron saint of the guild of coachmen of Milan 1253 • St Burgundofara • St Pancras of Taormina.

Holidays etc   Hilary Law Term ends (began 11 January).

Saints' days   St Isidore Bp of Seville – 'The schoolmaster of the Middle Ages' – patron saint of farmers 606 • St Plato ab 813 • St Ambrose (see also 1207) • St Benedict the Black.

Holidays etc   Maundy Thursday • Fourth Full Moon of the Gregorian year; first month of the Theravadan Buddhist year • Theravadan Buddhist Uposatha (Observance Day) = Sri Lankan Poya Day • Theravadan Buddhist New Year (Burma, Cambodia, Laos, Sri Lanka, Thailand) • Jewish observance: 15–22 Nisan – Pesach (Passover) • National Day: Senegal • PH: Argentina, China, Colombia, Denmark, HK, Iceland, Israel, Mexico, Norway, Peru, Philippines, Taiwan, Venezuela.

Saints' days   St Tigernach of Ireland 550 • St Becan of Ireland ab C6 • St Gerald ab of Seauve nr Bordeaux 1095 • St Vincent Ferrer of Spain confessor 1419.

Holidays etc   Good Friday • Jewish observance: 16 Nisan–5 Sivan – Sefirat Ha'Omer (the 7-week Count of the Omer) • PH: Argentina, Australia, Bolivia, Brazil, Bulgaria, Canada, Chile, Colombia, Denmark, Estonia, Finland, Germany, Ghana, HK, Iceland, Kenya, Republic of Korea, Latvia, Mexico, Netherlands, New Zealand, Nigeria, Norway, PNG,

Paraguay, Peru, Philippines, Portugal, Singapore, South Africa, Spain, Sweden, Switzerland, UK, Venezuela.

Week number 14 Day number 96–269 (97–269)   **Saturday 6 April**

Saints' days   St Sixtus Pope M C2 • 120 Ms of Hadiab in Persia 345 • St Celestine Pope 432 • St Prudentius Bp of Troyes 861 • St Celsus Abp of Armagh 1129 • St William ab of Eskille confessor 1203.

Holidays etc   Latter Lady Day • PH: Australia, Bulgaria, Chile, Ghana, HK, Thailand.

Week number 14 Day number 97–268 (98–268)   **Sunday 7 April**

Saints' days   St Hagesippus primitive father C2 • St Aphraates anchoret C4 • St Finan of Ireland • St Aibert recluse 1140 • St Herman Joseph confessor 1226.

Holidays etc   Easter Day (Western churches) • Daylight Saving Time begins: USA, Canada • PH: Finland, Italy, Latvia, Lithuania, Norway.

Week number 15 Day number 98–267 (99–267)   **Monday 8 April**

Saints' days   St Dionysius of Corinth C2 • St Ædesius of Corinth M 306 • St Perpetuus Bp of Tours 491 • St Walter, ab of St Martin's nr Pontoise 1099 • B Albert patriarch of Jerusalem 1214.

Holidays etc   Easter Monday • PH: Australia, Austria, Belgium, Canada, Denmark, Finland, France, Germany, Ghana, HK, Hungary, Iceland, Republic of Ireland, Italy, Kenya, Netherlands, New Zealand, Nigeria, Norway, PNG, Poland, South Africa, Sweden, Switzerland, UK (except Scotland).

Week number 15 Day number 99–266 (100–266)   **Tuesday 9 April**

Saints' days   Roman captives Ms in Persia 362 • St Mary of Egypt C5 • Massylitan Ms in Africa • St Eupsychius M • St Dotto ab in Orkney C6 • St Waltrude 686 • St Gautier ab in Limousin 1130.

Holidays etc   Easter Tuesday • PH: Tasmania.

Week number 15 Day number 100–265 (101–265)   Wednesday 10 April

Saints' days   St Bademus ab M 376 • B Mechtildes V and abs C14.

Holidays etc   PH: Israel.

Week number 15 Day number 101–264 (102–264) Thursday 11 April

Saints' days St Leo the Great Pope 461 • St Antipas M C5 • St Maccai ab C5 • St Aid ab in Ireland • St Guthlac hermit patron of the Abbey of Croyland (Crowland) 716 • St Gemma Galgani.

Holidays etc Moon's last quarter • The latest date for Passion 𝕾; the earliest is 8 March • Theravadan Buddhist Uposatha (Observance Day) = Sri Lankan Poya Day.

Week number 15 Day number 102–263 (103–263) Friday 12 April

Saints' days St Victor of Braga M • St Julius Pope 352 • St Sabas the Goth. M 372 • St Zeno Bp of Verona 380.

Holidays etc PH: Greece, Romania.

Week number 15 Day number 103–262 (104–262) Saturday 13 April

Saints' days St Hermengild M 586 • St Guinoch of Scotland C9 • St Caradoc priest and M 1124 • SS Carpus and Papylus.

Holidays etc Baisakhi Mela (Hindu new year) • PH: Thailand.

Week number 15 Day number 104–261 (105–261) Sunday 14 April

Saints' days SS Maximus, Tiburtius and Valerian Ms in Rome 229 • St Carpus of Thyatria *et al* 251 • St Benezet patron of Avignon 1184 • SS Antony, Eustachius and John Ms c1342 • B Lidwina of Sciedam 1433 • St Justin.

Holidays etc Low 𝕾; 1st after Easter • Easter Day (Christian-Eastern Orthodox observance) • PH: Romania • By the Easter Act of 1928, the 1st 𝕾 after the 2nd S in April would be Easter Day • Iraq: Overthrow of the Ba'ath regime of Saddam Hussein • Japanese observance (two days): Takayama Matsuri.

Week number 16 Day number 105–260 (106–260) Monday 15 April

Saints' days SS Anastasia and Basilissa Ms C1 • St Paternus Bp of Avranches 563 • St Ruadhan ab 584 • St Munde ab 962 • St Peter Gonzales 1246.

Holidays etc Buddhist observance: Songkran (purification; lasts several days) • PH: Egypt, Greece, Romania.

Week number 16 Day number 106–259 (107–259)   Tuesday 16 April

Saints' days   18 Ms of Saragossa 304 • St Turibius Bp of Astorga c420 • St Fructuosus Abp of Braga 665 • St Benedict Labre • St Bernadette – the visionary of Lourdes • St Magnus of Orkney M 1104 • St Druon recluse patron of shepherds 1186 • St Joachim of Sienna 1305.

Holidays etc   Easter Law Term begins (ends 24 May) • Jewish observance: 27 Nisan – Yom ha-Shoa (Holocaust Remembrance Day).

Week number 16 Day number 107–258 (108–258)   Wednesday 17 April

Saints' days   St Donnan • St Robert of Chaise-Dieu • St Stephen Harding • St Anicetus Pope and M 173 • St Simeon Bp of Ctesiphon 341 • St Stephen ab of Citeaux 1134.

Holidays etc   Fourth New Moon of the year • Theravadan Buddhist Uposatha (Observance Day) = Sri Lankan Poya Day • Chinese Clear and Bright Festival (for the dead) • National Day: Syria.

Week number 16 Day number 108–257 (109–257)   Thursday 18 April

Saints' days   St Apollonius the Apologist M 186 • St Laserian Bp of Leighlin, Ireland 638 • St Galdin Abp of Milan 1176.

Holidays etc   The latest date for Palm ☾; the earliest is 15 March • Independence Day: Zimbabwe.

Week number 16 Day number 109–256 (110–256)   Friday 19 April

Saints' days   St Ursmar Bp and ab 713 • St Alphege or Elphege Abp – 'the first martyr of Canterbury' 1012 • St Expeditus • St Leo IX Pope 1054.

Holidays etc   National Holiday: Venezuela • Zodiac: last day of Aries – The Ram (21 March–19 April).

Week number 16 Day number 110–255 (111–255)   Saturday 20 April

Saints' days   St Serf, or Servanus, of Scotland C5 • St Agnes of Monte Pulciano 1317 • St James of Sclavonia 1485.

Holidays etc   The fair-day in Tenbury, Worcestershire, there is a belief in that county that you never hear the cuckoo till Tenbury fair-day, or after Pershore fair-day (26th June) • Jewish calendar: Sivan 1 AM5756 • Muslim calendar: 1 Dhû'l-Hijja 1416AH • Zodiac: first day of Taurus – The Bull (20 April–20 May).

Week number 16 Day number 111–254 (112–254) Sunday 21 April

Saints' days St Anselm Abp of Canterbury – 'the father of scholasticism' 1109 • St Simeon Barsabba'e • St Eingan or Enean King of Scots 590 • St Anastasius the Younger – 'Patriarch of Antioch' 610 • St Anastasius the Sinaite • St Beuno Ab of Clynog in Caernarvonshire • St Malrubius of Ireland 721.

Holidays etc 2nd 𝕾 after Easter • HM Queen Elizabeth II: Birthday • PH: Saudi Arabia.

Week number 17 Day number 112–253 (113–253) Monday 22 April

Saints' days St Conrad of Parzham • St Pherbutha • St Theodore of Syketheon • SS Epipodius and Alexander, Martyrs at Lyons C2 • SS Soter and Caius C2 and C3 • St Leonides 202 • St Rufus or Rufin of Glendalough in Ireland • St Theodorus of Siceon 613 • St Opportuna abs of Montreuil 770 • St Azades or Rufin.

Holidays etc Hock-tide – a fortnight after Easter – occupied the Monday and Tuesday following the second Sunday after Easter. On the Monday, the men went out into the roads and streets with cords, and bound all those they met of the opposite sex, holding them till they purchased their release by a small contribution of money. On the Tuesday – the principal day – the women went out for the same purpose. Hock-tide can be traced as far back as the thirteenth century • PH: Brazil.

Week number 17 Day number 113–252 (114–252) Tuesday 23 April

Saints' days St George – The archetype of Christian chivalry – patron saint of England, Portugal, soldiers, armourers and archers, invoked against plague, leprosy and syphilis – St George slayed the dragon in Libya in the third century, and became the patron saint of England when he appeared in the sky during the Crusades 303 • St Ibar or Ivor Bp in Ireland 500 • St Gerard Bp of Toul 994 • St Adalbert Bp of Prague – The apostle of the Prussians – patron saint of Prussia and Poland 997.

Holidays etc St George's Day • Supposed birthday of William Shakespeare • Jewish observance: 4 Iyyar – Israel Memorial Day • PH: Saudi Arabia, Turkey.

Week number 17 Day number 114–251 (115–251)   Wednesday 24 April

Saints' days St Euphrasia Pelletier • St Ivo • St Mellitus Abp of Canterbury 624 • SS Beuve and Doda of Rheims C7 • St Fidelis 1622 • St Robert of Chaise-dieu 1067.

Holidays etc St Mark's Eve – apparitions of those to die in the coming year are said to appear at midnight in churchyards • Jewish observance: 5 Iyyar – Israel Independence Day • PH: Israel, Saudi Arabia.

Week number 17 Day number 115–250 (116–250)   Thursday 25 April

Saints' days St Mark – The first Gospel-writer – patron saint of Venice, glaziers and notaries, invoked by captives 68 • St William of Monte Vergine • St Anianus 2nd Bp of Alexandria 86 • St Kebius of Cornwall C4 • St Phæbadius Bp of Agen 392 • St Maughold or Macallius of the Isle of Man C6 • St Ivo C7.

Holidays etc Moon's first quarter • Theravadan Buddhist Uposatha (Observance Day) = Sri Lankan Poya Day • Anzac Day, commemorating the 1915 Gallipoli landing by heroic Australian and New Zealand troops; first celebrated 1916 • PH: Australia, Egypt, Iceland, Italy, New Zealand, Portugal, Saudi Arabia,

---

Week number 17 Day number 116–249 (117–249)   Friday 26 April

Saints' days SS Cletus (or Anacletus) and Marcellinus C1 and C3 • St Stephen of Perm • St Riquier or Ricardus Fr anchoret 645 • St Paschasius Radbert ab of Corwei in Saxony 865.

Holidays etc Union Day: Tanzania • PH: Egypt, Saudi Arabia.

Week number 17 Day number 117–248 (118–248)   Saturday 27 April

Saints' days St Anthimus Bp + Ms at Nicodemia 303 • St Anastasius Pope and con 401 • St Maughold • St Peter Canisius • St Toribio of Lima • St Zita V of Lucca 1272.

Holidays etc Eid-Al-Addha AH1416 (Islamic observance) • Independence Day: Sierra Leone • Freedom Day: South Africa • National Day: Serbia and Montenegro; Togo • PH: Bahrain, Egypt, Indonesia, Nigeria, Pakistan, South Africa, Turkey, Saudi Arabia, UAE.

Week number 17 Day number 118–247 (119–247)   Sunday 28 April

Saints' days St Louis Grignion • St Paul of the Cross • St Peter Chanel • St Vitalis M *c*62 • SS Didymus and Theodore Ms 304 • St Pollio *et al* Ms in

Pannonia 304 • St Patricius Bp of Pruse in Bithynia M • St Cronan ab of Roscrea in Ireland c640.

Holidays etc 3rd ☙ after Easter • PH: Bahrain, Egypt, Nigeria, Pakistan, Saudi Arabia, Singapore, Turkey, UAE.

Week number 18 Day number 119–246 (120–246)   Monday 29 April

Saints' days St Hugh ab of Cluny 1109 • St Robert ab of Molesme 1110 • St Peter M 1252 • St Fiachna of Ireland C7.

Holidays etc National Day: Japan (Greenery Day) • PH: Bahrain, Brazil, Egypt, Malaysia, Saudi Arabia, Turkey, UAE • Apparently this is the day that Noah left his ark.

Week number 18 Day number 120–245 (121–245)   Tuesday 30 April

Saints' days St Catherine of Siena – one of the greatest Christian mystics – patron saint of Italy V 1380 • St Erconwals or Erkonwald Bp of London c686 • St Joseph Cottolengo • SS Marian, James *et al* Ms in Numidia 259 • St Maximus M 251 • St Sophia V M C3 • St Adjutre recluse Vernon in Normandy 1131.

Holidays etc Earliest date for Ascension Day; latest is 3 June • PH: Egypt, Finland, Saudi Arabia, Turkey, UAE • National Day of the Netherlands • Walpurgisnacht in Germany – the Witch's Sabbath is held in the Harz Mountains, the Spectre of the Brocken is rife, bonfires are lit; it is considered to be a time of great evil.

May

Takes its name from the goddess Maia; daughter of Atlas, mother of Hermes.
Birthstone Emerald.

Week number 18 Day number 121–244 (122–244) Wednesday 1 May

Saints' days St Philip – Follower of Jesus – patron saint of Uruguay and St James the Less apostles • St Andeolus M 208 • SS Acius and Andeolus Ms of Amiens c290 • St Amator Bp of Auxerre 418 • St Briocus of Wales c502 • St Sigismund K of Burgundy c517 • St Marcon ab of Nanteu in Normandy 558 • St Asaph ab and Bp of Llanelwy in N Wales c590.

Holidays etc   May Day was a Roman Festival that began on 28 April and lasted several days to mark the beginning of Summer. In England, the middle and lower classes would gather flowers – 'go a-maying' – and the prettiest village maid was crowned Queen of the May, celebrated with dancing around the maypole • Labour Day, the annual holiday of the Labour movement, is held on the first Monday each May, and linked to 1 May, became an official Bank Holiday in England from 1978. (In the US, Labor Day is celebrated on the first Monday in September.) Independence Day: Marshall Islands • PH: Argentina, Austria, Belgium, Bolivia, Bulgaria, Chile, China, Colombia, Cuba, Egypt, Estonia, Finland, France, Germany, Ghana, Greece, Hungary, Iceland, Italy, Kenya, Lithuania, Malaysia, Mexico, Nigeria, Norway, Paraguay, Peru, Philippines, Poland, Portugal, Romania, Russian Federation, Saudi Arabia, Singapore, South Africa, Sweden, Venezuela • Japanese observance (early in the month): Ombashira Matsuri (Sacred Post Festival).

Week number 18 Day number 122–243 (123–243)   **Thursday 2 May**

Saint's Day   St Athanasius – the champion of orthodoxy 373.

Holidays etc   National Day: Cameroon • PH: Bulgaria, Cameroon, Russian Federation, Saudi Arabia.

Week number 18 Day number 123–242 (124–242)   **Friday 3 May**

Saint's Day   St Theodosius of the caves.

Holidays etc   Invention (or discovery) of the Holy Cross • Fifth Full Moon of the Gregorian year; second month of the Theravadan Buddhist year • Theravadan Buddhist Uposatha (Observance Day) = Sri Lankan Poya Day • Buddhist observance: Anapanasati Day; Wesak Day • Jewish observance: 14 Iyyar – Pesach Sheni (Second Pesach). National Day: Poland • Constitution Memorial Day: Japan • PH: Denmark, Indonesia, Japan, Poland • Japanese observances (3–5 May): Hakata Dontaku (Hataka Holiday); Hamamatsu Tokoage Matsuri (Hamamatsu Kite-Flying Festival).

Week number 18 Day number 124–241 (125–241)   **Saturday 4 May**

Saints' days   St Florian – patron saint of blacksmiths and firemen • St Monica widow 387 • St Godard Bp 1038 • St Pleagia of Tarsus.

Holidays etc   National Holiday: Japan • PH: Indonesia, Japan, Singapore.

Week number 18 Day number 125–240 (126–240)   Sunday 5 May

Saints' days St Hilary Abp Arles 449 • St Mauront ab 706 • St Avertin con c1189 • St Angelus Carmelite friar M 1225 • St Jutta • St Pius V Pope 1572.

Holidays etc 4th ⛪ after Easter • Children's Day: Japan • PH: Japan, Korea, Mexico, Thailand.

Week number 19 Day number 126–239 (127–239)   Monday 6 May

Saints' days St John before the Latin Gate 95 • St Eadbert Bp of Lindisfarne con c698 • St John Damascene 780.

Holidays etc May Day: Australia NT, UK • Spring holiday in Scotland • May Holiday: Ireland • Labour Day: QLD • PH: Australia NT, Eire, Japan, Spain, UK.

Week number 19 Day number 127–238 (128–238)   Tuesday 7 May

Saints' days St Benedict II Pope con 686 • St John of Beverley 721 • St Stanislaus Bp of Cracow M 1079.

Holidays etc Jewish observance: 18 Iyyar – Lag B'Omer (33rd day of the Omer Count).

Week number 19 Day number 128–237 (129–237)   Wednesday 8 May

Saints' days Apparition of St Michael • St Victor M 303 • St Odrian of Waterford • St Wiro of Ireland C7 • St Gybrian of Ireland C8 • St Peter Abp of Tarentaise in Savoy 1174.

Holidays etc PH: France.

Week number 19 Day number 129–236 (130–236)   Thursday 9 May

Saints' days St Hermas C1 • St Gregory Nazianzen 389 • St Brynoth Bp of Scara in Sweden 1317 • St Nicholas Bp of Lincopen in Sweden 1391.

Holidays etc Half Quarter Day • Liberation Day: Channel Islands • USA: Mother's Day • National Day of Czechoslovakia.

Week number 19 Day number 130–235 (131–235)   Friday 10 May

Saints' days St Antoninus Abp of Florence – the people's prelate 1459 • SS Gordian and Epimachus Ms C3 and C4 • St Comgall ab 601 • St Cataldus Bp of Tarentum C7 • St Isidore patron of Madrid labourer 1170.

Holidays etc Earliest date for Pentecost (Whit 𝔖); latest is 13 June • Moon's last quarter • Theravadan Buddhist Uposatha (Observance Day) = Sri Lankan Poya Day • PH: Mexico.

Week number 19 Day number 131–234 (132–234) Saturday 11 May

Saints' days St Mamertius Abp Vienna 447 • St Maieul ab Cluni 994 • St Asaph • St Comgall • St Francis di Girolamo • St James the Less and Philip (RC 0105).

Week number 19 Day number 132–233 (133–233) Sunday 12 May

Saints' days St Pancras – child martyr (*aet* 14) – patron saint of children, invoked against cramp, headaches and perjury 304 • St Epiphanius of Salamis • St Germanus of Constantinople • St Ignatius of Laconi • SS Nereus and Achilleus Ms C2 • St Flavia Domitilla C2.

Holidays etc 5th 𝔖 after Easter; Rogation 𝔖 • Mother's Day: Australia, Canada, USA.

Week number 20 Day number 133–232 (134–232) Monday 13 May

Saints' days St Gervatius or Servatius Bp of Tongres 384 • St Andrew Fournet • St Erconwald (see also 30 April) • St Euthymius the Enlightener • St Robert Bellarmine • St John the Silent Armenian anchoret 559 • St Peter Regalati con 1456.

Week number 20 Day number 134–231 (135–231) Tuesday 14 May

Saints' days St Michael Garicoïts • St Mary Mazzarello • St Pachomius ab 348 • St Carthagh Bp Lismore *c*637 • St Pontius M *c*258 • St Boniface M *c*307.

Holidays etc National Day of Paraguay, marking this day, 1811, when she claimed her independence from Spain • PH: Paraguay.

Week number 20 Day number 135–230 (136–230) Wednesday 15 May

Saints' days St Dympna – patron saint of the insane – invoked against mental illness and epilepsy – thought to have been an Irish princess who was slain by her incestuous father V M C7 • SS Peter and Andrew and companions Ms 250 • St Genebrard M C7 • St Hallvard • St John-Baptiste de la Salle.

Holidays etc National Day: Paraguay • PH: Philippines • Japanese observances: Kanda Matsuri and Aoi Matsuri.

Week number 20 Day number 136–229 (137–229) Thursday 16 May

Saints' days St Brendan the Navigator (or Voyager) the elder – travelling abbot of Clonfert – patron saint of sailors and travellers 578 • St Andrew Bobola • St Fructuosus of Braga • St Honorius of Amiens • St Simon Stock con of Kent 1265 • St Ubaldus Bp Gubio 1160 • St John of Nepomuc 1383 • St Abdjasus Bp M • St Abdas Bp Cascar M.

Holidays etc Ascension Day, or Holy Thursday – in commemoration of the glorious ascension of the Messiah into heaven – DO • PH: Austria, Belgium, Denmark, Finland, France, Germany, Iceland, Indonesia, Lithuania, Netherlands, Norway, Sweden, Switzerland.

Week number 20 Day number 137–228 (138–228) Friday 17 May

Saints' days St Possidius C5 • St Maden of Brittany • St Maw • St Cathan C7 • St Silave 1100 • St Paschal Baylon 1592.

Holidays etc Earliest date of Trinity 𝕾; latest is 30 June • Fifth New Moon of the Gregorian year • Fourth month of the Chinese year • Theravadan Buddhist Uposatha (Observance Day) = Sri Lankan Poya • Jewish observance: 28 Iyyar – Yom Yerushalayim (Jerusalem Reunification Day) • Constitution Day: Norway • PH: Austria, Norway.

Week number 20 Day number 138–227 (139–227) Saturday 18 May

Saints' days St Eric • St Felix of Cantalice • St Venantius M 250 • St Theodotus vintner and 7Vs Ms 303 • St Potamon M 341 • St Eric K of Sweden M 1151.

Holidays etc PH: Bahrain, Egypt, Indonesia, UAE • Japanese observance (S or 𝕾 nearest 17–18): Sanja Matsuri

Week number 20 Day number 139–226 (140–226) Sunday 19 May

Saints' days St Dunstan – reviver of monasticism in Britain – patron saint of goldsmiths, jewellers, locksmiths, blacksmiths, musicians and the blind – Anglo-Saxon saint and Archbishop of Canterbury 988 • St Peter Celestine V Pope 1296 • St Prudentiana V C1.

Holidays etc 1st 𝕾 after Ascension Day • Muslim calendar: New Year's Day 1 Muharram AH1417 • PH: Malaysia, Turkey.

Week number 21 Day number 140–225 (141–225) Monday 20 May

Saints' days St Bernardino of Siena – the people's preacher – patron saint of advertisers, invoked against hoarseness • St Ethelbert K of the East Angles 793 • St Yves (or Ivo) Bp of Chartres 1115

Holidays etc Adelaide Cup Day: SA • PH: Canada, Colombia • Zodiac: Taurus – The Bull ends (20 April–20 May).

Week number 21 Day number 141–224 (142–224) Tuesday 21 May

Saints' days St Godric hermit of Finkley nr Durham 1170 • St Felix of Cantalicio 1587 • St Hospitius recluse of Provence 881.

Holidays etc Earliest date for Corpus Christi; latest is 24 June • Sikh observance: Martyrdom of Guru Arjan Dav Ji • Zodiac: Gemini – The Twins (21 May–21 June).

Week number 21 Day number 142–223 (143–223) Wednesday 22 May

Saints' days St Rita of Cascia – the reluctant wife – patron saint of desperate cases, invoked by childless women and the infertile • SS Castus and Æmilius Ms 250 • St Basiliscus Bp of Comana in Pontius M 312 • St Bobo con 985 • St Conall ab • St Yvo con 1353

Holidays etc National Day: Yemen.

Week number 21 Day number 143–222 (144–222) Thursday 23 May

Saints' days St Julia M C5 • St Desiderius Bp of Langres M 411 • St Desiderius Bp of Vienne M 612 • St Euphrosyne of Polotsk • St Ivo of Chartres • St William of Rochester.

Week number 21 Day number 144–221 (145–221) Friday 24 May

Saints' days St David of Scotland – The great Scottish king • SS Donatian and Rogatian Ms c287 • St Vincent of Lerins 450 • St John de Prado priest M • St Simeon Stylites the Younger.

Holidays etc Empire Day (celebrated for Queen Victoria's birthday, 1817) • Easter Law Term ends (began 16 April) • Jewish observance: 6&7 Sivan – Shavuot (Feast of Weeks) • Independence Day: Eritrea • PH: Bulgaria, Israel, Republic of Korea.

Week number 21 Day number 145–220 (146–220)   Saturday 25 May

Saints' days St Aldhelm Bp Sherburn – the first great English scholar 709 • St Dumhade ab Iona 717 • St Bede, the Venerable – the father of English history • St Urban Pope M 230? • SS Maximus (Meuxe) and Venerand in Normandy C5? • St Madeleine Sophie Barat – Foundress of the Society of the Sacred Heart • St Gregory VII Pope (Hildebrand) 1085 • The Three St Marys • St Mary Magdalen of Pazzi 1607.

Holidays etc Moon's first quarter • Theravadan Buddhist Uposatha (Observance Day) = Sri Lankan Poya Day • Buddhist observance: Raek Na; Ploughing Festival • Independence Day: Jordan • National Day: Argentina.

Week number 21 Day number 146–219 (147–219)   Sunday 26 May

Saints' days St Augustine (or Austin) of Canterbury – apostle of the English 605? • St Mariana of Quito • St Philip Neri 1595 • St Quadratus Bp Athens C2 • St Eleutherius Pope M 192 • St Oduvald ab Melrose 698.

Holidays etc Pentecost or Whit ☙ • Independence Day: Georgia, Guyana (see also 23 February) • PH: Bahrain, Finland, Norway.

Week number 22 Day number 147–218 (148–218)   Monday 27 May

Saints' days St Bede – 'father of the church' con 735 • St Julius of Durostorum M c302 • St John Pope M 526.

Holidays etc Spring Holiday (last M in May): UK • May Day in Scotland • Muslim observance: Ashura • PH: Bahrain, Belgium. Denmark, France, Germany, Hungary, Iceland, Lithuania, Netherlands, Norway, Sweden, Switzerland, USA.

Week number 22 Day number 148–217 (149–217)   Tuesday 28 May

Saints' days St Bernard of Montjoux • St Germanus Bp of Paris 576 • St Caraunus (Cheron) M C5.

Holidays etc Whitsunday – Scottish Quarter Day; date varies • Removal Term in Scotland • Independence Day: Azerbaijan • National Day: Ethiopia.

Week number 22 Day number 149–216 (150–216)   Wednesday 29 May

Saints' days St Mary-Magdalen dei Pazzi • St Cyril M C3? • St Conon of Iconia in Asia and son Ms c275 • St Maximinus Bp of Thiers 349 • SS Alexander, Martyrus and Sisinnius Ms in the territory of Trent 397.

Holidays etc Oak Apple (or Royal Oak) Day, commemorating King Charles II finding safety in an oak tree in the ground of Boscobel House, Shropshire, after the Battle of Worcester (1651), because it was too dangerous for him to remain in the house while Parliamentary troops searched for him.

Week number 22 Day number 150–215 (151–215)   **Thursday 30 May**

Saints' days St Joan of Arc – The Maid of Orléans – second patron saint of France, soldiers – burnt at the stake in Rouen in 1431, she was canonised by Pope Benedict XV in 1921 on the anniversary of her death • St Felix Pope and M 274 • St Maguil recluse of Picardy c685 • St Walstan farm labourer of Taverham in Norfolk 1016 • St Ferdinand III K of Castile and Léon in union 1252

Holidays etc Corpus Christi – held on the Thursday after Whit Sunday, in honour of the doctrine of transubstantiation • Statehood Day: Ethiopia.

Week number 22 Day number 151–214 (152–214)   **Friday 31 May**

Saints' days St Petronilla C1 • SS Cantius, Cantianus (bros) and Cantianilla (sis) Ms 304 • US: Memorial Day • National Day: South Africa • PH: Malaysia.

June

Takes its name from the god Juno, wife of Zeus and queen of heaven.
Birthstone   Pearl, Agate, Moonstone or Alexandrite.

Week number 22 Day number 152–213 (153–213)   **Saturday 1 June**

Saints' days St Justin the philosopher 167 • St Angela of Brescia • St Nicomedes • St Pamphilus priest M 309 • St Caprias ab 430 • St Wistan Pr of Mecia M 849 • St Peter of Pisa founder of the Hermits of St Jerome 1435.

Holidays etc Sixth Full Moon of the Gregorian year • Third month of the Theravadan Buddhist year • Theravadan Buddhist Uposatha (Observance Day) = Sri Lankan Poya Day • Buddhist observance: Vesak or Visakah Puja (Buddha('s birth)Day – night of full moon in June for a leap year; otherwise May full moon) • Independence Day: Samoa • PH: China, Kenya, Malaysia.

Week number 22 Day number 153–212 (154–212)   Sunday 2 June

Saints' days   SS Pothinus Bp of Lyons, Sanctus, Attalus, Blandina *et al* Ms of Lyons 177 • St Erasmus – the sailor's friend – patron saint of sailors, invoked against birth-pains, colic and danger at sea – also known as St Elmo's Day – Bp and M 303 • St Blandina • SS Marcellinus and Peter Ms *c*304 • St Nicephorus of Constantinople.

Holidays etc   Pentecost (Christian-Eastern Orthodox observance) • Anniversary of the 1953 Coronation of HM Queen Elizabeth II • National Day: Italy

Week number 23 Day number 154–211 (155–211)   Monday 3 June

Saints' days   St Cecilius con 211 • St Clotildis or Clotilda Q of France 545 • St Laifard ab nr Orleans C6 • St Coemgen or Keivin Bp and con in Ireland 618 • St Genesius Bp and con *c*622.

Holidays etc   Queen's Birthday: New Zealand • Foundation Day: West Australia • PH: Republic of Ireland.

Week number 23 Day number 155–210 (156–210)   Tuesday 4 June

Saints' days   St Quirinus Bp of Siscia M 304 • St Optatus Bp of Milevum con C4 • St Breaca or Breague of Ireland • St Nenooc or Nennoca V of Britain 467 • St Burian of Ireland • St Petroc ab and con *c*564 • St Walter ab of Fontanelle or St Vandrilles 1150 • St Walter ab in San-Serviliano C13 • St Francis Caracciolo.

Holidays etc   Trinity Law Term begins (ends 31 July) • Emancipation Day: Tonga • PH: Ghana

Week number 23 Day number 156–209 (157–209)   Wednesday 5 June

Saints' days   St Boniface of Crediton – The apostle to the Germans – patron saint of brewers and tailors Abp Mentz, M 755 • St Dorotheus of Tyre M C4 • St Dorotheus the Theban ab C4 • St Illidius Bp of Auvergne con *c*385.

Holidays etc   Constitution Day: Denmark.

Week number 23 Day number 157–208 (158–208)   Thursday 6 June

Saints' days   St Philip the Deacon C1 • St Gudwall Bp of Maloi con C6/7 • St Clause Abp Besancon con 696 or 703 • St Jarlath of Tuam • St Norbert Abp Magdeburg founder of Premonstratensian Order con 1134.

Holidays etc   Corpus Christi: DO England, Wales and Ireland • Day of the Swedish Flag • PH: Austria, Bolivia, Brazil, Chile, Republic of Korea, Poland, Portugal.

Week number 23 Day number 158–207 (159–207)   Friday 7 June

Saints' days   St Paul Bp of Constantinople M 350 • St Colman Bp of Dromore con c610 • St Godeschalc Pr of the Western Vandals *et al* Ms 1066 • St Meriadec Bp of Vannes con 1302 • St Robert ab of Newminster 1159.

Holidays etc   Sette Guigno Riots: Malta.

Week number 23 Day number 159–206 (160–206)   Saturday 8 June

Saints' days   St Maximus first Abp Aix con C1/2 • St Gildard of Goldard Bp Rouen con C6 • St Medard Bp Noyon con C6 • St Syra V of Ireland C7 • St Clou or Clodulphus Bp of Metz con 696 • St Melania the Elder • St William Abp of York con 1154.

Holidays etc   Moon's last quarter • Theravadan Buddhist Uposatha (Observance Day) = Sri Lankan Poya Day • PH: Hong Kong.

Week number 23 Day number 160–205 (161–205)   Sunday 9 June

Saints' days   St Vincent M C2/3 • SS Primus and Felicianus Ms 286 • St Pelagia of Antioch V and M 311 • St Columba (or Colmcille) – 'Pilgrim for Christ' ab and Apostle of the Picts 597 • St Richard Bp of Andria con cC8.

Week number 24 Day number 161–204 (162–204)   Monday 10 June

Saints' days   St Getulius and companions Ms C2 • St Landry or Landericus Bp of Paris con C7 • St Margaret Q of Scotland 1093 • Blessed Henry or Rigo of Treviso con 1315.

Holidays etc   Duke of Edinburgh's birthday • National Day: Portugal • PH: Argentina, Australia (not WA), Colombia, HK, PNG • Time Observance Day in Japan, when people are supposed to be especially punctual • Japanese observance (10–16): Sanno Matsuri.

Week number 24 Day number 162–203 (163–203)   Tuesday 11 June

Saints' days   St Barnabas – Barnaby's Day – the Apostle, companion of St Paul – patron saint of Cyprus, invoked against hailstorms and as a peacemaker C1 • St Tochumra V of Ireland • Another St Tochumra V • St Benedict – The founder of western monasticism – patron saint of Europe, coppersmiths and schoolchildren, invoked against fever and poison, and by the dying and servants who have broken their master's belongings.

Week number 24 Day number 163–202 (164–202)   Wednesday 12 June

Saints' days SS Basilides, Quirinus or Cyrinus, Nabor and Nazarius Ms • St Onuphrius hermit • St Ternan Bp of the Picts con C5 • St Eskil of Sweden Bp M C11 • St John of Sahagun con 1479 • St Leo III.

Holidays etc Independence Day: Philippines (1898); Russia • PH: Paraguay, Philippines, Russian Federation.

Week number 24 Day number 164–201 (165–201)   Thursday 13 June

Saints' days St Antony of Padua – 'The hammer of heretics' – patron saint of Portugal, lost articles, the poor, lower animals and harvests con 1231 • St Damhnade of Ireland V.

Holidays etc Today or tomorrow: latest sunset.

Week number 24 Day number 165–200 (166–200)   Friday 14 June

Saints' days St Basil the Great Abp of Cæsarea con 379 • SS Rufinus and Valerius Ms • St Docmael or Toël con C6 • St Nennus or Nehemias ab C7 • St Psalmodius hermit C7 • St Methodius con Patriarch of Constantinople 846.

Holidays etc Today or yesterday: latest sunset.

Week number 24 Day number 166–199 (167–199)   Saturday 15 June

Saints' days St Bonaventure – the seraphic doctor • St Vitus or Guy – Patron saint of nervous disorders – patron saint of dogs, dancers, actors, and comedians, invoked against epilepsy, St Vitus's dance and snakebites Crescentia and Modestus Ms C4 • St Vaughe or Vorech hermit in Cornwall 585 • St Landelin ab of Crespin 686 • St Bernard of Menthon con 1008 • St Edburga of Winchester • St Germaine of Pibrac • Blessed Gregory Lewis Barbadigo Cardinal Bp of Padua con 1697.

Holidays etc Official Birthday of HM Queen Elizabeth II • Japanese observances (mid-June): Hana Taue (Rice-Planting Festival); Peiron Boat race.

Week number 24 Day number 167–198 (168–198)   Sunday 16 June

Saints' days   SS Ferreolus or Pargeau and Fewrrutius Ms 211/212 • SS Quiricus, Cyricus or Cyr and Julitta Ms 304 • St Aurelian Abp of Arles con 552 • St John Francis Regis con 1640 • St Lutgard • St Tikhon of Amathus.

Holidays etc   Father's Day • Sixth New Moon of the Gregorian year • Fifth month of the Chinese year • Theravadan Buddhist Uposatha (Observance Day) = Sri Lankan Poya Day • Bloomsday – 16 June 1904, the day on which Stephen Dedalus and Leopold Bloom wander round Dublin and finally meet, in James Joyce's *Ulysses* (1918). It was the very day on which Joyce and Nora Barnacle (later Mrs Joyce) first walked out together • PH: South Africa.

Week number 25 Day number 168–197 (169–197)   Monday 17 June

Saints' days   SS Nicander and Marcian Ms c303 • St Prior hermit in Egypt C4 • St Avitus or Avy or Harvey ab nr Orleans c530 • St Alban (see also 22 June) • St Botolph or Botulf ab of Ikanho 655 • St Molingus or Dairchilla Bp and con in Ireland 697.

Holidays etc   National Day: Iceland • PH: Colombia, Iceland • Japanese observance: Saikusa no Matsuri (Lily Festival).

Week number 25 Day number 169–196 (170–196)   Tuesday 18 June

Saints' days   St Elizabeth of Schonauge or Schönau V and abs 1165 • St Ephraem • SS Mark or Marcus and Marcellianus M 286 • St Armand Bp of Bordeaux • St Marina of Bithynia V C8.

Holidays etc   Waterloo Day (1815) • Jewish calendar: Tammuz 1 AM5756 • Muslim calendar: 1 Safar 1417AH • National Day: Seychelles • PH: Egypt.

Week number 25 Day number 170–195 (171–195)   Wednesday 19 June

Saints' days   SS Gervasius and Protasius Ms C1 • St Die or Deodatus Bp of Nevers and ab of Jointures 679/680 • St Boniface (or Bruno) Abp of Magdeburg Apostle to Russia M 1009 • St Juliana Falconieri V 1340.

Holidays etc   The Fête Dieu – kept by the Roman Catholics as one of their highest festivals; held as a celebration of God.

Week number 25 Day number 171–194 (172–194)   Thursday 20 June

Saints' days St Silverius Pope M 538 • St Gobain priest and M C7 • St Idaberga or Edburge of Mercia V cC7 • St Adalbert of Magdeburg • St Bain Bp of Terouanne or St Omer c711.

Holidays etc USA: Father's Day • PH: China, HK, Taiwan.

Week number 25 Day number 172–193 (173–193)   Friday 21 June

Saints' days St Eusebius Bp of Samosata M 379 • St Aaron ab in Brittany C6 • St Méen or Mevinus or Melanus ab in Brittany c617 • St Leufredus or Leufrol ab 738 • St Ralph Abp of Bourges con 866 • St Aloysius or Lewis Gonzaga – Patron of Catholic youth – patron saint of Jesuit students con 1591.

Holidays etc Longest Day • Chinese Fifth Moon Festival; also called Upright Sun Festival and Dragon-boat Festival (for the living) • PH: Finland.

Week number 25 Day number 173–192 (174–192)   Saturday 22 June

Saints' days St Alban – the first martyr of Britain (see also 17 June) 303 • St John Fisher – Bp and M • St Thomas Moore – 'The King's good servant, but God's first' – patron saint of lawyers • St Nicetas of Remesiana • St Paulinus Bp of Nola con 431.

Holidays etc PH: Finland, Sweden.

Week number 25 Day number 174–191 (175–191)   Sunday 23 June

Saints' days St Etheldreda or Audrey – V Queen and abs of Ely 679 – patron saint of Cambridge University (the day celebrated in the Romish calendar – see also 1017) • St Joseph Cafasso • St Mary of Oignies 1213.

Holidays etc Midsummer's Eve • National Day: Luxembourg • PH: Estonia, Lithuania, Luxembourg.

Week number 26 Day number 175–190 (176–190)   Monday 24 June

Saints' days St John the Baptist – Herald of Christ – patron saint of motorways, farriers, tailors and the Knights Hospitallers • The Ms of Rome under Nero C1 • St Bartholomew of Dunelm.

Holidays etc Midsummer Day – quarter-day in England, Wales and Northern Ireland • Moon's first quarter • Theravadan Buddhist Uposatha

(Observance Day) = Sri Lankan Poya Day • PH: Argentina, Estonia, Latvia, Lithuania, Venezuela.

Week number 26 Day number 176–189 (177–189)   Tuesday 25 June

Saints' days   SS Agoard and Agilbert Ms nr Paris c400 • St Prosper of Aquitaine con 463 • St Maximus Bp of Turin con C5 • St Moloc Bp and con in Scotland C7 • St Adelbert of Northumberland con c740 • St William of Monte-Vergine 1142 • St Febronia • St Prosper of Reggio.

Holidays etc   Independence Day: Mozambique • Statehood Day: Slovenia.

Week number 26 Day number 177–188 (178–188)   Wednesday 26 June

Saints' days   St Anthelm – Carthusian monk and Bp of Bellay con 1178 • SS John and Paul Ms in Rome c362 • St Vigilius Bp of Trent 400/405 • St Maxentius ab in Poitou c515 • St Babolan ab in France C7 • The Venerable Raingarda of Auvergne widow 1135.

Holidays etc   Independence Day: Madagascar • Pershore Fair day – see 20 April.

Week number 26 Day number 178–187 (179–187)   Thursday 27 June

Saints' days   St John of Moutier and Chinon priest and con C6 • St Cyril of Alexandria – Bishop and theologian • St Ladislas I K of Hungary con 1095.

Holidays etc   Independence Day: Djibouti.

Week number 26 Day number 179–186 (180–186)   Friday 28 June

Saints' days   St Irænius Bp of Lyons M 202 • S Plutarch, Serenus, Hero *et al* Ms C3 • SS Potamiana or Potamiena and Basilides Ms C3 • St Leo II Pope and con 683.

Week number 26 Day number 180–185 (181–185)   Saturday 29 June

Saints' days   St Peter – Leader of the Apostles – patron saint of fishermen and many other trades, invoked for a long life 68 • St Hemma widow 1045.

Holidays etc   PH: Chile, Peru.

Saints' days St Paul – Apostle of the Gentiles – patron saint of tent-makers and saddlers, invoked against poisonous snakes 68 • St Martial Bp of Limoges C3.

Holidays etc SS Peter and Paul: DO England, Wales and Scotland • Independence Day: Democratic Republic of Congo.

July

Takes its name from Julius Cæsar.
Birthstone Cornelian or Ruby.

Saints' days SS Julius and Aaron Ms c303 • St Thierri ab of Mpnt-d'Hor 533 • St Calais or Carilephus ab of Anille 542 • St Gal 1st Bp of Clermont c533 • St Cybar recluse at Angouleme 581 • St Simeon Salus C6 • St Leonorus or Lunaire Bp • St Rumold patron of Mechlin Bp and M 775 • St Theobald or Thibault con 1066.

Holidays etc National Day of Canada – in 1867 the Dominion of Canada was established • Buddhist observance: Dharma Day • Seventh Full Moon of the Gregorian year • Fourth month of the Theravadan Buddhist year • Theravadan Buddhist Uposatha (Observance Day) = Sri Lankan Poya Day • National Day: Burundi, Rwanda • PH: Colombia, Ghana.

Saints' days St Swithin – Bp of Winchester • St Mary's Day: the visitation of the Blessed V • SS Processus and Martinian Ms C1 • St Monegondes recluse at Tours 570 • St Oudoceus Bp of Llandaff C6 • St Otho Bp of Bamberg con 1139.

Saints' days St Phocas M 303 • St Gunthiern ab in Brittany C6 • St Bertran Bp of Mans 623 • St Guthagon recluse at Oostkerk C8 • St Thomas – The apostle of India – patron saint of builders, architects and theologians, invoked against blindness.

Holidays etc Independence Day: Belarus.

Week number 27 Day number 185–180 (186–180)   **Thursday 4 July**

Saints' days St Finbar ab • St Bolcan ab • St Sisoes or Sisoy anchoret in Egypt c429 • St Bertha widow ab of Blangy in Artois c725 • St Ulric Bp of Augsburg con 973 • St Odo the good Abp of Canterbury con C10 • St Elizabeth of Portugal – The peacemaker – invoked in time of war • St Andrew of Crete • St Martin of Tours.

Holidays etc US Independence Day – in 1776 the American Congress voted for independence from Britain, with Thomas Jefferson later signing the Declaration of Independence • Birthday of John Calvin Coolidge in 1872, 30th US President • Moreover, the anniversary of the deaths of 3 US Presidents; John Adams, 2nd US President, 1826, and Thomas Jefferson, 3rd US President, died on the same day. Both men wanted to live until the 50th anniversary of the Declaration. Jefferson died at one o'clock on the afternoon of the 4th, Adams a few hours later. Five years later to the day, James Monroe, the 5th President, died • Jewish observance: 17 Tammuz – Shivah Asar B'Tammuz (Fast commemorating the breaching of the walls of Jerusalem).

Week number 27 Day number 186–179 (187–179)   **Friday 5 July**

Saints' days St Modwena V of Ireland C9 • St Edana or Edæne V of Ireland • St Peter of Luxembourg con cardinal and Bp of Metz 1387 • St Antony Zaccaria • St Anthanasius the Athonite • St Philomena of San Severino.

Holidays etc US Independence Day observed • National Day of Venezuela – in 1811 Simón Bolívar declared independence from Spain • Independence Day: Cape Verde Islands • Day of the Slav Missionaries: Slovakia.

Week number 27 Day number 187–178 (188–178)   **Saturday 6 July**

Saints' days St Julian anchoret c370 • St Palladus apostle of the Scots Bp and con c450 • St Moninna of Ireland V 518 • St Goar priest and con 575 • St Mary Goretti • St Sexburga abs of Ely C7.

Holidays etc Independence Day: The Comoros, Malawi.

Week number 27 Day number 188–177 (189–177)   **Sunday 7 July**

Saints' days St Pantinus or Pantænus father of the church C3 • St Felix Bp of Nantes con 584 • St Edelburga V of Kent • St Hedda Bp of the West

Saxons con 705 • St Willibald Bp of Aichstadt con 790 • St Benedict XI Pope and con 1304.

Holidays etc Moon's last quarter • Theravadan Buddhist Uposatha (Observance Day) = Sri Lankan Poya Day • Independence Day: Solomon Islands.

Week number 28 Day number 189–176 (190–176)   Monday 8 July

Saints' days St Procopius M c303 • SS Kilian, Colman and Totnan Ms 688 • St Withburge V of Norfolk 743 • St Grimbald ab of New Minstre 903 • Blessed Theobalt ab of Vaux and Cernay 1247 • St Elizabeth Q of Portugal 1336.

Week number 28 Day number 190–175 (191–175)   Tuesday 9 July

Saints' days St Ephrem of Edessa doctor and con 378 • St Everildis V of England C7 • The Ms of Gorcum 1572 • St John of Rochester and Thomas More • St Veronica Giuliani

Holidays etc National Day of Argentina commemorating its declaration of independence from Spain in 1816.

Week number 28 Day number 191–174 (192–174)   Wednesday 10 July

Saints' days The seven bros Ms C2 • SS Rufina and Secunda Vs and Ms C3 • St Alexandra • St Amalburga • St Antony of the caves.

Holidays etc Independence Day: Bahamas.

Week number 28 Day number 192–173 (193–173)   Thursday 11 July

Saints' days St Pius I Pope and M 157 • St James Bp of Nisibis con 350 • St Hidulphus Bp and ab 707 • St Drostan ab of Daleongaile c809 • St Olga.

Week number 28 Day number 193–172 (194–172)   Friday 12 July

Saints' days SS Nabor and Felix Ms c304 • St Veronica – Woman of pity – patron saint of washerwomen • St John the Iberian • St John Gualberto ab 1073.

Holidays etc Battle of the Boyne; Orangeman's Day: Northern Ireland; if it fall on a Sunday, it is celebrated on the Monday • Independence Day: Kiribati, São Tomé and Príncipe.

Week number 28 Day number 194–171 (195–171)   **Saturday 13 July**

Saints' days St Anacletus M C2 • St Eugenius Bp of Carthage and companions Ms 505 • St Turiaf, Turiave or Thivisiau Bp of Dol in Brittany c749 • St Francis Solano • St Mildred • St Silas.

Holidays etc First day of 3-day Japanese Buddhist observance: Obon.

Week number 28 Day number 195–170 (196–170)   **Sunday 14 July**

Saints' days St Idus Bp of Ath-Fadha in Leinster • St Processus' Day • St Martin's Day • St Bonaventure cardinal and Bp 1274 • St Camillus de Lellis con 1614 • St Madalgaire • St Nicodemus of the Holy Mountain • St Phocas • St Ulric of Zell.

Holidays etc Bastille Day – National Day of France; in 1789 the hated Bastille prison in Paris was stormed and razed to the ground; the French Revolution had begun • The National Day of Iraq: in 1958, King Faisal was assassinated in a military coup led by General Kassem, and Iraq became a republic.

Week number 29 Day number 196–169 (197–169)   **Monday 15 July**

Saints' days St Swithun or Swithin con Bp and patron of Winchester 862. Anglo-Saxon saint who asked to be buried outside Winchester Cathedral, as he said he wanted to be exposed to 'the feet of passers-by and the drops falling from above' which led to the meteorological superstition that if its rains on 15 July it will rain for 40 days • St Plechelm Bp and con apostle of Guelderland 732 • SS Edith of Polesworth and Edith of Tamworth • St Henry II Emperor of Germany 1024 • St James of Nisibus • St Vladimir.

Holidays etc Seventh New Moon of the Gregorian year • Sixth month of the Chinese year • Theravadan Buddhist Uposatha (Observance Day) = Sri Lankan Poya Day • Jewish calendar: Ab 1 AM5756 • Muslim calendar: 1 Rabia I 1417AH

Week number 29 Day number 197–168 (198–168)   **Tuesday 16 July**

Saints' days St Eustathius con patriarch of Antioch 338 • St Elier or Helier hermit and M • St Mary Magdalen Postel • St Rainald.

Holidays etc The traditional starting day of the Islamic Era in AD622 when a persecuted Muhammad fled from Mecca to Medina, and known as the *hegira*, Arabic for 'flight'.

Week number 29 Day number 198–167 (199–167) **Wednesday 17 July**

Saints' days SS Speratus and his companions Ms C3 • St Marcellina eldest sis of St Ambrose c400 • St Alexis or Alexius con C5 • St Ennodius Bp of Pavia con 521 • St Turninus con C8 • St Kenelm • St Leo IV Pope and con 855 • St Narses of Lampron.

Holidays etc PH: Republic of Korea • Japanese observance: Gion Matsuri.

Week number 29 Day number 199–166 (200–166) **Thursday 18 July**

Saints' days St Symphorosa and her seven sons Ms 120 • St Philastrius Bp of Brescia con C4 • St Arnoul M c534 • St Arnoul Bp of Metz con 640 • St Frederic Bp of Utrecht con C9 • St Odulph canon of Utrecht con C9 • St Bruno Bp of Segni con 1125.

Holidays etc National Day of Spain

Week number 29 Day number 200–165 (201–165) **Friday 19 July**

Saints' days St Arsenius – the weeping monk anchoret 449 • St Macrina the younger V 379 • St Symmachus Pope and con 514 • St Vincent de Paul founder of the Lazarites con 1660.

Week number 29 Day number 201–164 (202–164) **Saturday 20 July**

Saints' days St Joseph Barsabbus con C1 • SS Justa and Rufina Ms 304 • St Margaret of Antioch – 'The very great martyr, Mariana' – patron saint of women, nurses and peasants, invoked in childbirth and against barrenness or loss of milk V&M early C4 • St Aurelius Abp of Carthage con 423 • St Ulmar or Vulmar ab of Samer 710 • St Ceslas con of the order of St Dominic 1242 • St Jerome Aemiliani con 1537 • St Jacob's Day • St Wilgefortis.

Holidays etc Independence Day: Colombia.

Week number 29 Day number 202–163 (203–163) **Sunday 21 July**

Saints' days St Praxides V C2 • St Zoticus Bp and M c204 • St Lawrence of Brindisi • St Victor of Marseilles M early C4 • St Barhadbeschiabas deacon and M 354 • St Abrogastus Bp of Strasburg con c678.

Holidays etc National Day of Belgium: in 1831 Belgium broke from the Netherlands and became a separate kingdom under King Leopold.

Week number 30 Day number 203–162 (204–162) Monday 22 July

Saints' days   St Mary Magdalene – Loyal follower of Christ – patron saint of repentent sinners and the contemplative life • St Joseph of Palestine (Count Joseph) c356 • St Vandrille or Wandregisilus ab of Fontanelles 666 • St Meneve ab of Menat 720 • St Dabius or Davius of Ireland con.

Holidays etc   National Day of Poland.

Week number 30 Day number 204–161 (205–161) Tuesday 23 July

Saints' days   St Apollinaris Bp of Ravenna M C1 • St Liborius Bp of Mans con c397 • St Bridget – Founder of the Bridgettines – patron saint of Sweden • St John Cassian.

Holidays etc   Moon's first quarter • Theravadan Buddhist Uposatha (Observance Day) = Sri Lankan Poya Day • Egypt: Anniversary of the 1952 revolution • The National Days of Ethiopia and the United Arab Republic • Remembrance Day: PNG • Japanese observance (23–25): Soma Nomaoi Matsuri (Soma Wild Horse Chase festival).

Week number 30 Day number 205–160 (206–160) Wednesday 24 July

Saints' days   St Christina V&M early C4 • St Lewine of Britain V&M • St Declan 1st Bp of Ardmore Ireland C5 • St Lupus Bp of Troyes con 478 • SS Wulfhad and Ruffin Ms c670 • SS Romanus and David patrons of Muscovy Ms 1010 • St Kinga or Cunegundes of Poland 1292 • St Francis Solano con C16 • St Boris and Gleb • St Christine.

Holidays etc   PH: Venezuela • Japanese observance: Temma Tenjin Matsuri.

Week number 30 Day number 206–159 (207–159) Thursday 25 July

Saints' days   St Christopher – The Christ-bearer – patron saint of travellers, especially motorists and sailors M C3 • St James the Greater – Friend of Christ – patron saint of Spain, pilgrims, labourers and furriers • St Cucufas M in Spain 304 • SS Thea and Valentina Vs and St Paul Ms 308 • St Nissen ab of Mountgarret Ireland.

Holidays etc   Jewish observance: 9 Ab – Tisha B'Ab (Fast commemorating the destruction of the First and Second Temples).

Week number 30 Day number 207–158 (208–158) Friday 26 July

Saints' days St Anne – The mother of Mary – patron saint of miners • St Germanus Bp of Auxerre con 448 • St Bartholomea Capitanio.

Holidays etc National Day: Liberia, the first African colony to gain independence (1847) • National Day: The Maldives • PH: Cuba.

Week number 30 Day number 208–157 (209–157) Saturday 27 July

Saints' days SS Maximian, Malchus, Martinian, Dionysius, John Serapion and Constantine Ms commonly called 'the seven sleepers' 250 • St Aurelius and Natalia • St Celestine I • St Clement Slovensky • St Pantaleon M 303 • St Congall ab of Iabhnallivin Ireland • St Lucian con of Ireland.

Holidays etc Milad-al-Nabi (The Prophet's birthday) • Buddhist observance: Asalha Puja or Dhamma Day • PH: Bahrain, Egypt, Indonesia, Nigeria, Pakistan, UAE • Festival of the Seven Sleepers – Emperor Decius, having set up a statue in the city of Ephesus (250CE), commanded all the inhabitants to worship it. Seven young men disobeying this mandate, and being unambitious of the honour of martyrdom, fled to Mount Cœlius, where they concealed themselves in a cavern. Decius, enraged, caused all the caverns on the mount to be closed up, and nothing was heard of them until 479, when someone digging foundations for a stable broke into the cavern, and discovered them. Disturbed by the unwanted noise, the young men, who been asleep all the time, awakened; feeling very hungry, and thinking they had slept but one night, they despatched one of their number into Ephesus to learn the news, and purchase some provisions. The antiquity of the coin proffered by the messenger at a baker's shop attracted suspicion, and the notice of the authorities. After an investigation, the whole affair was declared to be a miracle, and in its commemoration the festival was instituted.

Week number 30 Day number 209–156 (210–156) Sunday 28 July

Saints' days SS Nazarius and Celsus M c68 • St Victor Pope and M 201 • St Innocent I Pope and con 417 • St Samson – Missionary to Cornwall Bp and con c584.

Holidays etc National Day of Peru – when in 1821, San Martin's soldiers liberated the country and declared its independence from Spain • PH: Peru, Malaysia.

Week number 31 Day number 210–155 (211–155) Monday 29 July

Saints' days St Martha – patron saint of housewives V sis of Mary and Lazarus • SS Simplicius and Faustinus bros and sis Beatrice Ms 303 • St Olaus K of Sweden M • St Olaus or Olave Pirate K of Norway patron saint of Norway M 1030 • St William Bp of Brieuc in Brittany con c1234.

Holidays etc PH: Peru.

Week number 31 Day number 211–154 (212–154) Tuesday 30 July

Saints' days SS Abdon and Sennen Ms 250 • St Julitta M c303.

Holidays etc Eighth Full Moon of the Gregorian year • Fifth month of the Theravadan Buddhist year • Theravadan Buddhist Uposatha (Observance Day) = Sri Lankan Poya Day • Buddhist observance: Asalha Puja or Dhamma Day • Anniversary of the Throne: Morocco • Independence Day: Vanuatu.

Week number 31 Day number 212–153 (213–153) Wednesday 31 July

Saints' days St Helen of Skofde in Sweden M c1160 • St John Columbini con founder of the order of the Jesuati 1367 • St Ignatius Loyola – Founder of the Society of Jesus – patron saint of retreats and spiritual exercises 1556.

Holidays etc Trinity Law Term ends (began 4 June).

August

Takes its name from Augustus Cæsar.
Birthstone Sardonyx or Peridot.

Week number 31 Day number 213–152 (214–152) Thursday 1 August

Saints' days St Peter ad Vincula or St Peter's chains • The Seven Machabees, bros and their mother Ms • SS Faith, Hope and Charity Vs and Ms C2 • St Pellegrini or Peregrinus hermit 643 • St Ethelwold 'The Father of monks' Bp of Winchester con 984.

Holidays etc The National Day of Switzerland • Lammas or Loaf-Mass Day – one of the four great pagan festivals of Britain. The festival of the *Gule of August*, probably celebrated the realisation of the first-fruits of the earth, and most particularly that of the grain-harvest • 1834 – the emancipation of British slaves – the day on which slaves in Britain's colonies were assigned, not to their immediate freedom, but to a so-called 'apprenticeship' supposed to precede and prepare them for freedom • Japanese observance (1–7): Nebuta Matsuri

---

Week number 31 Day number 214–151 (215–151)   Friday 2 August

Saints' days   St Stephen Pope and M 257 • St Etheldritha or Alfrida V c834 • St Alfonso Maria de Liguori – Founder of the Redemptorists – patron saint of confessors and moral theologians • St Eusebius Bp of Vercelli • St Alphonsus Liguori • St Basil the Blessed.

Week number 31 Day number 215–150 (216–150)   Saturday 3 August

Saints' days   St Nicodemus • St Gamaliel • The Invention of St Stephen, or the Discovery of his Relics 415 • St Walthen or Waltheof con and ab of Melrose 1160 • St Peter Eymard.

Holidays etc   1492 – at the eighth hour on the morning of Friday 3 August, Columbus, with his little squadron of three ships, sailed from the port of Palos in Spain with the intention of reaching India by a westerly course. The result of this voyage was, as is well known, the discovery of the continent now known as America.

Week number 31 Day number 216–149 (217–149)   Sunday 4 August

Saints' days   St Jean-Baptiste Vianney – The beloved curé of Ars – patron saint of Parish priests • St Luanus or Lugid, sometimes called Molua ab in Ireland 622 • St Dominic con and founder of the friar preachers 1221.

Holidays etc   Birthday of HM Queen Elizabeth, the Queen Mother (1900).

Week number 32 Day number 217–148 (218–148)   Monday 5 August

Saints' days   St Memmius or Menge 1st Bp and apostle of Chalons-sur-Marne end C3 • St Afra – The saintly prostitute – patron saint of penitent women and her companions Ms 304 • St Oswald K of Northumbria 642 • The Dedication of St Mary ad Nives c435.

Holidays etc   Summer holiday in Scotland • Picnic Day: Northern Territories • Bank Holiday: New South Wales • PH: Iceland, Republic of Ireland • Japanese observance (5–7): Kanto (Lantern festival).

Week number 32 Day number 218–147 (219–147)   Tuesday 6 August

Saints' days St Xystus or Sixtus II Pope and M c258 • SS Justus and Pastor Ms 304.

Holidays etc The Transfiguration of Our Lord • Moon's last quarter • Theravadan Buddhist Uposatha (Observance Day) = Sri Lankan Poya Day • National Day of Bolivia – when it freed itself from 300 years of Spanish rule in 1825 • Independence Day: Jamaica • PH: UAE.

Week number 32 Day number 219–146 (220–146) Wednesday 7 August

Saints' days   St Donatus Bp of Arezzo in Tuscany M 361 • St Cajetan of Thienna reformer and founder of the Theatines con 1547 • St Victricius.

Holidays etc   National Day: Côte d'Ivoire • PH: Colombia.

Week number 32 Day number 220–145 (221–145)   Thursday 8 August

Saints' days   St Dominic founder of the Dominicans; patron saint of astronomers • SS Cyriacus, Largus Smaragdus and their companions Ms 303 • St Hormidz or Hormisdad M • St John-Baptist Vianney.

Holidays etc In 1988, according to the Chinese, this became the luckiest date of the century because it is a palindrome – 8.8.88 • In Kentucky a town called Eighty-Eight with only 300 inhabitants, was visited by 6,000 people who wanted to buy postcards to have 8.08am stamped on them with an 88 postmark. One couple drove to the town to be married at 8.08 on the eighth step of the church. The town was named by one of the founders who discovered he only had 88 cents in his pocket.

Week number 32 Day number 221–144 (222–144)   Friday 9 August

Saints' days   St Romanus M • St Nathy or David priest in Ireland • St Fedlimid or Felimy Bp of Kilmore con C6.

Holidays etc   National Day: Singapore • Day of Our Lady of Victories: Malta • PH: Singapore, South Africa.

Week number 32 Day number 222–143 (223–143)   Saturday 10 August

Saints' days   St Lawrence M 258 • St Deusdedit con • St Blaan Bp of Kinngaradha among the Picts in Scotland c440.

Holidays etc   Independence Day: Ecuador.

Week number 32 Day number 223–142 (224–142)   Sunday 11 August

Saints' days St Tiburtius M 286 • St Chromatius con 286 • St Susan or Susanna V&M c295 • St Gery or Gaugericus con 619 • St Equitius ab c540 • St Clare of Assisi – Founder of the 'Poor Clares' – patron saint of television V and abs 1253.

Week number 33 Day number 224–141 (225–141)   Monday 12 August

Saints' days St Francis of Assisi – 'Il Poverello' – patron saint of merchants, animals, animal welfare societies and ecology • St Euplius M 304 • St Muredach 1st Bp of Killala in Ireland C5.

Holidays etc The 'Glorious Twelfth' in Britain when the grouse shooting season officially opens • PH: Thailand • Japanese observance (12–15): Awa Odori (Awa Dance).

Week number 33 Day number 225–140 (262–140)   Tuesday 13 August

Saints' days St Hippolytus – the sainted antipope – patron saint of horses and prison officers M 252 • St Cassian of Imola M • St Narses the Gracious • St Radegundes Q of France 587 • St Tikhon of Zadonsk • St Wigbert ab and con c747.

Week number 33 Day number 226–139 (227–139) Wednesday 14 August

Saints' days St Eusebius priest and M end C3 • St Eusebius priest and con at Rome C4.

Holidays etc Eighth New Moon of the Gregorian year • Seventh month of the Chinese year • Theravadan Buddhist Uposatha (Observance Day) = Sri Lankan Poya Day • Independence Day: Pakistan.

Week number 33 Day number 227–138 (228–138)   Thursday 15 August

Saints' days The Assumption of the Blessed Virgin Mary • St Alipius Bp and con C5 • St Mac-cartin Aid or Aed Bp and con in Ireland 506 • St Arnoul or Arnulphus con and Bp of Soissons 1087 • St Tarsicius.

Holidays etc The Assumption: DO • Princess Anne, the Princess Royal's birthday • PH: Austria, Belgium, Chile, France, Greece, India, Italy, Lithuania, Paraguay, Philippines, Poland, Portugal • National Day: Republic of Congo-Brazzaville • Liberation Day: Republic of Korea.

Week number 33 Day number 228–137 (229–137)   **Friday 16 August**

Saints' days   St Stephen of Hungary – The first king of Hungary – patron saint of Hungary • St Joachim • St Hyacinth of Cracow con 1257 • St Rock or Roch con C14.

Holidays etc   Japanese observance: Daimonji Okuribi • Jewish observance: 1–29 Elul – Teshuvah (Repentance); ends 13 September • Jewish calendar: Elul 1 AM5756 • Muslim calendar: 1 Rabia II 1417AH

Week number 33 Day number 229–136 (230–136)   **Saturday 17 August**

Saints' days   St Mamas M c275 • SS Liberatus ab and six monks Ms 483.

Holidays etc   National Day of Indonesia marking its independence in 1945 following Japanese occupation • National Day: Gabon • PH: Argentina.

Week number 33 Day number 230–135 (231–135)   **Sunday 18 August**

Saints' days   St Agapetus M c275 • St Helena – Mother of the first Christian emperor 328 • SS Florus and Laurus • St Clare of Montefalco V 1308.

Week number 34 Day number 231–134 (232–134)   **Monday 19 August**

Saints' days   SS Timothy, Agapius and Theela Ms 304 • St Mochteus Bp and con 535 • St Cumin Bp in Ireland C7 • St Lewis Bp of Toulouse con 1297 • St Arnulf of Metz • St John Eudes.

Holidays etc   National Day: Afghanistan • PH: Colombia.

Week number 34 Day number 232–133 (233–133)   **Tuesday 20 August**

Saints' days   St Oswin K or Deira and M 651 • St Bernard ab of Clairvaux patron saint of Gibraltar, beekeepers and wax-melters 1153 • St Amadour • St Philibert.

Holidays etc   National Day: Hungary.

Week number 34 Day number 233–132 (234–132)   **Wednesday 21 August**

Saints' days   SS Bonosus and Maximilian Ms 363 • St Richard Bp of Andria con C12 • St Bernard Ptolemy founder of the Olivetans 1348 • St Abraham of Smolensk • St Jane Frances de Chantal widow and abs 1641 • St Sidonius Apollinaris.

Week number 34 Day number 234–131 (235–131)   Thursday 22 August

Saints' days   St Symphorian M c178 • St Hippolytus Bp and M C3 • St Timothy M 311 • St Philibert ab of Jumiège 684 • St Andrew deacon and con 880.

Holidays etc   Moon's first quarter • Theravadan Buddhist Uposatha (Observance Day) = Sri Lankan Poya Day.

Week number 34 Day number 235–130 (236–130)   Friday 23 August

Saints' days   SS Claudius, Asterius, Neon, Domnina and Theonilla Ms c285 • St Theonas Abp of Alexandria 300 • St Justinian hermit and M c529 • St Apollinaris Sidonius con Bp of Clermont 482 • St Eugenius Bp in Ireland 618 • St Rose of Lima – The flower of Lima – patron saint of Peru, New World, India, florists and gardeners • St Philip Benizi or Beniti con 1285.

Week number 34 Day number 236–129 (237–129)   Saturday 24 August

Saints' days   St Bartholomew – the enigmatic apostle – patron saint of Florentine salt and cheese merchants, tanners and leather-workers, invoked against nervous diseases and twitching • The Ms of Utica or The White Mass 258 • St Ouen or Audoen Abp of Rouen con 683 • St Irehard or Erthad Bp and con in Scotland C10 • St Emily de Vialar • St Joan Thouret.

Holidays etc   Independence Day: Ukraine • PH: Hong Kong.

Week number 34 Day number 237–128 (238–128)   Sunday 25 August

Saints' days   St Ebba or Tabbs V and abs 683 • St Gregory of Utrecht ab and con 776 • St Louis IX – The model mediaeval ruler – patron saint of French monarchs and soldiers, and of stonemasons and sculptors – he died this day in 1270, near Tunis while leading a Crusade • St Genesius.

Holidays etc   The National Day of Uruguay, marking its independence from Spain in 1825.

Week number 35 Day number 238–127 (239–127)   Monday 26 August

Saints' days   St Zephyrinus Pope and M 219 • St Gelasinus M 297 • St Genesius (a comedian) M end C3 • St Genesius of Arles M • St Ninian – Traditionally known as the apostle of the Picts • St Elizabeth Bichier des Âges.

Holidays etc   UK: Late Summer Holiday – last Monday in August • Liberation Day: Hong Kong.

Week number 35 Day number 239–126 (240–126) **Tuesday 27 August**

Saints' days St Poemen or Pastor ab c451 • St Caesarius Abp of Arles con 542 • St Syagrius Bp of Autun 600 • St Malrubius hermit and M in Scotland c1040 • St Hugh of Lincoln M 1255 • St Joseph Calasanctius con 1648.

Holidays etc Independence Day: Moldova.

Week number 35 Day number 240–125 (241–125) **Wednesday 28 August**

Saints' days St Augustine – Greatest of the Latin Fathers – the patron saint of theologians • St Hermes M c132 • St Julian M at Brioude • St Augustine or Austin Bp of Hippo con and doctor of the church 430 • St Joaquina • St Moses the Black.

Holidays etc Lammas – Scottish Quarter Day; used to be 1 August • Buddhist observance: Kandy (Sri Lanka) Festival of the Tooth • Chinese Fourteenth Day of the Seventh Moon Festival (for the dead) • Ninth Full Moon of the Gregorian year; sixth month of the Theravadan Buddhist year • Theravadan Buddhist Uposatha (Observance Day) = Sri Lankan Poya Day • Raksha-bandhan.

Week number 35 Day number 241–124 (242–124) **Thursday 29 August**

Saints' days The Decollation of St John the Baptist • St Sabina M C2 • St Sebbi or Sebba K of Essex 697 • St Merri or Medericus ab of St Martin's c700.

Holidays etc Day of the Slovak National uprising.

Week number 35 Day number 242–123 (243–123) **Friday 30 August**

Saints' days St Fiaker, Fefre or Fiacre – the gardener saint – patron saint of gardeners, florists and taxi-drivers, invoked against fistula haemorrhoids, veneral disease and sterility anchoret and con c650 • St Agilus or Aile ab of Rebais c650 • SS Felix and Adauctus Ms c303 • St Pammachius con 410 • St Rose of Lima. V 1617.

Holidays etc PH: Peru, Turkey.

Week number 35 Day number 243–122 (244–122) **Saturday 31 August**

Saints' days St Aidan or Aedan Bp of Lindisfarne the apostle of Northumbria con 651 • St Cuthburge Q of Northumbria V and abs early C8 • St Paulinus of Trier • St Raymund Nonnatus con 1240 • St Isabel V 1270.

Holidays etc Independence Day: Kyrgyzstan, Trinidad and Tobago •
Hari Kebangsaan: Malaysia.

September

Takes its name from the Latin *septem* = seven (named when it was the
seventh month).
Birthstone   Sapphire or Chrysolite.

Week number 35 Day number 244–121 (245–121) Sunday 1 September

Saints' days SS Felix, Donatus, Arontius, Honoratus, Fortunatus,
Sabinianus, Septimus, Januarius, Felix, Vitalis, Satyrus, and Repositus 12
bros Ms at Benevento in Italy • St Firminius II Bp and con C4 • St Lupus or
Lew Abp of Sens con *c*623 • St Giles the protector-saint – patron saint of
beggars, cripples and blacksmiths ab *c*700.

Holidays etc National Day of Libya, commemorating the overthrow of
King Idris I by Colonel Gaddafi in 1969 • Constitution Day: Slovakia •
Independence Day: Uzbekistan • Father's Day: Australia and New
Zealand.

Week number 36 Day number 245–120 (246–120)   Monday 2 September

Saints' days   St Justus Abp of Lyon con *c*390 • St Brocard • St Stephen K
of Hungry con 1038 • St William Bp of Roschild con 1067 • Blessed
Margaret V&M C13.

Holidays etc   1666 – Great Fire of London – only a few months freed
from a desolating pestilence, suffering from the ill-conducted war with
Holland, when on the evening of 2 September 1666 a fire began by which
about two-thirds of it were burned down, including the cathedral of St
Paul, the Royal Exchange, about 100 parish churches, and a vast number
of public buildings. The conflagration broke out in the house of a baker
named Farryner, at Pudding Lane, near the Tower and, being favoured by
high wind, it continued for three nights and days, spreading gradually
eastward, till it ended at a spot called Pye Corner, in Giltspur Stret • Labor
Day: USA, Canada (first Monday in September; analogous to UK May Day)
• National Day: Vietnam.

Week number 36 Day number 246–119 (247–119) Tuesday 3 September

Saints' days St Mansuet 1st Bp of Toul, in Lorraine, *c*375 • St Macnisius 1st Bp of Connor in Ireland 513 • St Simeon Stylites the Younger 592 • St Remaclus Bp of Mæstricht con *c*664 • St Cuthburga • St Puis X.

Holidays etc Oliver Cromwell died 1658 • Britain entered World War II 1939 • National Day: Qatar, San Marino.

Week number 36 Day number 247–118 (248–118) Wednesday 4 September

Saints' days SS Marcellus and Valerian Ms 179 • St Ultan 1st Bp of Ardbraccan in Meath 656 • St Ida widow C9 • The Translation of St Cuthbert *c*995 • St Rosalia V 1160 • St Rosa of Viterbo V *c*1252 • St Marinus of San Marino.

Holidays etc Moon's last quarter • Theravadan Buddhist Uposatha (Observance Day) = Sri Lankan Poya Day • Janmashtani.

Week number 36 Day number 248–117 (249–117) Thursday 5 September

Saints' days St Alto ab • St Bertin ab 709 • St Lawrence Justinian or Giustiniani con 1st patriarch of Venice 1455.

Week number 36 Day number 249–116 (250–116) Friday 6 September

Saints' days St Pambo of Nitria 385 • St Macculindus Bp of Lusk 497 • St Eleutherius ab *c*585 • St Bega or Bees V C7 • St Lawrence Justinian – confessor, first patriarch of Venice, 1455 • St Cagnoald.

Holidays etc Independence Day: Swaziland • PH: Pakistan.

Week number 36 Day number 250–115 (251–115) Saturday 7 September

Saints' days St Regina or Reine V&M C3 • St Evurtius Bp of Orléans con *c*340 • St Grimonia or Germana V&M • St Eunan 1st Bp of Raphoe in Ireland • St Cloud con 560 • St Madelberte V *c*705 • SS Alchmund and Tilberth cons C8.

Holidays etc The National Day of Brazil: on this day 1822 it declared itself independent from Portugal with Pedro I as its emperor.

Week number 36 Day number 251–114 (252–114) Sunday 8 September

Saints' days The Nativity of the Blessed Virgin Mary observed in the West since AD600 • St Sidronius M C3 • SS Eusebius, Nestablus, Zeno and

Nestor Ms C4 • St Disen or Disibode Bp and con c700 • St Cerbinian Bp of Frisingen con 730 • St Adrian.

Holidays etc National Day: Andorra.

Week number 37 Day number 252–113 (253–113) Monday 9 September

Saints' days SS Gorgonius, Dorotheus and companions Ms 304 • St Ciaren or Kiaran ab in Ireland 549 • St Omer Bp and con 670 • St Osmanna V cC7 • St Bettelin hermit and con • St Peter Claver 'The Slave of the Negroes'.

Holidays etc Independence Day: Tajikistan.

Week number 37 Day number 253–112 (254–112) Tuesday 10 September

Saints' days SS Nemesianus, Felix, Lucius, another Felix, Litteus, Polianus, Victor, Jader and Dativus Bps and their companions pt Ms, pt cons C3 • St Pulcheria virgin and empress 435 • St Aubert of Avranches • St Finnian or Winin Bp and con of Moville C6 • St Salvius Bp of Albi C6 • St Nicholas of Tolentino con 1306.

Week number 37 Day number 254–111 (255–111) Wednesday 11 September

Saints' days St Patiens – archbishop of Lyon, confessor, about 480 • St Deiniol • St Paphnutius Bp and con C4 • St Protus and Hyacinthus Ms.

Holidays etc Infamous day, particularly in the American calendar, but with echoes round the world • PH: Pakistan.

Week number 37 Day number 255–110 (256–110) Thursday 12 September

Saints' days St Albeus Bp and con 525 • St Eanswide V and abs C7 • St Guy of Anderlecht con C11.

Week number 37 Day number 256–109 (257–109) Friday 13 September

Saints' days St Maurilius Bp of Angers con C5 • St Eulogius con and patriarch of Alexandria 608 • St Amatus ab and con c627 • St Amatus (another) Bp and con c690 • St John Chrysostom – The golden-mouthed saint – patron saint of preachers, invoked against epilepsy • St Notburga.

Holidays etc Ninth New Moon of the Gregorian year • Eighth month of the Chinese year • Theravadan Buddhist Uposatha (Observance Day) = Sri Lankan Poya Day.

Week number 37 Day number 257–108 (258–108) Saturday 14 September

Saints' days St Cormac Bp of Cashel 908 • St Catherine of Genoa widow 1510.

Holidays etc 629 – The Exaltation of the Holy Cross – the discovery of the cross on which Christ was supposed to have suffered, by the Empress Helena • Jewish calendar: Tishri 1 AM5757 • Jewish observance: 1&2 Tishri – Rosh Hashanah (New Year); second day 15 September • Jewish observance: 1–10 Tishri – Days of Penitence; last day 23 September • Muslim calendar: 1 Jumâda I 1417AH • PH: Israel.

Week number 37 Day number 258–107 (259–107) Sunday 15 September

Saints' days St John the Dwarf – anchoret of Scete • St Nicetas the Goth M C4 • St Nicomedes M c90 • St Aper or Evre Bp and con C5 • St Aicard or Achart ab and con c687.

Holidays etc Battle of Britain Day: the most active day of the battle when the RAF claimed to have shot down 185 German aircraft • 1830 – opening of the Liverpool and Manchester Railway • National Day: Costa Rica, El Salvador, Guatemala, Honduras, Nicaragua • PH: Israel • Respect for the Aged Day: Japan.

Week number 38 Day number 259–106 (260–106) Monday 16 September

Saints' days St Cornelius Pope and martyr patron saint of cattle and domestic animals, invoked against earache, epilepsy, fever and twitching 252 • St Cyprian Abp of Carthage M 258 • SS Lucia and Geminianus Ms c303 • St Euphemia V&M c307 • St Ninian or Ninyas Bp and con and apostle of the southern Picts 432 • St Editha of Wilton V 984.

Holidays etc Ganesh Chaturthi (first day) • Jewish observance: 3 Tishri – Feast of Gedaliah • Proclamation Day of Mexico marking the revolt against Spanish rule which began in 1810 • Proclamation of Independence Day: Mexico • Independence Day: PNG • Japanese observance: Tsurugaoka Hachimangu Yabusame.

Week number 38 Day number 260–105 (261–105) Tuesday 17 September

Saints' days SS Socrates and Stephen Ms early C4 • St Rouin, Rodingus or Chrodingus ab of Beaulieu c680 • St Lambert Bp of Mæstricht and patron of Liège M 709 • St Columba V&M 853 • St Hildegardis V and abs 1179 • St Robert Bellarmine – a great Catholic apologist • St Columba of Córdoba.

Week number 38 Day number 261–104 (262–104) Wednesday 18 September

Saints' days   St Ferreol M c304 • St Methodius of Olympus Bp of Tyre M C4 • St Thomas of Villanova con Abp of Valentia c1555 • St Joseph of Cupertino con 1663.

Holidays etc   The National Day of Chile, marking the start, two days after Mexico, of the Chilean revolt against Spanish rule.

Week number 38 Day number 262–103 (263–103) Thursday 19 September

Saints' days   St Januarius Bp of Benevento and companions Ms 305 • SS Peleus Pa-Termuthes and companions Ms early C4 • St Eustochius Bp of Tours 461 • St Sequanus or Seine ab c580 • St Theodore of Tarsus Abp of Canterbury con organiser of the English Church 690 • St Lucy V 1090 • St Emily de Rodat.

Holidays etc   1356 – Battle of Poitiers – fought by English on French soil • 1665 – Great Plague of London • Independence Day: St Christopher and Nevis • PH: Chile.

Week number 38 Day number 263–102 (264–102) Friday 20 September

Saints' days   St Eustachius and companions Ms C2 • St Agapetus Pope and con 536 • St Eustace.

Holidays etc   Moon's first quarter • Theravadan Buddhist Uposatha (Observance Day) = Sri Lankan Poya Day.

Week number 38 Day number 264–101 (265–101) Saturday 21 September

Saints' days   St Matthew author of the first Gospel patron saint of accountants, bookkeepers, tax-collectors, customs officers and security guards • St Maura V 850 • St Lo or Laudus Bp of Constances 568.

Holidays etc   Autumnal Equinox • National Day of Malta, marking its independence in 1964 from Britain after 164 years • Independence Day: Armenia, Belize.

Week number 38 Day number 265–100 (266–100) Sunday 22 September

Saints' days   St Maurice and his companions Ms 286 • St Emmeran Bp of Poitiers, and patron of Ratisbon, M 653 • The Martyrs of Agaunum • St Phocas • St Thomas of Villanueva.

Holidays etc   National Day: Mali.

Week number 39 Day number 266–99 (267–99)   Monday 23 September

Saints' days   St Adomnan supporter of the Roman tradition ab 705 • St Linus Pope and M C1 • St Thecla of Iconium V&M C1.

Holidays etc   Autumn (Fall) between Autumnal Equinox and Winter Solstice • Jewish observance: 10 Tishri – Yom Kippur (Day of Atonement) • The National Day of Saudi Arabia: proclamation and unification of the Kingdom (Hejaz + Njed – 1932) • Autumn Equinox Holiday: Japan • PH: Israel • Libra

Week number 39 Day number 267–98 (268–98)   Tuesday 24 September

Saints' days   St Rusticus or Rotiri Bp of Auvergne C5 • St Chuniald or Conald priest and missionary • St Germer or Geremar ab 658 • St Gerard Bp of Chonad M 1046.

Holidays etc   Independence Day: Guinea–Bissau • PH: South Africa.

Week number 39 Day number 268–97 (269–97)   Wednesday 25 September

Saints' days   St Firmin Bp of Amiens M • St Finbar/Finbarr or Barr founder of Cork patron saint of Barra in Scotland and Cork, Ireland con C6 • St Aunaire Bp of Auxerre c605 • St Colfrid ab 716 • St Cadoc • St Euphrosyne • St Francis of Camporosso • St Sergius of Radonezh • St Vincent Strambi.

Week number 39 Day number 269–96 (270–96)   Thursday 26 September

Saints' days   St Cyprian and Justina Ms 304 • St Eusebius Pope and con 310 • St Nilus the Younger – abbot, 1005 • St Colman of Lann Elo ab and con 610 • St Cornelius • St Nilus of Rossano the younger ab 1005 • The Martyrs of North America.

Holidays etc   Ganesh Chaturthi (last day) • PH: Republic of Korea.

Week number 39 Day number 270–95 (271–95)   Friday 27 September

Saints' days   St Cosmas and Damian Ms c303 • St Augustine of Canterbury – the original archbishop of Canterbury • St Vincent de Paul – philanthropist and founder – patron saint of all charitable societies, hospitals and prisoners, invoked to find lost articles and for spiritual help • St Elzear Count of Arian and his wife St Delphina C14.

Holidays etc   Tenth Full Moon of the Gregorian year • Seventh month of the Theravadan Buddhist year • Theravadan Buddhist Uposatha (Observance Day) = Sri Lankan Poya Day • PH: China, Republic of Korea.

Week number 39 Day number 271–94 (272–94)   Saturday 28 September

Saints' days   St Eustochium V c419 • St Exuperius Bp of Toulouse early C5 • St Lioba abs c779 • St Wenceslas 'Good King Wenceslas' Duke of Bohemia patron saint of Czechoslovakia and brewers attempted to Christianise his nation and was murdered by his brother 938.

Holidays etc   Chinese Mid-Autumn Festival (for the living) • Jewish observance: 15–21 Tishri – Succot (Feast of Tabernacles); ends 4 October • PH: Hong Kong, Israel, Republic of Korea, Taiwan.

Week number 39 Day number 272–93 (273–93)   Sunday 29 September

Saints' days   St Michael the Archangel – Captain of the heavenly host – patron saint of Brussels, the sick and battle, invoked when tempted, or when storm-tossed at sea • St Cyriacus the Recluse • St Theodora M 642.

Holidays etc   Michaelmas Day – quarter-day in England, Wales and Northern Ireland.

Week number 40 Day number 273–92 (274–92)   Monday 30 September

Saints' days   St Jerome of Aquileia the learned, irascible doctor of the church patron saint of librarians 420 • St Gregory apostle of Armenia and Bp early C4 • St Honorius Abp of Canterbury con 653 • St Otto of Bamberg • St Sophia.

Holidays etc   The National Day of Botswana, formerly Bechuanaland, which became independent in 1966 with Sir Seretse Khama as its first President • The Revolution of 1399 marks an epoch of some moment in English history – the transference of the crown from the House of Plantagenet to that of Lancaster • Queen's Birthday: Western Australia.

October

Takes its name from Latin *octo* = eight.
Birthstone   Opal or Tourmaline.

Week number 40 Day number 274–91 (275–91)   Tuesday 1 October

Saints' days   St Piat apostle of Tournay M c286 • St Emigius con Abp of Rheims 533 • St Wasnulf or Wasnon con patron of Condé c651 • St Thérèse of Lisieux – The little flower – patron saint of France, mission and florists • Agnes of Lisieux – patron saint of florists • St Bavo anchoret patron of Ghent C7 • St Fidharleus of Ireland ab 762 • St Gregory the Enlightener • St Nicetius of Trier • St Remi • St Romanus the Melodist.

Holidays etc   The Festival of the Rosary • Michaelmas Law Term begins (ends 1221) • National Day of China marking the formation in 1949 of the People's Republic with Mao Tse-tung as chairman • The National Day of Nigeria which became independent within the Commonwealth in 1960, and became a republic this day in 1963 • Independence Day: Cyprus, Tuvalu • PH: Chile

Week number 40 Day number 275–90 (276–90)   Wednesday 2 October

Saints' days   The Feast of the Holy Angel-Guardians • St Leodegarius or Leger Bp and M 678 • St Thomas Bp of Hereford (the only excommunicated saint) con 1282.

Holidays etc   Anniversary of the Proclamation of Independence: Guinea • PH: India.

Week number 40 Day number 276–89 (277–89)   Thursday 3 October

Saints' days   St Dionysius the Aeropagite Bp of Athens M C1 • The two Ewalds or Hewalds, Ms c695 • St Gerard of Brogne ab 959 • St Josepha Rossello • St Teresa of Lisieux.

Holidays etc   Anniversary of the Reunification (1990): Germany • PH: Republic of Korea.

Week number 40 Day number 277–88 (278–88)   Friday 4 October

Saints' days   SS Marcus and Martian and their companions Ms early C4 • The Ms of Trier C4 • St Ammon hermit founder of the Hermitages of Nitria, C4 • St Petronius Bp of Bologna con C5 • St Edwin K of Northumberland M 633 • St Aurea V and abs 666 • St Francis of Assisi con founder of the Friar Minors 1226.

Holidays etc   Moon's last quarter • Theravadan Buddhist Uposatha (Observance Day) = Sri Lankan Poya Day • Jewish observance: 21 Tishri – Hoshana Rabba • Independence Day: Lesotho.

Week number 40 Day number 278–87 (279–87)   Saturday 5 October

Saints' days   St Placidus ab and companions Ms 546 • St Galla widow c550 • St Maurus.

Holidays etc   Jewish observance: 22 Tishri – Shemeni Atzeret (Eighth Day of the Solemn Assembly) • PH: Israel, Portugal.

Week number 40 Day number 279–86 (280–86)   Sunday 6 October

Saints' days   St Faith or Fides V and her companions Ms C4 • St Bruno con founder of the Carthusian monks 1101.

Holidays etc   Jewish observance: 23 Tishri – Simhat Torah (Rejoicing of the Law) • Summertime begins: Tasmania • PH: Egypt.

Week number 41 Day number 280–85 (281–85)   Monday 7 October

Saints' days   St Justina of Padua V&M • SS Marcellus and Apuleius Ms at Rome • SS Sergius and Bacchus Ms C4 • St Mark Pope and con 336 • St Osyth or Osith V c870.

Holidays etc   Labour Day: ACT, NSW, SA • Japanese observance (7–9): Nagasaki Suwa Matsuri (Festival of the Nagasaki Suwa Shrine).

Week number 41 Day number 281–84 (282–84)   Tuesday 8 October

Saints' days   St Thais the penitent c348 • St Pelagia the penitent C5 • St Keyna V C5 or 6 • St Bridget widow 1373 • St Demetrius.

Week number 41 Day number 282–83 (283–83)   Wednesday 9 October

Saints' days   St Dionysius or Denis 1st Bp of Paris patron saint of France, invoked against headaches, frenzy and strife and his companions Ms 272 • St Domninus M 374 • St Guislain ab 681 • St Lewis Bertrand con 1581 • St John Leonardi.

Holidays etc   National Day of Uganda celebrating its independence in 1962 after 70 years of British rule. Milton Obote became first prime minister.

Week number 41 Day number 283–82 (284–82)   Thursday 10 October

Saints' days   St Paulinus Abp of York con 644 • St John of Bridlington con 1379 • St Francis Borgia second founder of the Jesuits con 1572 • St Gereon.

Holidays etc   Fiji Day • National Day: Taiwan • Sports Day: Japan • PH: Cuba, Kenya.

Week number 41 Day number 284–81 (285–81)   Friday 11 October

Saints' days   SS Tarachus, Probus and Andronicus Ms 304 • St Canicus or Kenny ab in Ireland 599 • St Ethelburge or Edilburge V and ab c664 • St Gummar or Gomer con 774 • St Peter of Alcantara – a celebrated Spanish mystic – patron saint of Brazil and Estremadura • St Alexander Sauli • St Bruno • St Canice.

Holidays etc   US: Columbus Day.

Week number 41 Day number 285–80 (286–80)   **Saturday 12 October**

Saints' days   St Wilfird Bp of York con 709 • St Ethelburga of Barking • St Serafino.

Holidays etc   Tenth New Moon of the Gregorian year • Ninth month of the Chinese year • Theravadan Buddhist Uposatha (Observance Day) = Sri Lankan Poya Day • Columbus Day in Spain commemorating this day in 1492 when Columbus sighted the New World • National Day: Equatorial Guinea, Spain • PH: Argentina, Chile, Mexico.

Week number 41 Day number 286–79 (287–79)   **Sunday 13 October**

Saints' days   SS Faustus, Januarius and Martialis Ms 304 • Translation of the relics of St Edward the Confessor, last of the Old English Kings • St Gerald Count of Aurillac or Orillac con 909 • St Colman M 1012 • Seven Friar Minors Ms in Morocco 1220.

Holidays etc   Hindu observance: Navrati.

Week number 42 Day number 287–78 (288–78)   **Monday 14 October**

Saints' days   St Calixtus or Callistus I the slave who became Pope and M 222 • St Donatian con Bp of Rheims and patron of Bruges 389 • St Burckard con 1st Bp of Wurtzburg 752 • St Dominic surnamed Loricatus con 1060 • St Justus of Lyons.

Holidays etc   1066 – Battle of Hastings (fought on a Saturday) • Jewish calendar: Marcheshvan 1 AM5757 • Muslim calendar: 1 Jumâda II 1417AH • PH: Brazil, Canada, Colombia, USA.

Week number 42 Day number 288–77 (289–77)   **Tuesday 15 October**

Saints' days   St Hospicus or Hospis anchoret c580 • St Tecla of Kitzingen V and ab •St Teresa of Ávila V 'The eagle and the dove' – patron saint of lace-makers, invoked by those in need of grace – foundress of the Reformation of the Barefooted Carmelites, 1582 • St Euthymius the Younger

Week number 42 Day number 289–76 (290–76)   Wednesday 16 October

Saints' days   St Gall or Gallus the apostle of Switzerland patron saint of birds ab 646 • St Mummolin or Mommolin Bp of Noyon con C7 • St Lullus or Lullon Abp of Mentz con 787 • St Gerald Majella • St Hedwig

Week number 42 Day number 290–75 (291–75)   Thursday 17 October

Saints' days   St Margaret Mary Alacoque – Saint of the Sacred Heart • St Etheldreda or Audry the d of the K of East Anglia abs of Ely (as celebrated in the English calendar) in celebration of the translation of her relics from the common cemetery of the nuns to a splendid marble coffin within the church of Ely • St Anstrudis abs at Laon 688 • St Andrew of Crete 761 • St Hedwiges or Avoice Duchess of Poland widow 1248 • St Shushanik.

Week number 42 Day number 291–74 (292–74)   Friday 18 October

Saints' days   St Luke the learned doctor; the Evangelist; patron saint of butchers, bookbinders, doctors, painters, sculptors, glassworkers and surgeons • St Justin M in France C4 • St Julian Sabas hermit • St Monan M C7.

Week number 42 Day number 292–73 (293–73)   Saturday 19 October

Saints' days   St Paul of the Cross – Priest of the Passion • SS Ptolemy, Lucius and a companion 166 • St Ethbin or Egbin ab end C6 • St Frideswide V and patroness of Oxford C8 • St John of Rila • St Peter of Alcántara con 1562.

Holidays etc   Moon's first quarter • Theravadan Buddhist Uposatha (Observance Day) = Sri Lankan Poya Day • Durga-puja.

Week number 42 Day number 293–72 (294–72)   Sunday 20 October

Saints' days   St Barsabius and his companions Ms in Persia 342 • St Artemius M 362 • St Zenobius Bp of Florence con C5 • St Sindulphus or Sendou of Rheims C7 • St Aidan Bp of Mayo 768 • St Andrew of Crete • St Bertilla Boscardin • St John of Kanti.

Holidays etc   Sarasvati-puja • PH: Kenya.

Week number 43 Day number 294–71 (295–71)   Monday 21 October

Saints' days   St Hilarion the first hermit of Palestine ab c371 • St Ursula leader of 11,000 companions, Vs and Ms C5 • St Vintan or Fintan of

Taghmon surnamed Munnu or Mundus ab in Ireland 634 • St John of Bridlington • St Viator.

Holidays etc   1805 – Trafalgar Day, commemorating Nelson's victory and his death • Chinese Double-Nine Festival (ninth day of the ninth moon) (for the dead) • Dasara • PH: Kenya.

Week number 43 Day number 295–70 (296–70)   **Tuesday 22 October**

Saints' days   St Mark Bp of Jerusalem con C2 • St Philip Bp of Heraclea and companions Ms 304 • St Mello or Meanius Bp of Rouen con early C4 • SS Nunilo and Alodia Vs and Ms in Spain C9 • St Donatus Bp of Fiesoli in Tuscany con C9.

Holidays etc   Inauguration of the present pontiff: Vatican City State • PH: Egypt • Japanese observances: Kurama Hi Matsuri; Jidai Matsuri

---

Week number 43 Day number 296–69 (297–69)   **Wednesday 23 October**

Saints' days   St Theodoret priest and M 362 • St Severin Abp of Cologne con 400 • St Severin (another) or Surin Bp • St Romanus Abp of Rouen con 639 • St Ignatius patriarch of Constantinople, con 878 • St Antony Claret • St John Capistran con 1456.

Holidays etc   National Day: Hungary • PH: Thailand.

Week number 43 Day number 297–68 (298–68)   **Thursday 24 October**

Saints' days   St Felix of Thibiuca Bp and M 303 • St Proclus con Abp of Constantinople 447 • St Magloire Bp and con c575 • St Raphael.

Holidays etc   United Nations Day commemorating this day in 1945 when the UN Charter came into force • The National Day of Zambia. In 1964, Northern Rhodesia became independent and was renamed Zambia • Scorpio.

Week number 43 Day number 298–67 (299–67)   **Friday 25 October**

Saints' days   SS Chrysanthus and Daria Ms C3 • SS Crispin and Crispinian the shoemaking bros – patron saints of shoemakers, cobblers and leather-workers – a craft they practised in Soissons, France, after fleeing persecution in Rome. In 287, they were martyred when, according to one version, they were both thrown into molten lead, but more probably were beheaded. A Kentish claim was that their bodies were cast into the sea and floated ashore at Romney Marsh. St Crispin's Day is also the anniversary of the Battle of Agincourt in 1415 • St Gaudentius of

Brescia Bp and con c420 • St Boniface I Pope and con 422 • St Edmund Arrowsmith Jesuit priest and M • St Margaret Clitherow – The pearl of York • St Isidore the Farm-servant • St John of Beverley.

Holidays etc   Republic Day: Kazakhstan • PH: Taiwan.

Week number 43 Day number 299–66 (300–66)   Saturday 26 October

Saints' days   St Evaristus Pope and M 112 • SS Lucian and Marcian Ms 250.

Holidays etc   Eleventh Full Moon of the Gregorian year • Eighth month of the Theravadan Buddhist year • Theravadan Buddhist Uposatha (Observance Day) = Sri Lankan Poya Day • Mahayana Buddhist observance: Ulambana (Ancestor Day) celebrated for 15 days • Buddhist observance: Abhidhamma Day • National Day of Austria.

Week number 43 Day number 300–65 (301–65)   Sunday 27 October

Saints' days   St Frumentius apostle of Ethiopia Bp and con C4 • St Abban ab in Ireland c500 • St Elsbaan K of Ethiopia con C6.

Holidays etc   Summertime begins: ACT, NSW, SA, Vic • BST ends • Independence Day: St Vincent, Turkmenistan.

Week number 44 Day number 301–64 (302–64)   Monday 28 October

Saints' days   St Simon the Canaanite apostle • St Jude 'Judas, not Iscariot' apostle patron saint of hopeless causes • St Neot Anchoret and con C9 • St Demetrius of Rostov • SS Jude and Simon.

Holidays etc   Labour Day: New Zealand • National Day: Czech Republic • PH: Greece, Republic of Ireland.

Week number 44 Day number 302–63 (303–63)   Tuesday 29 October

Saints' days   St Narcissus Bp of Jerusalem C2 • St Chef or Theuderius ab c575 • St Colmon of Kilmacduagh.

Holidays etc   National Day of Turkey. Kemal Atatürk proclaimed Turkey a republic and became its first President.

Week number 44 Day number 303–62 (304–62)   Wednesday 30 October

Saints' days   St Marcellus the Centurion M 298 • St Germanus Bp of Capua con c540 • St Asterius Bp of Amasea in Pontus early C5 • St Alphonsus Rodriguez.

Holidays etc 1841 – the Burning of the Tower of London – the cause appeared to have been overheating of the flue of a stove.

Week number 44 Day number 304–61 (305–61)	Thursday 31 October

Saints' days St Quintin M 287 • St Foillan M 655 • St Wolfgang Bp of Ratisbon, 994 • St Bee.

Holidays etc Halloween, Hallowe'en (All Hallows' Eve), the day the souls of the dead were supposed to revisit their homes • PH: Taiwan.

November

Takes its name from Latin *novem* = nine.
Birthstone Topaz.

Week number 44 Day number 305–60 (306–60)	Friday 1 November

Saints' days The Festival of All Saints • St Benignus apostle of Burgundy M C3 • St Austremonius C3 • St Cæsarius M 300 • St Mary M C4 • St Marcellus Bp of Paris con early C5 • St Harold K of Denmark M 980.

Holidays etc All Saints' Day DO England, Wales, Ireland and Scotland • National Day: Algeria • PH: Austria, Belgium, Chile, France, Italy, Lithuania, Mexico, Peru, Poland, Portugal, Singapore, Spain.

Week number 44 Day number 306–59 (307–59)	Saturday 2 November

Saints' days St Victorinus Bp and M c304 • St Marcian anchoret and con c387 • St Vulgan con C7.

Holidays etc All Souls' Day – Commemoration of the Faithful Departed • PH: Brazil, Finland, Mexico, Sweden.

Week number 44 Day number 307–58 (308–58)	Sunday 3 November

Saints' days St Papoul or Papulus priest and M C3 • St Flour Bp and con c389 • St Rumald or Rumbald con patron of Brackley and Buckingham • St Wenefrede or Winifred V&M in Wales • St Hubert 1st Bp of Liège – patron saint of hunting and huntsmen, invoked against rabies and hydrophobia con 727 • St Malachy – the pioneer of Gregorian reform in Ireland Abp of Armagh con 1148 • St Martín de Porres.

Holidays etc Moon's last quarter • Theravadan Buddhist Uposatha (Observance Day) = Sri Lankan Poya Day • Independence Day: Dominica • Culture Day: Japan • National Day: Panama.

Week number 45 Day number 308–57 (309–57)   **Monday 4 November**

Saints' days SS Vitalis and Agricola Ms c3204 • St Joannicus ab 845 • St Clarus M 894 • St Brinstan Bp of Winchester 934 • St Emeric Hungarian Pr C11; son of St Stephen C11 K of Hungary • St Carlo Borromeo aka Charles Borromeo – the pattern for prelates cardinal Abp of Milan con 1584.

Holidays etc Recreation Day: N Tasmania • PH: Colombia, Japan.

Week number 45 Day number 309–56 (310–56)   **Tuesday 5 November**

Saints' days St Bertille abs of Chelles 692 • SS Zachary and Elizabeth.

Holidays etc 1605 – The Gunpowder Plot discovered • Melbourne Cup Day: Melbourne.

Week number 45 Day number 310–55 (311–55)   **Wednesday 6 November**

Saints' days St Leonard hermit and con C6 • St Winoc or Winnoc ab C8 • St Illtyd.

Holidays etc PH: Thailand.

Week number 45 Day number 311–54 (312–54)   **Thursday 7 November**

Saints' days St Prosdecimus 1st Bp of Padua con C2 • St Werenfrid priest and con • St Willibrod con 1st Bp of Utrecht 738 • St Engelbert.

Holidays etc The National Day of Russia, when, in 1917, Lenin's Bolsheviks led the overthrow of the moderate Kerensky socialist government.

Week number 45 Day number 312–53 (313–53)   **Friday 8 November**

Saints' days Feast of the Four Crowned Ones (bros) still marked by some English freemasons commemorating four masons martyred by Emperor Diocletian for refusing to sculpt a pagan god 304 • St Cuby • St Godfrey Bp of Amiens con 1118 • St Willehad con Bp of Bremen and apostle of Saxony end C8.

Week number 45 Day number 313–52 (314–52)   Saturday 9 November

Saints' days   The Dedication of the Church of Our Saviour or St John Lateran • St Mathurin priest and con C3 • St Theodorus (surnamed Tyro) M 306 • St Benignus or Binen Bp 468 • St Vanne or Vitonius Bp of Verdun con c525 • St Nectarius Kephalas.

Holidays etc   The Lord Mayor of London's Show • 15th and last day of Mahayana Buddhist observance Ulambana • Independence Day: Cambodia • PH: Pakistan.

Week number 45 Day number 314–51 (315–51)   Sunday 10 November

Saints' days   SS Trypho and Respicius Ms and Nympha V C3 and C5 • SS Milles Bp of Susa, Arbrosimus priest and Sina deacon Ms in Persia 341 • St Leo the Great – Inheritor of the authority of Peter • St Andrew Avellino con 1608 • St Justus Abp of Canterbury con 627.

Holidays etc   Remembrance Sunday • St Martinmas Eve • Diwali (Hindu Festival of Lights – first day) • PH: Bolivia, India.

Week number 46 Day number 315–50 (316–50)   Monday 11 November

Saints' days   St Martin Bp of Tours symbol of charity patron saint of France, soldiers, beggars and innkeepers con 397 • St Menas or Mannas believed by the Greeks to have the power to locate lost objects, especially sheep M c304 • St Bartholomew of Grottaferrata • St Theodore the Studite.

Holidays etc   Eleventh New Moon of the Gregorian year • Tenth month of the Chinese year • US: Veterans' Day • Theravadan Buddhist Uposatha (Observance Day) = Sri Lankan Poya Day • Martinmas or Hollantide: half-quarter day • Signing of the Armistice that ended the First World War • Hindu New Year • 1630 – The Day of Dupes: Triumph of Cardinal Richelieu • Independence Day: Angola • PH: Belgium, Canada, Colombia, France, Malaysia, Poland, USA.

Week number 46 Day number 316–49 (317–49)   Tuesday 12 November

Saints' days   St Nilus anchoret father of the church and con C5 • St Livin or Lebwin patron of Daventer con end C8 • St Martin I Pope and M 655.

Holidays etc   Diwali (Hindu Festival of Lights – last day) • Jewish calendar: Kislev 1 AM5757 • Muslim calendar: 1 Rajab 1417AH • 1381 – The Order of Fools – founded by Adolphus Count of Cleves • PH: Taiwan.

Week number 46 Day number 317–48 (318–48) Wednesday 13 November

Saints' days   St Mitrius M early C4 • St Brice Bp of Tours and con 444 • St Chillen or Killian priest C7 • St Constant 777 • St Homobonus merchant con 1197 • St Didacus con 1463 • St Stanislas Kostka con 1568 • St Frances Xavier Cabrini the first American citizen to be canonized; patroness of immigrants • St Diego • St Francis Cabrini • St Nicholas I

Holidays etc   1831–1833 – Fall of Shooting Stars.

Week number 46 Day number 318–47 (319–47) Thursday 14 November

Saints' days   St Dubricius 'Chief of the Church in Britain' Bp and con C6 • St Laurence con Abp of Dublin 1180 • St Gregory Palamas • St Josephat of Polotsk.

Holidays etc   1948 – Birthday of HRH Prince Charles.

Week number 46 Day number 319–46 (320–46) Friday 15 November

Saints' days   St Eugenius M 275 • St Malo or Maclou 1st Bp of Aleth in Brittany 565 • St Leopold Marquis of Austria con 1136 • St Gertrude V and ab 1292 • St Albertus Magnus – The universal doctor – patron saint of students, scientists and all the natural sciences • St Fintan of Rheinau.

Holidays etc   1682 – Halley's Comet • PH: Brazil.

Week number 46 Day number 320–45 (321–45) Saturday 16 November

Saints' days   St Eucherius Bp of Lyon con 450.• St Edmund of Abingdon con Abp Canterbury critic of the king 1242 • St Gerturde of Helfta – A life of spiritual experiences – patron saint of the West Indies • St Margaret of Scotland a civilising influence patron saint of Scotland.

Holidays etc   Buddhist observance: Thai Elephant Festival (third Saturday in November).

Week number 46 Day number 321–44 (322–44) Sunday 17 November

Saints' days   St Dionysius Abp of Alexandria con 265 • St Gregory Thaumaturgus 'The wonder-worker' patron saint of those in desperate situations, invoked against earthquake and flood Bp and con 270 • St Anian or Agnan Bp of Orleans con 453 • St Gregory Bp of Tours 596 • St Hugh Bp of Lincoln the 1st canonised Carthusian patron saint of sick children con 1200 • St Elizabeth Q of Hungary who served beggars – patron saint of bakers, Sisters of Mercy, charities and lace-makers, invoked against toothache • St Hilda 'Mother Hilda' patron saint of business and professional women.

Holidays etc   Queen Elizabeth's Day – commemorating the ascension of Queen Elizabeth to the throne in 1558; 1679, after King Charles II.

Week number 47 Day number 322–43 (323–43)   Monday 18 November

Saints' days   The dedication of the churches of SS Peter and Paul at Rome • SS Alphæus, Zachæus, Romanus and Barulas Ms *c*304 • St Hilda or Hild abs 680 • St Odo 2nd ab of Cluny con 942 • St Mawes • St Romanus of Antioch.

Holidays etc   Moon's first quarter • Theravadan Buddhist Uposatha (Observance Day) = Sri Lankan Poya Day • National Day: Latvia, Oman • PH: India.

Week number 47 Day number 323–42 (324–42)   Tuesday 19 November

Saints' days   St Pontian Pope and M *c*235 • St Barlaam M early C4 • St Elizabeth of Hungary widow 1231 • St Mechtilde of Hackeborn • St Narses I.

Holidays etc   National Day: Monaco.

Week number 47 Day number 324–41 (325–41)   Wednesday 20 November

Saints' days   St Maxentia V&M • St Edmund K of East Anglia patron saint of Richard II invoked against plague M 870 • St Humbert Bp of the East Angles M C9 • St Bernard Bp of Hildesheim con 1021 • St Felix of Valois con 1212.

Holidays etc   Wedding Anniversary of Queen Elizabeth II 1947 • PH: Germany, Mexico.

Week number 47 Day number 325–40 (326–40)   Thursday 21 November

Saints' days   The Presentation of the Blessed Virgin Mary • St Columban the younger ab and con 615 • St Gelasius Pope and con 496.

Week number 47 Day number 326–39 (327–39)   Friday 22 November

Saints' days   SS Philemon and Appia • St Cecilia or Cecily patron saint of poets, singers, music and musicians, V&M 230 • St Theodorus the Studite ab C9.

Holidays etc   National Day: Lebanon • Sagittarius.

Week number 47 Day number 327–38 (328–38)   Saturday 23 November

Saints' days   St Clement 1st of the apostolic fathers Pope and M 100 •
St Amphilochius Bp of Iconium con 100 • St Daniel Bp and con 545 • St
Tron con 693 • St Alexander Nevsky • St Columban • St Felicity.

Holidays etc   Labour Thanksgiving Day: Japan.

Week number 47 Day number 328–37 (329–37)   Sunday 24 November

Saints' days   St Chrysogonus M early C4 • St Cianan or Kenan Bp of
Duleek in Ireland 489 • SS Flora and Mary – Vs and Ms 851 • St John of the
Cross con 1591 • St Colman of Cloyne.

Holidays etc   Thanksgiving Day in America – always celebrated on
Thursday – thanksgiving for the blessings of the year, and especially the
bounties of the harvest.

Week number 48 Day number 329–36 (330–36)   Monday 25 November

Saints' days   St Catherine of Alexandria – 'The bride of Christ' – patron
saint of philosophers, preachers, librarians, young girls and craftsmen
working with a wheel (*eg* potters, spinners *etc*) V&M C4 • St Erasmus or
Elme Bp and M C4 • St Mercury.

Holidays etc   Twelfth Full Moon of the Gregorian year • Ninth month of
the Theravadan Buddhist year • US: Thanksgiving • Theravadan Buddhist
Uposatha (Observance Day) = Sri Lankan Poya Day • Some biblical
scholars claim this was the day in 2348BC when the Floods began • Sikh
observance: Birthday of Guru Nanak Dev Ji • National Day: Suriname.

Week number 48 Day number 330–35 (331–35)   Tuesday 26 November

Saints' days   St Peter Bp of Alexandria M 311 • St Conrad Bp of
Constance con 976 • St Nicon surnamed Metanoite con 998 • St
Sylvester Gozzolini ab of Osimo instituter of the Sylvestrian monks 1267
• St John Berchmans • St Leonard of Porto Maurizio.

Week number 48 Day number 331–34 (332–34)   Wednesday 27 November

Saints' days   St James surnamed Intersicus M 421 • St Maharsapor M
421 • St Secundin or Seachnal Bp of Dunseachlin or Dunsaghlin in Meath
447 • St Maximus Bp of Riez con *c*460 • SS Barlaam and Josephat • St
Gregory of Sinai • St Virgil Bp of Salzburg con 784.

Holidays etc   The Great Storm occurred early in the morning of
Saturday 27 November 1703 a tremendous hurricane of a week's

duration; much of the British fleet recently returned from the Mediterranean was lost.

Week number 48 Day number 332–33 (333–33)   Thursday 28 November

Saints' days   St Stephen the Younger M 764 • St James of La Marca of Ancona con 1476 • St Katherine Lobourné.

Week number 48 Day number 333–32 (334–32)   Friday 29 November

Saints' days   St Saturninus Bp of Toulouse M 257 • St Radbod Bp of Utrecht con 918.

Holidays etc   *The Times* was the first newspaper to be printed by steam, on this day in 1814.

Week number 48 Day number 334–31(335–31)   Saturday 30 November

Saints' days   St Andrew – first disciple and first missionary of Christ – patron saint of Scotland, Russia, Achaia, golfers, fishermen and old maids, invoked against gout and sore throats • SS Sapor and Isaac Bps, Mahanes, Abraham and Simeon Ms 339 • St Narses Bp and companions Ms 343.

December

Takes its name from Latin *decem* = ten.
Birthstone   Turquoise or Zircon.

Week number 48 Day number 335–30 (336–30)   Sunday 1 December

Saints' days   St Eloi, Eloy or Elligus the apostle of Flanders patron saint of smiths and metalworkers Bp of Noyon con 659 • St Natalia.

Holidays etc   National Day: Central African Republic, Romania • PH: Chad, Portugal, Romania.

Week number 49 Day number 336–29 (337–29)   Monday 2 December

Saints' Day   St Bibiana or Viviana V&M 363.

Holidays etc   National Day: Laos, UAE.

Week number 49 Day number 337–28 (338–28)   Tuesday 3 December

Saints' days St Lucius K and con end C2 • St Birinus Bp and con 650 • St Sola hermit 790 • St Francis Xavier Apostle of the Indies patron saint of RC foreign missions con 1552 • St Cassian of Tangier.

Holidays etc Moon's last quarter • Theravadan Buddhist Uposatha (Observance Day) = Sri Lankan Poya Day • PH: UAE • Japanese observance: Chichibu Yo Matsuri (Chichibu Night Festival).

Week number 49 Day number 338–27 (339–27) Wednesday 4 December

Saints' days St Clement of Alexandria father of the church early C3.• St Barbara, a romantic heroine patron saint of architects, builders, artillerymen, firemen, military engineers and miners, invoked against sudden death, lightning, fIre and impenitence – her father is said to have beheaded her for her faith and was immediately struck down by lightning and died V&M c306 • St Maruthus Bp and con C5 • St Peter Chrysologus Abp of Ravenna con 450 • St Siran or Sigirannus ab in Berry con 655 • St Anno Abp of Cologne con 1075 • St Osmund Bp and con 1099.

Week number 49 Day number 339–26 (340–26)   Thursday 5 December

Saints' days St Crispina M 304 • St Sabas ab 532 • St Nicetius Bp of Trier, con c566 • St Birinus.

Holidays etc PH: The King's Birthday: Thailand.

Week number 49 Day number 340–25 (341–25)   Friday 6 December

Saints' days St Theophilus Bp of Antioch con 190 • St Nicholas the children's saint – popularly known as Santa Claus – patron saint of Russia, children, pawnbrokers, unmarried girls, perfumiers and sailors – also of merchants, thieves and travellers con Abp of Myra 342 • SS Dionysia, Dativa, Aemilianus, Boniface, Leontia, Tertius and Majoricus Ms 484 • St Peter Paschal Bp and M 1300 • St Abraham of Kratia.

Holidays etc Jewish observance: 25 Kislev – Hanukkah (Festival of Lights) begins • The National Day of Finland marking the day in 1917 when it proclaimed its independence from Russia • PH: Finland, Ghana, Spain.

Week number 49 Day number 341–24 (342–24)   Saturday 7 December

Saints' days St Ambrose patron saint of Milan, bee keepers, wax refiners, domestic animals and the French Commissariat, doctor of the church Bp and con 397 • St Fara V and ab 655.

Holidays etc Muslim observance: Lailat Al-Isra wa Al-Miraj • PH: Indonesia, UAE.

Week number 49 Day number 342–23 (343–23)   Sunday 8 December

Saints' days The Conception of the Blessed Virgin Mary • St Romaric ab 653 • St Budoc.

Holidays etc Immaculate conception: DO Ireland • PH: Argentina. Austria, Chile, Colombia, Italy, Paraguay, Peru, Philippines, Portugal, Spain.

Week number 50 Day number 343–22 (344–22)   Monday 9 December

Saints' days The Seven Martyrs at Samosata 297 • St Leoncadia V&M 304 • St Wulfhilde V and ab 990 • SS Hipparchus and Philotheus • St Peter Fourier.

Holidays etc The National Day of Tanzania, celebrating its independence in 1961. Originally Tanganyika, it became a republic on the first anniversary of independence, remaining within the Commonwealth and with Julius Nyerere as the first President • PH: Peru, Spain.

Week number 50 Day number 344–21 (345–21)   Tuesday 10 December

Saints' days St Eulalia V&M c304 • St Melchiades Pope 314.

Holidays etc Twelfth New Moon of the Gregorian year • Eleventh month of the Chinese year • Theravadan Buddhist Uposatha (Observance Day) = Sri Lankan Poya Day • PH: Thailand.

Week number 50 Day number 345–20 (346–20)   Wednesday 11 December

Saints' days SS Fuscian, Victoricus and Gentian Ms c287 • St Damasus I Pope and con 384 • St Daniel the Stylite (Successor to Simeon Stylite) con c494.

Holidays etc Jewish calendar: Tebet 1 AM5757 • National Day: Burkina Faso.

Week number 50 Day number 346–19 (347–19)   Thursday 12 December

Saints' days   SS Epimachus, Alexander *et al* Ms 250 • St Corentin Bp and con C5 • St Columba ab in Ireland 548 • St Finian or Finan the teacher of Irish saints, Bp of Clonard in Ireland C6 • St Cormac ab in Ireland 659 • St Eadburge abs of Menstrey in Thanet 751 • St Vicelin.

Holidays etc   Jewish observance: 2/3 Tebet – Hanukkah (Festival of Lights) ends • Muslim calendar: 1 Shaabân 1417AH • The National Day of Kenya marking its independence, with Jomo Kenyatta as the first Prime Minister, in 1963. He became President when Kenya became a republic in 1964 • PH: Kenya, Mexico.

Week number 50 Day number 347–18 (348–18)   Friday 13 December

Saints' days   St Lucy V&M 304 • St Jodoc or Josse con 666 • St Aubert Bp of Cambray and Arras 669 • St Othilia or Odilia abs of Odilienberg and Niedermünster patron saint of Alsace and the blind V 772 • St Kenelm K&M 820 • Blessed John Marioni con 1562.

Holidays etc   The Ember Days – periodical fasts originally instituted by Pope Calixtus in C3 • Earliest sunset • Republic Day: Malta.

Week number 50 Day number 348–17 (349–17)   Saturday 14 December

Saints' days   St Spiridion Bp and con 348 • SS Nicasius Abp of Rheims & his companions Ms C5 • St John of the Cross – Poet, mystic and theologian

Holidays etc   The *Halcyon Days* begin – according to the ancients, the seven days preceding and the seven days following the shortest day, or the winter solstice – a period of tranquillity and happiness. Legend has it that the sea was always calm when the halcyon bird, or kingfisher, laid her eggs in a floating nest thereon.

Week number 50 Day number 349–16 (350–16)   Sunday 15 December

Saints' days   St Eusebius Bp of Vercelli 371 • St Mary di Rosa • St Nino.

Holidays etc   Sikh observance: Martyrdom of Guru Tegh Bahadur Ji.

Week number 51 Day number 350–15 (351–15)   Monday 16 December

Saints' days   St Ado Abp of Vienne con 875 • St Adelaide or Alice the beloved empress of Germany 999.

Holidays etc   National Day: Bahrain • PH: Bahrain, South Africa.

Week number 51 Day number 351–14 (352–14)   Tuesday 17 December

Saints' days   St Olympias widow *c*410 • St Begga widow and abs 698 •
St Sturm.

Holidays etc   Moon's first quarter • Theravadan Buddhist Uposatha
(Observance Day) = Sri Lankan Poya Day • PH: Bhutan, Venezuela •
Japanese observance: Kasuga Wakamiya Ommatsuri (Kasuga Wakamiya
Grand Festival).

Week number 51 Day number 352–13 (353–13)   Wednesday 18 December

Saints' days   SS Rufus and Zozimus Ms 116 • St Gatian 1st Bp of Tours
con *c*300 • St Winebald ab and con 760.

Holidays etc   National Day: Niger • PH: Niger.

Week number 51 Day number 353–12 (354–12)   Thursday 19 December

Saints' days   St Emesion or Nemesion *et al* Ms 250 • St Samthana V and
ab 738.

Week number 51 Day number 354–11 (355–11)   Friday 20 December

Saints' days   St Philogonius Bp of Antioch con 322 • St Paul of Latrus or
Latra hermit 956.

Week number 51 Day number 355–10 (356–10)   Saturday 21 December

Saints' days   St Thomas the Apostle patron saint of Portugal and of
architects • St Edburge V C9.

Holidays etc   Michaelmas Law Term ends (began 1001).

Week number 51 Day number 356–9 (357–9)   Sunday 22 December

Saints' days   St Ischyrion M 253 • SS Cyril and Methodius cons end C9.

Holidays etc   Winter, the season between the Winter Solstice and the
Vernal Equinox • Capricorn (the Goat) 22 December – 19 January.

Week number 52 Day number 357–8 (358–8)   Monday 23 December

Saints' days   St Servulus con 590 • The Ten Martyrs of Crete C3 • St
Victoria V&M 250 • St Thorlac.

Holidays etc   Emperor's Birthday: Japan • PH: Egypt, Japan.

Week number 52 Day number 358–7 (359–7)   Tuesday 24 December

Saints' days   St Gregory of Spoleto M 304 • SS Thrasilla and Emiliana Vs.

Holidays etc   Christmas Eve • Thirteenth Full Moon of the Gregorian year • Tenth month of the Theravadan Buddhist year • Theravadan Buddhist Uposatha (Observance Day) = Sri Lankan Poya Day • PH: Finland, Mexico.

Week number 52 Day number 359–6 (360–6)   Wednesday 25 December

Saints' days   The Nativity of Jesus Christ • St Eugenia V&M c257 • St Anastasia M 304 • Another St Anastasia.

Holidays etc   Christmas Day • Quarter-day in England, Wales and Northern Ireland. DO • PH: Australia, Austria, Belgium, Bolivia, Brazil, Bulgaria, Canada, Chile, Colombia, Denmark, Eire, Estonia, Finland, France, Germany, Ghana, Greece, Hungary, Iceland, Indonesia, India, Italy, Kenya, Korea, Latvia, Lithuania, Malaysia, Mexico, Netherlands, New Zealand, Nigeria, Norway, PNG, Pakistan, Paraguay, Peru, Philippines, Poland, Portugal, Romania, Singapore, South Africa, Spain, Sweden, Switzerland, Taiwan, UK, USA, Venezuela.

Week number 52 Day number 360–5 (361–5)   Thursday 26 December

Saints' days   St Stephen the 1st Christian M – patron saint of deacons, invoked against headaches • St Dionysius Pope and con 269 • St Iarlath con 1st Bp of Tuam in Ireland C6.

Holidays etc   Boxing Day – if 26 December is a Sunday, the PH is the following day • The traditional starting day for English pantomimes, the first in 1717, *Harlequin Executed* presented by John Rich at Lincoln's Inn Fields Theatre, London. The BBC presented the first televised panto, *Dick Whittington*, in 1932 • Proclamation Day: South Africa • PH: Australia, Austria, Canada, Denmark, Eire, Estonia, Finland, Germany, Ghana, Greece, Hungary, Iceland, Italy, Kenya, Latvia, Lithuania, Netherlands, New Zealand, Nigeria, Norway, PNG, Poland, Romania, South Africa, Sweden, Switzerland, UK.

Week number 52 Day number 361–4 (362–4)   Friday 27 December

Saints' days   St John the Evangelist – he whom Jesus loved – patron saint of theologians, writers and all aspects of the book trade • St Theodorus Grapt con C9 • St Fabiola.

Week number 52 Day number 362–3 (363–3)   Saturday 28 December

Saints' days   The Holy Innocents • St Theodorus ab of Tabenna con 367.

Holidays etc   Innocents Day – Childermas Day or Childermas – a commemoration of the barbarous massacre of children in Bethlehem, ordered by King Herod, with the view of destroying among them the infant Saviour • The King's Birthday: Nepal • The Halcyon Days end.

Week number 52 Day number 363–2 (364–2)   Sunday 29 December

Saints' days   St Marcellus ab of the Acœmetes con c485 • St Evroul ab and con 596 • St Thomas Becket 'This turbulent priest' Abp of Canterbury 1170.

Week number 1 Day number 364–1 (365–1)   Monday 30 December

Saints' days   St Sabinus Bp of Assisium and his companions Ms 304 • St Egwin Founder of Evesham • St Anysia M 304 • St Maximus con c662.

Week number 1 Day number 365–0 (366–0)   Tuesday 31 December

Saints' days   St Sylvester Pope and con 335 • St Columba V&M C3 • St Melania the Younger 439.

Holidays etc   New Year's Eve • Scotland: Hogmanay • PH: Ghana, Latvia • Japanese observance: Gion Okera Matsuri.

Part 3
The Calendar

We will now look at some calendars as a means of recording the passage of time day by day. As mankind developed, people must have noted the recurrence of various events: the sun appearing and disappearing (and much effort was expended on 'explaining' this, and making sure that it kept happening), the moon waxing and waning, tides rising and falling, changes in the seasons, and many others.

Some people must have started recording the periodicity of such events; certainly as agriculture developed there was a need to understand the seasons and phenomena associated with them, particularly as they affected the supply of food, and this can still be seen in the Fijian local calendar below.

Unless it is a colossal coincidence, the alignment of Stonehenge seems to show that the Summer Solstice was well understood some 5,000 years ago, and thus the concept of the solar year. Compared with that, observation of the phases of the moon is child's play, and early calendars were indeed based on the moon's behaviour, combined with attempts to reconcile it with that of the sun. An important criterion for most calendars is to keep them in step with the seasons, primarily for agricultural reasons mentioned above.

In this section, we are concerned more with types of calendars and their present-day relationships than with their nuances and fine tuning. This is not the place to present the complex potted histories of what emerge as delicate mechanisms intertwined with the cultures from which they come. Instead, we give a flavour of a number of different calendars to show their similarities and differences. In this new millennium of rapid travel, and even more rapid communication, it is – like it or not – the Gregorian calendar that has emerged as the framework upon which commercial life is based. But many religions and nations understandably cling strongly to their traditions – including calendars – even as they acknowledge the wider world without.

Contents

The Chinese calendar

It is said the the Emperor Huang-di invented the calendar in 2637BCE. It is now in its 78th 60-year cycle as shown in the table below, with the corresponding Gregorian years.

Cycle	Start	BCE	Cycle	Start	BCE	Cycle	Start	CE	Cycle	Start	CE
1	1	2637	23	1321	1317	45	2641	4	67	3961	1324
2	61	2577	24	1381	1257	46	2701	64	68	4021	1384
3	121	2517	25	1441	1197	47	2761	124	69	4081	1444
4	181	2457	26	1501	1137	48	2821	184	70	4141	1504
5	241	2397	27	1561	1077	49	2881	244	71	4201	1564
6	301	2337	28	1621	1017	50	2941	304	72	4261	1624
7	361	2277	29	1681	957	51	3001	364	73	4321	1684
8	421	2217	30	1741	897	52	3061	424	74	4381	1744
9	481	2157	31	1801	837	53	3121	484	75	4441	1804
10	541	2097	32	1861	777	54	3181	544	76	4501	1864
11	601	2037	33	1921	717	55	3241	604	77	4561	1924
12	661	1977	34	1981	657	56	3301	664	78	4621	1984
13	721	1917	35	2041	597	57	3361	724	79	4681	2044
14	781	1857	36	2101	537	58	3421	784	80	4741	2304
15	841	1797	37	2161	477	59	3481	844	•	•	•
16	901	1737	38	2221	417	60	3541	904	•	•	•
17	961	1677	39	2281	357	61	3601	964	•	•	•
18	1021	1617	40	2341	297	62	3661	1024	•	•	•
19	1081	1557	41	2401	237	63	3721	1084	•	•	•
20	1141	1497	42	2461	177	64	3781	1144	•	•	•
21	1201	1437	43	2521	117	65	3841	1204	•	•	•
22	1261	1377	44	2581	57	66	3901	1264	•	•	•

Within the 60-year cycle, the years are given a two-part name; the first part consists of one of the 10 'celestial stems' (untranslatable), and the second part one of the 12 'terrestrial stems' (the well-known animals). Working on the current cycle that started on (2 February) 1984, the names are shown overleaf.

The same cycle of 60 names is applied also to days and months. As a starting point, the first day of jia-zi (below) was bing-yin, and its first month was gui-chou.

Year	CE	CStem	TStem	English
1	1984	jia	zi	rat
2	1985	yi	chou	ox
3	1986	bing	yin	tiger
4	1987	ding	mao	rabbit
5	1988	wu	chen	dragon
6	1989	ji	si	snake
7	1990	geng	wu	horse
8	1991	xin	wei	sheep
9	1992	ren	shen	monkey
10	1993	gui	you	rooster
11	1994	jia	xu	dog
12	1995	yi	hai	pig
13	1996	bing	zi	rat
14	1997	ding	chou	ox
15	1998	wu	yin	tiger
16	1999	ji	mao	rabbit
17	2000	geng	chen	dragon
18	2001	xin	si	snake
19	2002	ren	wu	horse
20	2003	gui	wei	sheep

Year	CE	CStem	TStem	English
21	2004	jia	shen	monkey
22	2005	yi	you	rooster
23	2006	bing	xu	dog
24	2007	ding	hai	pig
25	2008	wu	zi	rat
26	2009	ji	chou	ox
27	2010	geng	yin	tiger
28	2011	xin	mao	rabbit
29	2012	ren	chen	dragon
30	2013	gui	si	snake
31	2014	jia	wu	horse
32	2015	yi	wei	sheep
33	2016	bing	shen	monkey
34	2017	ding	you	rooster
35	2018	wu	xu	dog
36	2019	ji	hai	pig
37	2020	geng	zi	rat
38	2021	xin	chou	ox
39	2022	ren	yin	tiger
40	2023	gui	mao	rabbit

Year	CE	CStem	TStem	English
41	2024	jia	chen	dragon
42	2025	yi	si	snake
43	2026	bing	wu	horse
44	2027	ding	wei	sheep
45	2028	wu	shen	monkey
46	2029	ji	you	rooster
47	2030	geng	xu	dog
48	2031	xin	hai	pig
49	2032	ren	zi	rat
50	2033	gui	chou	ox
51	2034	jia	yin	tiger
52	2035	yi	mao	rabbit
53	2036	bing	chen	dragon
54	2037	ding	si	snake
55	2038	wu	wu	horse
56	2039	ji	wei	sheep
57	2040	geng	shen	monkey
58	2041	xin	you	rooster
59	2042	ren	xu	dog
60	2043	gui	hai	pig

The Fijian calendar

The Fiji Island calendar emerged from long observation of the recurrence of events; not surprisingly, it is based on lunar months, and natural phenomena. When, from time to time, the calendar became palpably out of step with nature, the Islanders merely inserted an appropriate period to realign it. They now use the Gregorian calendar for their dealings with the outside world, but the economic importance of the traditional calendar is not forgotten.

Gregorian	Fijian	What to do this month
June	vula ni werewere	Clear and weed.
		Gather kavika (*Syzygium malaccense*), wi (*Spondias dulcis*) and dawa (*Pomentia pinnata*).
		Dig kawai (a yam – *Dioscorea esculanta*), kaile (a wild yam – *Dioscorea bulbifera*).
		Catch and smoke fish.
July	vula i cukicuki	Prepare yam beds and leave until the ivi tree
August	vula i liliwa	(*Inocarpus fagiferus*) blooms.
September	vula i vavakada	Dig reeds into yam beds for yam runners to climb.
October	vula i balolo lailai	Small rising of the Pacific balolo (or palolo or paolo) worm (*Eunice viridis*); gather and eat.
		Gather breadfruit and kaile.
		Plant kawai.
November	vula i balolo levu	Great rising of the balolo; gather and eat.
		Gather bananas.
		Dig tivoli (a yam – *Dioscorea nummularia*).
December	vula ni nuqa lailai	Small rising of the reef fish nuqa; gather and eat.
January	vula i nuqa levu	Great rising of nuqa; gather and eat.
February	vula i sevu	Offer first fruits to God.
		Gather ripe ivi and dawa.
March	vula i kelikeli	Yams mature; gather and store.
		Oranges ripen.
April	vula i gasau	Use flourishing reeds to build and repair dwellings.
May	vula i doi	The Doi tree flowers.
		Tarawau (*Dracontomelon vitiense*) ripens.
		Plant yams.

The French Revolutionary calendar

One of the desired results of the French Revolution was that the Old Order should be completely swept away; one of the more sweeping proposals, for example, was for a temperature scale which took the boiling point of water as 0° and its freezing point as 100°.

Many people before and since have seen a need to revolutionise the calendar, but one of the most powerful arguments against any change has been the resistance of 'ordinary people' to learning something new, when the old seems perfectly serviceable (*eg* British metrication). The FRC didn't pull any punches.

The French mathematician Gilbert Romme proposed a system for the FRC, and Fabre d'Eglantine named the months which, it will be seen, fall into four groups of three (–aire, –ôse, –al and –idor), and the days, of which, it will be seen, there are 10 in each week. New Year's Day was supposed to be the Autumnal Equinox, but in course of time this gave rise to its own confusion.

The FRC ran for 13 years (I–XIII) from 22 September 1792, but was not adopted until 24 October 1793 (3 Brumaire II); here is Year I – which is the same as Year II:

Automne (Autumn)

	Vendémiaire (Vintage)		Brumaire (Mists)		Frimaire (Frosts)	
Primidi	1	1792 Sept 22	1	1792 Oct 22	1	1792 Nov 21
Duodi	2	23	2	23	2	22
Tridi	3	24	3	24	3	23
Quartidi	4	25	4	25	4	24
Quintidi	5	26	5	26	5	25
Sextidi	6	27	6	27	6	26
Septidi	7	28	7	28	7	27
Octidi	8	29	8	29	8	28
Nonidi	9	30	9	30	9	29
Décadi	10	1792 Oct 1	10	31	10	30
Primidi	11	2	11	1792 Nov 1	11	1792 Dec 1
Duodi	12	3	12	2	12	2
Tridi	13	4	13	3	13	3
Quartidi	14	5	14	4	14	4
Quintidi	15	6	15	5	15	5
Sextidi	16	7	16	6	16	6
Septidi	17	8	17	7	17	7
Octidi	18	9	18	8	18	8
Nonidi	19	10	19	9	19	9
Décadi	20	11	20	10	20	10
Primidi	21	12	21	11	21	11
Duodi	22	13	22	12	22	12
Tridi	23	14	23	13	23	13
Quartidi	24	15	24	14	24	14
Quintidi	25	16	25	15	25	15
Sextidi	26	17	26	16	26	16
Septidi	27	18	27	17	27	17
Octidi	28	19	28	18	28	18
Nonidi	29	20	29	19	29	19
Décadi	30	21	30	20	30	20

Hiver (Winter)

	Nivôse (Snows)		Pluviôse (Rainy)		Ventôse (Windy)	
Primidi	1	1792 Dec 21	1	1793 Jan 20	1	1793 Feb 19
Duodi	2	22	2	21	2	20
Tridi	3	23	3	22	3	21
Quartidi	4	24	4	23	4	22
Quintidi	5	25	5	24	5	23
Sextidi	6	26	6	25	6	24
Septidi	7	27	7	26	7	25
Octidi	8	28	8	27	8	26
Nonidi	9	29	9	28	9	27
Décadi	10	30	10	29	10	28
Primidi	11	31	11	30	11	1793 Mar 1
Duodi	12	1793 Jan 1	12	31	12	2
Tridi	13	2	13	1793 Feb 1	13	3
Quartidi	14	3	14	2	14	4
Quintidi	15	4	15	3	15	5
Sextidi	16	5	16	4	16	6
Septidi	17	6	17	5	17	7
Octidi	18	7	18	6	18	8
Nonidi	19	8	19	7	19	9
Décadi	20	9	20	8	20	10
Primidi	21	10	21	9	21	11
Duodi	22	11	22	10	22	12
Tridi	23	12	23	11	23	13
Quartidi	24	13	24	12	24	14
Quintidi	25	14	25	13	25	15
Sextidi	26	15	26	14	26	16
Septidi	27	16	27	15	27	17
Octidi	28	17	28	16	28	18
Nonidi	29	18	29	17	29	19
Décadi	30	19	30	18	30	20

Printemps (Spring)

	Germinal (Seed-time)		Floréal (Flowers)		Prairial (Meadows)	
Primidi	1	1793 Mar 21	1	1793 Apr 20	1	1793 May 20
Duodi	2	22	2	21	2	21
Tridi	3	23	3	22	3	22
Quartidi	4	24	4	23	4	23
Quintidi	5	25	5	24	5	24
Sextidi	6	26	6	25	6	25
Septidi	7	27	7	26	7	26
Octidi	8	28	8	27	8	27
Nonidi	9	29	9	28	9	28
Décadi	10	30	10	29	10	29
Primidi	11	31	11	30	11	30
Duodi	12	1793 Apr 1	12	1793 May 1	12	31
Tridi	13	2	13	2	13	1793 June 1
Quartidi	14	3	14	3	14	2
Quintidi	15	4	15	4	15	3
Sextidi	16	5	16	5	16	4
Septidi	17	6	17	6	17	5
Octidi	18	7	18	7	18	6
Nonidi	19	8	19	8	19	7
Décadi	20	9	20	9	20	8
Primidi	21	10	21	10	21	9
Duodi	22	11	22	11	22	10
Tridi	23	12	23	12	23	11
Quartidi	24	13	24	13	24	12
Quintidi	25	14	25	14	25	13
Sextidi	26	15	26	15	26	14
Septidi	27	16	27	16	27	15
Octidi	28	17	28	17	28	16
Nonidi	29	18	29	18	29	17
Décadi	30	19	30	19	30	18

Été (Summer)

	Messidor (Harvest)		Thermidor (Heat)		Fructidor (Fruits)	
Primidi	1	1793 June 19	1	1793 July 19	1	1793 Aug 18
Duodi	2	20	2	20	2	19
Tridi	3	21	3	21	3	20
Quartidi	4	22	4	22	4	21
Quintidi	5	23	5	23	5	22
Sextidi	6	24	6	24	6	23
Septidi	7	25	7	25	7	24
Octidi	8	26	8	26	8	25
Nonidi	9	27	9	27	9	16
Décadi	10	28	10	28	10	27
Primidi	11	29	11	29	11	28
Duodi	12	30	12	30	12	29
Tridi	13	1793 July 1	13	31	13	30
Quartidi	14	2	14	1793 Aug 1	14	31
Quintidi	15	3	15	2	15	1793 Sept 1
Sextidi	16	4	16	3	16	2
Septidi	17	5	17	4	17	3
Octidi	18	6	18	5	18	4
Nonidi	19	7	19	6	19	5
Décadi	20	8	20	7	20	6
Primidi	21	9	21	8	21	7
Duodi	22	10	22	9	22	8
Tridi	23	11	23	10	23	9
Quartidi	24	12	24	11	24	10
Quintidi	25	13	25	12	25	11
Sextidi	26	14	26	13	26	12
Septidi	27	15	27	14	27	13
Octidi	28	16	28	15	28	14
Nonidi	29	17	29	16	29	15
Décadi	30	18	30	17	30	16

And then the public holidays:

1	La Fête de la Vertu	Virtue Day	September 17
2	La Fête du Génie	Talent Day	September 18
3	La Fête du Travail	Labour Day	September 19
4	La Fête de l'Opinion	Opinion Day	September 20
5	La Fête des Récompenses	Rewards Day	September 21
6	La Fête de la Révolution	Revolution Day	Leap Year Day

12 months each of 30 days = 360 days. There was therefore great rejoicing at the end of Fructidor with five public holidays (wittingly or not akin to a harvest festival) and six in a leap year.

These days were known as Les Sans-Culottides (after the extreme republicans) in Years I and II, but as Les Jours Complémentaires from Year III onwards.

As 1792 was a leap year, and February was past when the FRC began, the first Fête de la Révolution didn't come round until 1796, Year III in the FRC (and then in VII, XI, XV and so on).

The FRC came to an end at midnight on 10 Nivôse XIV, or 31 December 1805, by the decree of the self-crowned Emperor Napoléon Bonaparte. It must have taken a dogged revolutionary spirit to put up with 10-day weeks, and their absence of an obvious day of worship did not appeal to the Church. It was partly to appease the Catholics that Bonaparte reverted to the conventional calendar, no doubt with enormous sighs of relief all round. Notwithstanding that, the FRC was briefly resurrected during the Paris Commune of 1871, but most people carried on as if nothing had happened.

The Gregorian calendar

Arithmetic decrees that neither 365 or 366 is divisible exactly by 7. Thus a year, whether ordinary or leap, may begin on any day of the week. By convention, a year is assigned a dominical letter (DL) (from A to G) according to the day upon which its first Sunday falls.

This is shown in the Table G1. Column 1 shows the day on which 1 January falls; this determines (Col 2) the date of the first Sunday of the year, and hence (Col 3O) the DL if it's an ordinary year, or (Col 5L) the DLs if it's a leap year. Col 4 shows the dominical letter or letters of the ordinary (or leap) year that may follow the ordinary year of Col 3O, and Col 6 shows the DL of the ordinary year that must follow a leap year. Leap years have two DLs because they start off in the ordinary way, but need another letter to show how all dates from 1 March are 'pushed forward' by the insertion of 29 February. With its missing 11 days, 1752 is unique in having three DLs (EDA).

Table G1 Types of year and their DLs

1	2	3O	4	5L	6
1st January	Date 1st ☉ in Jan	DL ord year	Following year's DL	DL leap year	Following year's DL
☉	1	A	G (GF)	AG	F
S	2	B	A (AG)	BA	G
F	3	C	B (BA)	CB	A
Th	4	D	C (CB)	DC	B
W	5	E	D (DC)	ED	C
Tu	6	F	E (ED)	FE	D
M	7	G	F (FE)	GF	E

With one year in four a leap year, and a choice of seven possible starting days, we can see that there must be a cycle of 28 years in which each of the seven types of leap year occurs once, and each of the seven types of ordinary year occurs thrice: Table G2.

Table G2 The 28-year cycle of years and their DLs

1	G	5	B	9	D	13	F	17	A	21	C	25	E
2	F	6	A	10	C	14	E	18	G	22	B	26	D
3	E	7	G	11	B	15	D	19	F	23	A	27	C
4	DC	8	FE	12	AG	16	CB	20	ED	24	GF	28	BA

Table G3 shows the starting days for each month in an ordinary or a leap year, given its DLs. The last column shows the day of the week on which 31 December falls, and this affords an easy step to the starting day, and hence the DL, of the following year.

Table G3 DLs and starting days of months

DL	J	F	M	A	M	J	J	A	S	O	N	D	31D
A	Su	W	W	S	M	Th	S	Tu	F	Su	W	F	Su
BA	S	Tu											
B	S	Tu	Tu	F	Su	W	F	M	Th	S	Tu	Th	S
CB	F	M											
C	F	M	M	Th	S	Tu	Th	Su	W	F	M	W	F
DC	Th	Su											
D	Th	Su	Su	W	F	M	W	S	Tu	Th	Su	Tu	Th
ED	W	S											
E	W	S	S	Tu	Th	Su	Tu	F	M	W	S	M	W
FE	Tu	F											
F	Tu	F	F	M	W	S	M	Th	Su	Tu	F	Su	Tu
GF	M	Th											
G	M	Th	Th	Su	Tu	F	Su	W	S	M	Th	S	M
AG	Su	W											

If we know the starting day of a month, we know the rest of the days for that month. Table G4 makes it easier to determine any given day in a month once the day on which the first of the month falls is known.

Table G4 The seven different sorts of month

1	M	Tu	W	Th	F	S	Su	1
2	Tu	W	Th	F	S	Su	M	2
3	W	Th	F	S	Su	M	Tu	3
4	Th	F	S	Su	M	Tu	W	4
5	F	S	Su	M	Tu	W	Th	5
6	S	Su	M	Tu	W	Th	F	6
7	Su	M	Tu	W	Th	F	S	7
8	M	Tu	W	Th	F	S	Su	8
9	Tu	W	Th	F	S	Su	M	9
10	W	Th	F	S	Su	M	Tu	10
11	Th	F	S	Su	M	Tu	W	11
12	F	S	Su	M	Tu	W	Th	12
13	S	Su	M	Tu	W	Th	F	13
14	Su	M	Tu	W	Th	F	S	14
15	M	Tu	W	Th	F	S	Su	15
16	Tu	W	Th	F	S	Su	M	16
17	W	Th	F	S	Su	M	Tu	17
18	Th	F	S	Su	M	Tu	W	18
19	F	S	Su	M	Tu	W	Th	19
20	S	Su	M	Tu	W	Th	F	20
21	Su	M	Tu	W	Th	F	S	21
22	M	Tu	W	Th	F	S	Su	22
23	Tu	W	Th	F	S	Su	M	23
24	W	Th	F	S	Su	M	Tu	24
25	Th	F	S	Su	M	Tu	W	25
26	F	S	Su	M	Tu	W	Th	26
27	S	Su	M	Tu	W	Th	F	27
28	Su	M	Tu	W	Th	F	S	28
29	M	Tu	W	Th	F	S	Su	29
30	Tu	W	Th	F	S	Su	M	30
31	W	Th	F	S	Su	M	Tu	31

Table G5 (in two parts) shows the DLs for the Gregorian years from 1582 (the year in which the Gregorian calendar was first adopted) to 2316CE.

Table G6 shows the special case of the Gregorian year 1752.

Table G5 Gregorian Perpetual Calendar – Dominical letters of years 1582–1876CE

DL												
G	•	1593	1621	1649	1677	1705	1733	1753	1781	•	1821	1849
F	•	1594	1622	1650	1678	1706	1734	1754	1782	•	1822	1850
E	•	1595	1623	1651	1679	1707	1735	1755	1783	•	1823	1851
DC	•	1596	1624	1652	1680	1708	1736	1756	1784	•	1824	1852
B	•	1597	1625	1653	1681	1709	1737	1757	1785	•	1825	1853
A	•	1598	1626	1654	1682	1710	1738	1758	1786	•	1826	1854
G	•	1599	1627	1655	1683	1711	1739	1759	1787	•	1827	1855
FE	•	1600	1628	1656	1684	1712	1740	1760	1788	•	1828	1856
D	•	1601	1629	1657	1685	1713	1741	1761	1789	1801	1829	1857
C	•	1602	1630	1658	1686	1714	1742	1762	1790	1802	1830	1858
B	•	1603	1631	1659	1687	1715	1743	1763	1791	1803	1831	1859
AG	•	1604	1632	1660	1688	1716	1744	1764	1792	1804	1832	1860
F	•	1605	1633	1661	1689	1717	1745	1765	1793	1805	1833	1861
E	•	1606	1634	1662	1690	1718	1746	1766	1794	1806	1834	1862
D	•	1607	1635	1663	1691	1719	1747	1767	1795	1807	1835	1863
CB	•	1608	1636	1664	1692	1720	1748	1768	1796	1808	1836	1864
A	•	1609	1637	1665	1693	1721	1749	1769	1797	1809	1837	1865
G	1582	1610	1638	1666	1694	1722	1750	1770	1798	1810	1838	1866
F	1583	1611	1639	1667	1695	1723	1751	1771	1799	1811	1839	1867
ED	1584	1612	1640	1668	1696	1724	•	1772	•	1812	1840	1868
C	1585	1613	1641	1669	1697	1725	•	1773	•	1813	1841	1869
B	1586	1614	1642	1670	1698	1726	•	1774	•	1814	1842	1870
A	1587	1615	1643	1671	1699	1727	•	1775	•	1815	1843	1871
GF	1588	1616	1644	1672	1700	1728	•	1776	•	1816	1844	1872
E	1589	1617	1645	1673	1701	1729	•	1777	1800	1817	1845	1873
D	1590	1618	1646	1674	1702	1730	•	1778	•	1818	1846	1874
C	1591	1619	1647	1675	1703	1731	•	1779	•	1819	1847	1875
BA	1592	1620	1648	1676	1704	1732	•	1780	•	1820	1848	1876

EDA	1752

Table G5 Gregorian Perpetual Calendar – Dominical letters of years 1877–2152CE

G	1877	•	1917	1945	1973	2001	2029	2057	2085	•	2125
F	1878	•	1918	1946	1974	2002	2030	2058	2086	•	2126
E	1879	•	1919	1947	1975	2003	2031	2059	2087	•	2127
DC	1880	•	1920	1948	1976	2004	2032	2060	2088	•	2128
B	1881	•	1921	1949	1977	2005	2033	2061	2089	2101	2129
A	1882	•	1922	1950	1978	2006	2034	2062	2090	2102	2130
G	1883	1900	1923	1951	1979	2007	2035	2063	2091	2103	2131
FE	1884	•	1924	1952	1980	2008	2036	2064	2092	2104	2132
D	1885	•	1925	1953	1981	2009	2037	2065	2093	2105	2133
C	1886	•	1926	1954	1982	2010	2038	2066	2094	2106	2134
B	1887	•	1927	1955	1983	2011	2039	2067	2095	2107	2135
AG	1888	•	1928	1956	1984	2012	2040	2068	2096	2108	2136
F	1889	1901	1929	1957	1985	2013	2041	2069	2097	2109	2137
E	1890	1902	1930	1958	1986	2014	2042	2070	2098	2110	2138
D	1891	1903	1931	1959	1987	2015	2043	2071	2099	2111	2139
CB	1892	1904	1932	1960	1988	2016	2044	2072	•	2112	2140
A	1893	1905	1933	1961	1989	2017	2045	2073	•	2113	2141
G	1894	1906	1934	1962	1990	2018	2046	2074	•	2114	2142
F	1895	1907	1935	1963	1991	2019	2047	2075	•	2115	2143
ED	1896	1908	1936	1964	1992	2020	2048	2076	•	2116	2144
C	1897	1909	1937	1965	1993	2021	2049	2077	2100	2117	2145
B	1898	1910	1938	1966	1994	2022	2050	2078	•	2118	2146
A	1899	1911	1939	1967	1995	2023	2051	2079	•	2119	2147
GF	•	1912	1940	1968	1996	2024	2052	2080	•	2120	2148
E	•	1913	1941	1969	1997	2025	2053	2081	•	2121	2149
D	•	1914	1942	1970	1998	2026	2054	2082	•	2122	2150
C	•	1915	1943	1971	1999	2027	2055	2083	•	2123	2151
BA	•	1916	1944	1972	2000	2028	2056	2084	•	2124	2152

Table G6 Gregorian Calendar for 1752 DLs: EDA

In 1752, England and Wales, Ireland, and the Colonies including North America, changed from the Julian to the Gregorian calendar (Scotland, always ahead of the game, had made the change in 1600). By this time, the Julian and Gregorian calendars were eleven days out of step, and so it was decreed that Wednesday 2 September would be followed by Thursday 14 September. Many people thought that they were being cheated of 264 hours of their lives – and, what was worse, of eleven days' wages. However rational one is, it's not difficult to see their point!

	Jan	Feb	Mar	Apr	May	Jun	Jul	Aug	Sep	Oct	Nov	Dec
W	1			1			1				1	
Th	2			2			2				2	
F	3			3	1		3				3	1
S	4	1		4	2		4	1			4	2
S	5	2	1	5	3		5	2		1	5	3
M	6	3	2	6	4	1	6	3		2	6	4
Tu	7	4	3	7	5	2	7	4	1	3	7	5
W	8	5	4	8	6	3	8	5	2	4	8	6
Th	9	6	5	9	7	4	9	6	14	5	9	7
F	10	7	6	10	8	5	10	7	15	6	10	8
S	11	8	7	11	9	6	11	8	16	7	11	9
S	12	9	8	12	10	7	12	9	17	8	12	10
M	13	10	9	13	11	8	13	10	18	9	13	11
Tu	14	11	10	14	12	9	14	11	19	10	14	12
W	15	AW12	11	15	13	10	15	12	20	11	15	13
Th	16	13	12	16	14	11	16	13	21	12	16	14
F	17	14	13	17	15	12	17	14	22	13	17	15
S	18	15	14	18	16	13	18	15	23	14	18	16
S	19	16	15	19	17	14	19	16	24	15	19	17
M	20	17	16	20	18	15	20	17	25	16	20	18
Tu	21	18	17	21	19	16	21	18	26	17	21	19
W	22	19	18	22	20	17	22	19	27	18	22	20
Th	23	20	19	23	21	18	23	20	28	19	23	21
F	24	21	20	24	22	19	24	21	29	20	24	22
S	25	22	21	25	23	20	25	22	30	21	25	23
S	26	23	22	26	24	21	26	23		22	26	24
M	27	24	23	27	25	22	27	24		23	27	CD25
Tu	28	25	24	28	26	23	28	25		24	28	26
W	29	26	25	29	27	24	29	26		25	29	27
Th	30	27	26	30	28	25	30	27		26	30	28
F	31	28	GF27		29	26	31	28		27		29
S		29	28		30	27		29		28		30
S			ED29		31	28		30		29		31
M			30			29		31		30		
Tu			31			30				31		

AW = Ash Wednesday   GF = Good Friday   ED = Easter Day   CD = Christmas Day

The Jewish calendar

Introduction

The Jewish calendar in its present form is thought to have been introduced by the Patriarch Hillel II (330–65CE). It is luni-solar – that is, the months (of 29 or 30 days) are lunar, but the years are solar. This arrangement allows agricultural festivals to be celebrated at about the same time each year. A lunar year is 354 days; a solar year 365.25 days. The Jewish calendar is kept roughly in step with the Gregorian calendar by intercalating (inserting) an extra month (Adar Sheni – Second Adar; Ve-Adar) in certain years – leap years – in the 19-year cycle: Table J1.

Table J1 The 19-year cycle

1		2		3	leap	4	
5		6	leap	7		8	leap
9		10		11	leap	12	
13		14	leap	15		16	
17	leap	18		19	leap		

The mean length of a year over the 19-year cycle is just over 365 days:

The Jewish year starts at the new moon of Tishri (September–October), but may be shifted by a day for various reasons – for example, that Yom Kippur (Day of Atonement) must not fall on a Friday or Sunday, nor the First Day of Sukkot (Tabernacles) on a Sabbath.

Table J2 The Jewish months

Month number*		Name	Days	Babylonian equivalent†	Equivalent Gregorian months
Ecclesi-astical	Civil				
1	7	Nisan	30	Nisannu	March/April
2	8	Iyyar	29	Ayara (Bud)	April/May
3	9	Sivan	30	Simânu	May/June
4	10	Tammuz	29	Du'ûzu (A god)	June/July
5	11	Ab (Av)	30	Abu	July/August
6	12	Elul	29	Ulûlu (Purification)	August/September
7	1	Tishri	30	Tashrêtu (Beginning)	September/October
8	2	Marcheshvan or Cheshvan or Heshvan	29/30	Arakhshama	October/November

9	3	Kislev	29/30	Kislîmu	November/December
10	4	Tebet (Tevet)	29	Tabêtu (Flooding)	December/January
11	5	Shebat (Shevat)	30	Shabâtu (Beating)	January/February
12	6	Adar	29/30	Addaru	February/March
13		Adar Sheni	30		

* Although Rosh Hashanah is the start of a new year, it is customary to count the months from Nisan.
† Compare with the principles of the French Revolutionary calendar.

Jewish years

Jewish years are counted from the supposed Creation of the World; year 1AM (Anno Mundi) = 3760BCE (Before the Common Era).

AM dates are customarily given using Hebrew letters for numbers, and omitting the thousands.

To find AM from 1240CE onwards, deduct 1240 from the CE year, and add 5000. For dates Sept/Oct to Dec, add 5001. For example, 1996CE is equivalent to 5756/7AM.

To find CE from AM, delete the 5 and add 1240. For dates Tishri–Tebet, add 1239. For example, 5760AM is equivalent to 1999/2000CE.

The year 5000AM began on 1 September 1239CE.

Table J3 Jewish festivals∗

The Bible mentions three pilgrim festivals – when every male was bound to appear in the Temple – Sukkot, Pesach and Shavuot. Rosh Hashanah and Yom Kippur are Days of Solemnity. Work is forbidden on all Holy Days though – except on Yom Kippur – the prohibition is not as rigid as that pertaining to the Sabbath in that fire may be used, food prepared and carrying is permitted.

Tishri	1&2	Rosh Hashanah	New Year
	3	Feast of Gedaliah	Commemorates Gedaliah's assassination
	10	Yom Kippur	Day of Atonement (for sins)
	1–10	Days of Penitence	On the Eve of Yom Kippur, eating and drinking are a duty; also an occasion for charity giving, visiting cemeteries and the graves of the pious (and, in some oriental traditions, flagellation)
	15–21	Sukkot∗∗	Tabernacles
	22	Shemeni Atzeret	Eighth Day of the Solemn Assembly
	23	Simhat Torah	Rejoicing of the Law
Kislev	25	Hanukkah† begins	Festival of Lights

Tebet	2/3	Hanukkah ends	
	10	Fast¶	Start of Siege of Jerusalem by Nebuchadnezzar
Shebat	15	New Year for Trees	
Adar	13	Fast of Esther	Decreed by Esther
	14–15	Purim†	Lots
Adar Sheni, Second Adar, Ve-Adar – Intercalated in leap years, when Adar holidays fall in Adar Sheni			
Nisan	15–22	Pesach**	Passover (Anniversary of the Exodus)
	27	Yom ha-Shoah‡	Holocaust Remembrance Day
Iyyar	5	Israel Independence Day	
	14	Pesach Sheni	Second Pesach (Celebrated by those impure or absent on a journey at Pesach)
Sivan	6&7	Shavuot	Pentecost, Feast of Weeks
Tammuz	17	Fast	Walls of Jerusalem breached by Nebuchadnezzar and Titus
Ab	9	Fast	Destruction of First and Second Temples

* The Sabbath, and feast and fast days, begin at sunset.

** The first and last days of Sukkot and Pesach are festive, but work is permitted on the intervening days.

† The post-Biblical festivals of Hanukkah and Purim are working days in Jewish law.

¶ Now the day on which to recite the Kaddish prayer in memory of the victims of the Holocaust.

• In Temple times, the Paschal Lamb was slaughtered on the eve of Pesach, and eaten on the first night. Strictly speaking, Pesach covers the sacrifice and the first day; the whole period is the Feast of the Unleavened Bread.

‡ Established in Israel in 1951; anniversary of the Warsaw Ghetto Uprising. Outside Israel, it may be marked on 19 April.

Table J4 The six Jewish years

Jewish years may be either Common years or Leap years; of each type there are Minimal, Regular and Full years. The arrangement looks like this:

Months	Common Years			Months	Leap Years			
	Minimal	Regular	Full		Minimal	Regular*	Full	
Tishri	30	30	30	Tishri	30	30	30	Sep–Oct
Cheshvan**	29	29	30	Cheshvan**	29	29	30	Oct–Nov
Kislev	29	30	30	Kislev	29	30	30	Nov–Dec
Tebet (Tevet)	29	29	29	Tebet (Tevet)	29	29	29	Dec–Jan
Shebat (Shevat)	30	30	30	Shebat (Shevat)	30	30	30	Jan–Feb

Month				Month				Range
Adar	29	29	29	Adar Rishon†	30	30	30	Feb–Mar
•	•	•	•	Adar Sheni§	29	29	29	Mar–Apr
Nisan	30	30	30	Nisan	30	30	30	Mar–Apr
Iyyar	29	29	29	Iyyar	29	29	29	Apr–May
Sivan	30	30	30	Sivan	30	30	30	May–Jun
Tammuz	29	29	29	Tammuz	29	29	29	Jun–Jul
Ab (Av)	30	30	30	Ab (Av)	30	30	30	Jul–Aug
Elul	29	29	29	Elul	29	29	29	Aug–Sep
Total days	353	354	355		383	384	385	
Frequency	10.04%	24.29%	28.82%		15.47%	5.26%	16.11%	
In 689,472 years	69,222	167,497	198,737		106,677	($\frac{1}{19}$) 36,288	111,051	

* Always begins on a Tuesday, and always followed by a Full Common year
** or Marcheshvan
† or 1st Adar
§ or 2nd Adar; or Ve-Adar

An edited extract shows the pattern of the six types of year much more clearly:

	Common			Leap		
	Min	Reg	Full	Min	Reg	Full
Cheshvan	29	29	30	29	29	30
Kislev	29	30	30	29	30	30
Adar I	29	29	29	30	30	30
Adar II	•	•	•	29	29	29

Table J5 The six Jewish year grids

The following grids show the six types of Jewish year in full. Continuing our close examination of the year 1996, we have used as examples of the Full Common year and the Minimal Leap year the actual years AM5756 and 5757, which (by good luck) are years of the desired types, and include 1996CE as shown. These six grids will enable you to construct any Jewish year, but the rules attached to determining Jewish dates are complex – so much so that there are telephone helplines dedicated to providing such information.

Minimal Common Year: 353 Days

Tis		Che		Kis		Teb		She		Ad	
1	1	3	1	4	1	5	1	6	1	1	1
2	2	4	2	5	2	6	2	7	2	2	2
3	3	5	3	6	3	7	3	1	3	3	3
4	4	6	4	7	4	1	4	2	4	4	4
5	5	7	5	1	5	2	5	3	5	5	5
6	6	1	6	2	6	3	6	4	6	6	6
7	7	2	7	3	7	4	7	5	7	7	7
1	8	3	8	4	8	5	8	6	8	1	8
2	9	4	9	5	9	6	9	7	9	2	9
3	10	5	10	6	10	7	10	1	10	3	10
4	11	6	11	7	11	1	11	2	11	4	11
5	12	7	12	1	12	2	12	3	12	5	12
6	13	1	13	2	13	3	13	4	13	6	13
7	14	2	14	3	14	4	14	5	14	7	14
1	15	3	15	4	15	5	15	6	15	1	15
2	16	4	16	5	16	6	16	7	16	2	16
3	17	5	17	6	17	7	17	1	17	3	17
4	18	6	18	7	18	1	18	2	18	4	18
5	19	7	19	1	19	2	19	3	19	5	19
6	20	1	20	2	20	3	20	4	20	6	20
7	21	2	21	3	21	4	21	5	21	7	21
1	22	3	22	4	22	5	22	6	22	1	22
2	23	4	23	5	23	6	23	7	23	2	23
3	24	5	24	6	24	7	24	1	24	3	24
4	25	6	25	7	25	1	25	2	25	4	25
5	26	7	26	1	26	2	26	3	26	5	26
6	27	1	27	2	27	3	27	4	27	6	27
7	28	2	28	3	28	4	28	5	28	7	28
1	29	3	29	4	29	5	29	6	29	1	29
2	30	• • •		• • •		• • •		7	30	• • •	
Tis		Che		Kis		Teb		She		Ad	

In this, and the grids for the Regular Common Year and the Full Leap Year, we have indicated the days of the week by the numbers 1–7, enabling users to make whatever is the appropriate substitution for a given year.

Minimal Common Year: 353 Days (continued)

Nis		Iya		Siv		Tam		Ab		El	
2	1	4	1	5	1	7	1	1	1	3	1
3	2	5	2	6	2	1	2	2	2	4	2
4	3	6	3	7	3	2	3	3	3	5	3
5	4	7	4	1	4	3	4	4	4	6	4
6	5	1	5	2	5	4	5	5	5	7	5
7	6	2	6	3	6	5	6	6	6	1	6
1	7	3	7	4	7	6	7	7	7	2	7
2	8	4	8	5	8	7	8	1	8	3	8
3	9	5	9	6	9	1	9	2	9	4	9
4	10	6	10	7	10	2	10	3	10	5	10
5	11	7	11	1	11	3	11	4	11	6	11
6	12	1	12	2	12	4	12	5	12	7	12
7	13	2	13	3	13	5	13	6	13	1	13
T	14	3	14	4	14	6	14	7	14	2	14
2	15	4	15	5	15	7	15	1	15	3	15
3	16	5	16	6	16	1	16	2	16	4	16
4	17	6	17	7	17	2	17	3	17	5	17
5	18	7	18	1	18	3	18	4	18	6	18
6	19	1	19	2	19	4	19	5	19	7	19
7	20	2	20	3	20	5	20	6	20	1	20
1	21	3	21	4	21	6	21	7	21	2	21
2	22	4	22	5	22	7	22	1	22	3	22
3	23	5	23	6	23	1	23	2	23	4	23
4	24	6	24	7	24	2	24	3	24	5	24
5	25	7	25	1	25	3	25	4	25	6	25
6	26	1	26	2	26	4	26	5	26	7	26
7	27	2	27	3	27	5	27	6	27	1	27
1	28	3	28	4	28	6	28	7	28	2	28
2	29	4	29	5	29	7	29	1	29	3	29
3	30	•	• •	6	30	•	• •	2	30	•	• •
Nis		Iya		Siv		Tam		Ab		El	

Regular Common Year: 354 Days

Tis		Che		Kis		Teb		She		Ad	
1	1	3	1	4	1	6	1	7	1	2	1
2	2	4	2	5	2	7	2	1	2	3	2
3	3	5	3	6	3	1	3	2	3	4	3
4	4	6	4	7	4	2	4	3	4	5	4
5	5	7	5	1	5	3	5	4	5	6	5
6	6	1	6	2	6	4	6	5	6	7	6
7	7	2	7	3	7	5	7	6	7	1	7
1	8	3	8	4	8	6	8	7	8	2	8
2	9	4	9	5	9	7	9	1	9	3	9
3	10	5	10	6	10	1	10	2	10	4	10
4	11	6	11	7	11	2	11	3	11	5	11
5	12	7	12	1	12	3	12	4	12	6	12
6	13	1	13	2	13	4	13	5	13	7	13
7	14	2	14	3	14	5	14	6	14	1	14
1	15	3	15	4	15	6	15	7	15	2	15
2	16	4	16	5	16	7	16	1	16	3	16
3	17	5	17	6	17	1	17	2	17	4	17
4	18	6	18	7	18	2	18	3	18	5	18
5	19	7	19	1	19	3	19	4	19	6	19
6	20	1	20	2	20	4	20	5	20	7	20
7	21	2	21	3	21	5	21	6	21	1	21
1	22	3	22	4	22	6	22	7	22	2	22
2	23	4	23	5	23	7	23	1	23	3	23
3	24	5	24	6	24	1	24	2	24	4	24
4	25	6	25	7	25	2	25	3	25	5	25
5	26	7	26	1	26	3	26	4	26	6	26
6	27	1	27	2	27	4	27	5	27	7	27
7	28	2	28	3	28	5	28	6	28	1	28
1	29	3	29	4	29	6	29	7	29	2	29
2	30	•	•	5	30	•	•	1	30	•	•
Tis		Che		Kis		Teb		She		Ad	

Regular Common Year: 354 Days (continued)

Nis		Iya		Siv		Tam		Ab		El	
3	1	5	1	6	1	1	1	2	1	4	1
4	2	6	2	7	2	2	2	3	2	5	2
5	3	7	3	1	3	3	3	4	3	6	3
6	4	1	4	2	4	4	4	5	4	7	4
7	5	2	5	3	5	5	5	6	5	1	5
1	6	3	6	4	6	6	6	7	6	2	6
2	7	4	7	5	7	7	7	1	7	3	7
3	8	5	8	6	8	1	8	2	8	4	8
4	9	6	9	7	9	2	9	3	9	5	9
5	10	7	10	1	10	3	10	4	10	6	10
6	11	1	11	2	11	4	11	5	11	7	11
7	12	2	12	3	12	5	12	6	12	1	12
1	13	3	13	4	13	6	13	7	13	2	13
2	14	4	14	5	14	7	14	1	14	3	14
3	15	5	15	6	15	1	15	2	15	4	15
4	16	6	16	7	16	2	16	3	16	5	16
5	17	7	17	1	17	3	17	4	17	6	17
6	18	1	18	2	18	4	18	5	18	7	18
7	19	2	19	3	19	5	19	6	19	1	19
1	20	3	20	4	20	6	20	7	20	2	20
2	21	4	21	5	21	7	21	1	21	3	21
3	22	5	22	6	22	1	22	2	22	4	22
4	23	6	23	7	23	2	23	3	23	5	23
5	24	7	24	1	24	3	24	4	24	6	24
6	25	1	25	2	25	4	25	5	25	7	25
7	26	2	26	3	26	5	26	6	26	1	26
1	27	3	27	4	27	6	27	7	27	2	27
2	28	4	28	5	28	7	28	1	28	3	28
3	29	5	29	6	29	1	29	2	29	4	29
4	30	•	• •	7	30	•	• •	3	30	•	• •
Nis		Iya		Siv		Tam		Ab		El	

Full Common Year: 355 Days (Example: AM5756)

		95			95			95			95			96			96
	Tis	*Sep*		*Che*	*Oct*		*Kis*	*Nov*		*Teb*	*Dec*		*She*	*Jan*		*Ad*	*Feb*
M	1	25	W	1	25	F	1	24	𝔖	1	24	M	1	22	W	1	21
Tu	2	26	Th	2	26	S	2	25	M	2	25	Tu	2	23	Th	2	22
W	3	27	F	3	27	𝔖	3	26	Tu	3	26	W	3	24	F	3	23
Th	4	28	S	4	28	M	4	27	W	4	27	Th	4	25	S	4	24
F	5	29	𝔖	5	29	Tu	5	28	Th	5	28	F	5	26	𝔖	5	25
S	6	30	M	6	30	W	6	29	F	6	29	S	6	27	M	6	26
𝔖	7	1	Tu	7	31	Th	7	30	S	7	30	𝔖	7	28	Tu	7	27
M	8	2	W	8	1	F	8	1	𝔖	8	31	M	8	29	W	8	28
Tu	9	3	Th	9	2	S	9	2	M	9	1	Tu	9	30	Th	9	29
W	10	4	F	10	3	𝔖	10	3	Tu	10	2	W	10	31	F	10	1
Th	11	5	S	11	4	M	11	4	W	11	3	Th	11	1	S	11	2
F	12	6	𝔖	12	5	Tu	12	5	Th	12	4	F	12	2	𝔖	12	3
S	13	7	M	13	6	W	13	6	F	13	5	S	13	3	M	13	4
𝔖	14	8	Tu	14	7	Th	14	7	S	14	6	𝔖	14	4	Tu	14	5
M	15	9	W	15	8	F	15	8	𝔖	15	7	M	15	5	W	15	6
Tu	16	10	Th	16	9	S	16	9	M	16	8	Tu	16	6	Th	16	7
W	17	11	F	17	10	𝔖	17	10	Tu	17	9	W	17	7	F	17	8
Th	18	12	S	18	11	M	18	11	W	18	10	Th	18	8	S	18	9
F	19	13	𝔖	19	12	Tu	19	12	Th	19	11	F	19	9	𝔖	19	10
S	20	14	M	20	13	W	20	13	F	20	12	S	20	10	M	20	11
𝔖	21	15	Tu	21	14	Th	21	14	S	21	13	𝔖	21	11	Tu	21	12
M	22	16	W	22	15	F	22	15	𝔖	22	14	M	22	12	W	22	13
Tu	23	17	Th	23	16	S	23	16	M	23	15	Tu	23	13	Th	23	14
W	24	18	F	24	17	𝔖	24	17	Tu	24	16	W	24	14	F	24	15
Th	25	19	S	25	18	M	25	18	W	25	17	Th	25	15	S	25	16
F	26	20	𝔖	26	19	Tu	26	19	Th	26	18	F	26	16	𝔖	26	17
S	27	21	M	27	20	W	27	20	F	27	19	S	27	17	M	27	18
𝔖	28	22	Tu	28	21	Th	28	21	S	28	20	𝔖	28	18	Tu	28	19
M	29	23	W	29	22	F	29	22	𝔖	29	21	M	29	19	W	29	20
Tu	30	24	Th	30	23	S	30	23	•	•	•	Tu	30	20	•	•	•
	Tis	*Oct*		*Che*	*Nov*		*Kis*	*Dec*		*Teb*	*Jan*		*She*	*Feb*		*Ad*	*Mar*

AM5756: a Full Common year (355 days) corresponding to the Gregorian period 25 September 1995 to 13 September 1996 (part of which corresponds to the year in Part 2).

Appropriate substitutions of the days of the week will have to be made when necessary.

Full Common Year: 355 Days (Example: AM5756 continued)

	96			96			96			96			96			96	
	Nis	Mar		Iya	Apr		Siv	May		Tam	Jun		Ab	Jul		El	Aug
Th	1	21	S	1	20	Ŝ	1	19	Tu	1	18	W	1	17	F	1	16
F	2	22	Ŝ	2	21	M	2	20	W	2	19	Th	2	18	S	2	17
S	3	23	M	3	22	Tu	3	21	Th	3	20	F	3	19	Ŝ	3	18
Ŝ	4	24	Tu	4	23	W	4	22	F	4	21	S	4	20	M	4	19
M	5	25	W	5	24	Th	5	23	S	5	22	Ŝ	5	21	Tu	5	20
Tu	6	26	Th	6	25	F	6	24	Ŝ	6	23	M	6	22	W	6	21
W	7	27	F	7	26	S	7	25	M	7	24	Tu	7	23	Th	7	22
Th	8	28	S	8	27	Ŝ	8	26	Tu	8	25	W	8	24	F	8	23
F	9	29	Ŝ	9	28	M	9	27	W	9	26	Th	9	25	S	9	24
S	10	30	M	10	29	Tu	10	28	Th	10	27	F	10	26	Ŝ	10	25
Ŝ	11	31	Tu	11	30	W	11	29	F	11	28	S	11	27	M	11	26
M	12	1	W	12	1	Th	12	30	S	12	29	Ŝ	12	28	Tu	12	27
Tu	13	2	Th	13	2	F	13	31	Ŝ	13	30	M	13	29	W	13	28
W	14	3	F	14	3	S	14	1	M	14	1	Tu	14	30	Th	14	29
Th	15	4	S	15	4	Ŝ	15	2	Tu	15	2	W	15	31	F	15	30
F	16	5	Ŝ	16	5	M	16	3	W	16	3	Th	16	1	S	16	31
S	17	6	M	17	6	Tu	17	4	Th	17	4	F	17	2	Ŝ	17	1
Ŝ	18	7	Tu	18	7	W	18	5	F	18	5	S	18	3	M	18	2
M	19	8	W	19	8	Th	19	6	S	19	6	Ŝ	19	4	Tu	19	3
Tu	20	9	Th	20	9	F	20	7	Ŝ	20	7	M	20	5	W	20	4
W	21	10	F	21	10	S	21	8	M	21	8	Tu	21	6	Th	21	5
Th	22	11	S	22	11	Ŝ	22	9	Tu	22	9	W	22	7	F	22	6
F	23	12	Ŝ	23	12	M	23	10	W	23	10	Th	23	8	S	23	7
S	24	13	M	24	13	Tu	24	11	Th	24	11	F	24	9	Ŝ	24	8
Ŝ	25	14	Tu	25	14	W	25	12	F	25	12	S	25	10	M	25	9
M	26	15	W	26	15	Th	26	13	S	26	13	Ŝ	26	11	Tu	26	10
Tu	27	16	Th	27	16	F	27	14	Ŝ	27	14	M	27	12	W	27	11
W	28	17	F	28	17	S	28	15	M	28	15	Tu	28	13	Th	28	12
Th	29	18	S	29	18	Ŝ	29	16	Tu	29	16	W	29	14	F	29	13
F	30	19	•	•	•	M	30	17	•	•	•	Th	30	15	•	•	•
	Nis	Apr		Iya	May		Siv	Jun		Tam	Jul		Ab	Aug		El	Sep

Minimal Leap Year: 383 Days (Example: AM5757)

	96			96			96			96			97			97	
Tis	Sep		Che	Oct		Kis	Nov		Teb	Dec		She	Jan		Ad1	Feb	
S	1	14	M	1	14	Tu	1	12	W	1	11	Th	1	9	S	1	8
☼	2	15	Tu	2	15	W	2	13	Th	2	12	F	2	10	☼	2	9
M	3	16	W	3	16	Th	3	14	F	3	13	S	3	11	M	3	10
Tu	4	17	Th	4	17	F	4	15	S	4	14	☼	4	12	Tu	4	11
W	5	18	F	5	18	S	5	16	☼	5	15	M	5	13	W	5	12
Th	6	19	S	6	19	☼	6	17	M	6	16	Tu	6	14	Th	6	13
F	7	20	☼	7	20	M	7	18	Tu	7	17	W	7	15	F	7	14
S	8	21	M	8	21	Tu	8	19	W	8	18	Th	8	16	S	8	15
☼	9	22	Tu	9	22	W	9	20	Th	9	19	F	9	17	☼	9	16
M	10	23	W	10	23	Th	10	21	F	10	20	S	10	18	M	10	17
Tu	11	24	Th	11	24	F	11	22	S	11	21	☼	11	19	Tu	11	18
W	12	25	F	12	25	S	12	23	☼	12	22	M	12	20	W	12	19
Th	13	26	S	13	26	☼	13	24	M	13	23	Tu	13	21	Th	13	20
F	14	27	☼	14	27	M	14	25	Tu	14	24	W	14	22	F	14	21
S	15	28	M	15	28	Tu	15	26	W	15	25	Th	15	23	S	15	22
☼	16	29	Tu	16	29	W	16	27	Th	16	26	F	16	24	☼	16	23
M	17	30	W	17	30	Th	17	28	F	17	27	S	17	25	M	17	24
Tu	18	1	Th	18	31	F	18	29	S	18	28	☼	18	26	Tu	18	25
W	19	2	F	19	1	S	19	30	☼	19	29	M	19	27	W	19	26
Th	20	3	S	20	2	☼	20	1	M	20	30	Tu	20	28	Th	20	27
F	21	4	☼	21	3	M	21	2	Tu	21	31	W	21	29	F	21	28
S	22	5	M	22	4	Tu	22	3	W	22	1	Th	22	30	S	22	1
☼	23	6	Tu	23	5	W	23	4	Th	23	2	F	23	31	☼	23	2
M	24	7	W	24	6	Th	24	5	F	24	3	S	24	1	M	24	3
Tu	25	8	Th	25	7	F	25	6	S	25	4	☼	25	2	Tu	25	4
W	26	9	F	26	8	S	26	7	☼	26	5	M	26	3	W	26	5
Th	27	10	S	27	9	☼	27	8	M	27	6	Tu	27	4	Th	27	6
F	28	11	☼	28	10	M	28	9	Tu	28	7	w	28	5	F	28	7
S	29	12	M	29	11	Tu	29	10	W	29	8	Th	29	6	S	29	8
☼	30	13	•	•	•	•	•	•	•	•	•	F	30	7	☼	30	9
Tis	Oct		Che	Nov		Kis	Dec		Teb	Jan		She	Feb		Ad1	Mar	

AM5757: a Minimal Leap Year (383 days) corresponding to the Gregorian period 14 September 1996 to 1 October 1997 (part of which corresponds to the year in Part 2).

Appropriate substitutions of the days of the week will have to be made when necessary.

Minimal Leap Year: 383 Days (Example: AM5757 continued)

	97			97			97			97			97			97			97	
	Ad2	Mar		Nis	Apr		Iya	May		Siv	Jun		Tam	Jul		Ab	Aug		El	Sep
M	1	10	Tu	1	8	Th	1	8	F	1	6	Ṡ	1	6	M	1	4	W	1	3
Tu	2	11	W	2	9	F	2	9	S	2	7	M	2	7	Tu	2	5	Th	2	4
W	3	12	Th	3	10	S	3	10	Ṡ	3	8	Tu	3	8	W	3	6	F	3	5
Th	4	13	F	4	11	Ṡ	4	11	M	4	9	W	4	9	Th	4	7	S	4	6
F	5	14	S	5	12	M	5	12	Tu	5	10	Th	5	10	F	5	8	Ṡ	5	7
S	6	15	Ṡ	6	13	Tu	6	13	W	6	11	F	6	11	S	6	9	M	6	8
Ṡ	7	16	M	7	14	W	7	14	Th	7	12	S	7	12	Ṡ	7	10	Tu	7	9
M	8	17	Tu	8	15	Th	8	15	F	8	13	Ṡ	8	13	M	8	11	W	8	10
Tu	9	18	W	9	16	F	9	16	S	9	14	M	9	14	Tu	9	12	Th	9	11
W	10	19	Th	10	17	S	10	17	Ṡ	10	15	Tu	10	15	W	10	13	F	10	12
Th	11	20	F	11	18	Ṡ	11	18	M	11	16	W	11	16	Th	11	14	S	11	13
F	12	21	S	12	19	M	12	19	Tu	12	17	Th	12	17	F	12	15	Ṡ	12	14
S	13	22	Ṡ	13	20	Tu	13	20	W	13	18	F	13	18	S	13	16	M	13	15
Ṡ	14	23	M	14	21	W	14	21	Th	14	19	S	14	19	Ṡ	14	17	Tu	14	16
M	15	24	Tu	15	22	Th	15	22	F	15	20	Ṡ	15	20	M	15	18	W	15	17
Tu	16	25	W	16	23	F	16	23	S	16	21	M	16	21	Tu	16	19	Th	16	18
W	17	26	Th	17	24	S	17	24	Ṡ	17	22	Tu	17	22	W	17	20	F	17	19
Th	18	27	F	18	25	Ṡ	18	25	M	18	23	W	18	23	Th	18	21	S	18	20
F	19	28	S	19	26	M	19	26	Tu	19	24	Th	19	24	F	19	22	Ṡ	19	21
S	20	29	Ṡ	20	27	Tu	20	27	W	20	25	F	20	25	S	20	23	M	20	22
Ṡ	21	30	M	21	28	W	21	28	Th	21	26	S	21	26	Ṡ	21	24	Tu	21	23
M	22	31	Tu	22	29	Th	22	29	F	22	27	Ṡ	22	27	M	22	25	W	22	24
Tu	23	1	W	23	30	F	23	30	S	23	28	M	23	28	Tu	23	26	Th	23	25
W	24	2	Th	24	1	S	24	31	Ṡ	24	29	Tu	24	29	W	24	27	F	24	26
Th	25	3	F	25	2	Ṡ	25	1	M	25	30	W	25	30	Th	25	28	S	25	27
F	26	4	S	26	3	M	26	2	Tu	26	1	Th	26	31	F	26	29	Ṡ	26	28
S	27	5	Ṡ	27	4	Tu	27	3	W	27	2	F	27	1	S	27	30	M	27	29
Ṡ	28	6	M	28	5	W	28	4	Th	28	3	S	28	2	Ṡ	28	31	Tu	28	30
M	29	7	Tu	29	6	Th	29	5	F	29	4	Ṡ	29	3	M	29	1	W	29	1
•	•	•	W	30	7	•	•	•	S	30	5	•	•	•	Tu	30	2	•	•	•
	Ad2	Apr		Nis	May		Iya	Jun		Siv	Jul		Tam	Aug		Ab	Sep		El	Oct

Regular Leap Year: 384 Days (always starting on a Tuesday)

Tis		Che		Kis		Teb		She		Ad1	
Tu	1	Th	1	F	1	Su	1	M	1	W	1
W	2	F	2	S	2	M	2	Tu	2	Th	2
Th	3	S	3	Su	3	Tu	3	W	3	F	3
F	4	Su	4	M	4	W	4	Th	4	S	4
S	5	M	5	Tu	5	Th	5	F	5	Su	5
Su	6	Tu	6	W	6	F	6	S	6	M	6
M	7	W	7	Th	7	S	7	Su	7	Tu	7
Tu	8	Th	8	F	8	Su	8	M	8	W	8
W	9	F	9	S	9	M	9	Tu	9	Th	9
Th	10	S	10	Su	10	Tu	10	W	10	F	10
F	11	Su	11	M	11	W	11	Th	11	S	11
S	12	M	12	Tu	12	Th	12	F	12	Su	12
Su	13	Tu	13	W	13	F	13	S	13	M	13
M	14	W	14	Th	14	S	14	Su	14	Tu	14
Tu	15	Th	15	F	15	Su	15	M	15	W	15
W	16	F	16	S	16	M	16	Tu	16	Th	16
Th	17	S	17	Su	17	Tu	17	W	17	F	17
F	18	Su	18	M	18	W	18	Th	18	S	18
S	19	M	19	Tu	19	Th	19	F	19	Su	19
Su	20	Tu	20	W	20	F	20	S	20	M	20
M	21	W	21	Th	21	S	21	Su	21	Tu	21
Tu	22	Th	22	F	22	Su	22	M	22	W	22
W	23	F	23	S	23	M	23	Tu	23	Th	23
Th	24	S	24	Su	24	Tu	24	W	24	F	24
F	25	Su	25	M	25	W	25	Th	25	S	25
S	26	M	26	Tu	26	Th	26	F	26	Su	26
Su	27	Tu	27	W	27	F	27	S	27	M	27
M	28	W	28	Th	28	S	28	Su	28	Tu	28
Tu	29	Th	29	F	29	Su	29	M	29	W	29
W	30	•	•	S	30	•	•	Tu	30	Th	30
Tis		Che		Kis		Teb		She		Ad1	

Note that, although a Regular Leap year is always followed by a Full Common year, a Full Common year is not always preceded by a Regular Leap year. We cannot therefore assume that a Full Common year always starts on a Monday.

Regular Leap Year: 384 Days (continued)

Ad2		Nis		Iya		Siv		Tam		Ab		El	
F	1	S	1	M	1	Tu	1	Th	1	F	1	Ṡ	1
S	2	Ṡ	2	Tu	2	W	2	F	2	S	2	M	2
Ṡ	3	M	3	W	3	Th	3	S	3	Ṡ	3	Tu	3
M	4	Tu	4	Th	4	F	4	Ṡ	4	M	4	W	4
Tu	5	W	5	F	5	S	5	M	5	Tu	5	Th	5
W	6	Th	6	S	6	Ṡ	6	Tu	6	W	6	F	6
Th	7	F	7	Ṡ	7	M	7	W	7	Th	7	S	7
F	8	S	8	M	8	Tu	8	Th	8	F	8	Ṡ	8
S	9	Ṡ	9	Tu	9	W	9	F	9	S	9	M	9
Ṡ	10	M	10	W	10	Th	10	S	10	Ṡ	10	Tu	10
M	11	Tu	11	Th	11	F	11	Ṡ	11	M	11	W	11
Tu	12	W	12	F	12	S	12	M	12	Tu	12	Th	12
W	13	Th	13	S	13	Ṡ	13	Tu	13	W	13	F	13
Th	14	F	14	Ṡ	14	M	14	W	14	Th	14	S	14
F	15	S	15	M	15	Tu	15	Th	15	F	15	Ṡ	15
S	16	Ṡ	16	Tu	16	W	16	F	16	S	16	M	16
Ṡ	17	M	17	W	17	Th	17	S	17	Ṡ	17	Tu	17
M	18	Tu	18	Th	18	F	18	Ṡ	18	M	18	W	18
Tu	19	W	19	F	19	S	19	M	19	Tu	19	Th	19
W	20	Th	20	S	20	Ṡ	20	Tu	20	W	20	F	20
Th	21	F	21	Ṡ	21	M	21	W	21	Th	21	S	21
F	22	S	22	M	22	Tu	22	Th	22	F	22	Ṡ	22
S	23	Ṡ	23	Tu	23	W	23	F	23	S	23	M	23
Ṡ	24	M	24	W	24	Th	24	S	24	Ṡ	24	Tu	24
M	25	Tu	25	Th	25	F	25	Ṡ	25	M	25	W	25
Tu	26	W	26	F	26	S	26	M	26	Tu	26	Th	26
W	27	Th	27	S	27	Ṡ	27	Tu	27	W	27	F	27
Th	28	F	28	Ṡ	28	M	28	W	28	Th	28	S	28
F	29	S	29	M	29	Tu	29	Th	29	F	29	Ṡ	29
•	•	Ṡ	30	•	•	•	W	30	•	•	•	S	30	•	•	•
Ad2		Nis		Iya		Siv		Tam		Ab		El	

Full Leap Year: 385 Days

Tis		Che		Kis		Teb		She		Ad1	
1	1	3	1	5	1	7	1	1	1	3	1
2	2	4	2	6	2	1	2	2	2	4	2
3	3	5	3	7	3	2	3	3	3	5	3
4	4	6	4	1	4	3	4	4	4	6	4
5	5	7	5	2	5	4	5	5	5	7	5
6	6	1	6	3	6	5	6	6	6	1	6
7	7	2	7	4	7	6	7	7	7	2	7
1	8	3	8	5	8	7	8	1	8	3	8
2	9	4	9	6	9	1	9	2	9	4	9
3	10	5	10	7	10	2	10	3	10	5	10
4	11	6	11	1	11	3	11	4	11	6	11
5	12	7	12	2	12	4	12	5	12	7	12
6	13	1	13	3	13	5	13	6	13	1	13
7	14	2	14	4	14	6	14	7	14	2	14
1	15	3	15	5	15	7	15	1	15	3	15
2	16	4	16	6	16	1	16	2	16	4	16
3	17	5	17	7	17	2	17	3	17	5	17
4	18	6	18	1	18	3	18	4	18	6	18
5	19	7	19	2	19	4	19	5	19	7	19
6	20	1	20	3	20	5	20	6	20	1	20
7	21	2	21	4	21	6	21	7	21	2	21
1	22	3	22	5	22	7	22	1	22	3	22
2	23	4	23	6	23	1	23	2	23	4	23
3	24	5	24	7	24	2	24	3	24	5	24
4	25	6	25	1	25	3	25	4	25	6	25
5	26	7	26	2	26	4	26	5	26	7	26
6	27	1	27	3	27	5	27	6	27	1	27
7	28	2	28	4	28	6	28	7	28	2	28
1	29	3	29	5	29	7	29	1	29	3	29
2	30	4	30	6	30	•	•	2	30	4	30
Tis		Che		Kis		Teb		She		Ad1	

Full Leap Year: 385 Days (continued)

Ad2		Nis		Iya		Siv		Tam		Ab		El	
5	1	6	1	1	1	2	1	4	1	5	1	7	1
6	2	7	2	2	2	3	2	5	2	6	2	1	2
7	3	1	3	3	3	4	3	6	3	7	3	2	3
1	4	2	4	4	4	5	4	7	4	1	4	3	4
2	5	3	5	5	5	6	5	1	5	2	5	4	5
3	6	4	6	6	6	7	6	2	6	3	6	5	6
4	7	5	7	7	7	1	7	3	7	4	7	6	7
5	8	6	8	1	8	2	8	4	8	5	8	7	8
6	9	7	9	2	9	3	9	5	9	6	9	1	9
7	10	1	10	3	10	4	10	6	10	7	10	2	10
1	11	2	11	4	11	5	11	7	11	1	11	3	11
2	12	3	12	5	12	6	12	1	12	2	12	4	12
3	13	4	13	6	13	7	13	2	13	3	13	5	13
4	14	5	14	7	14	1	14	3	14	4	14	6	14
5	15	6	15	1	15	2	15	4	15	5	15	7	15
6	16	7	16	2	16	3	16	5	16	6	16	1	16
7	17	1	17	3	17	4	17	6	17	7	17	2	17
1	18	2	18	4	18	5	18	7	18	1	18	3	18
2	19	3	19	5	19	6	19	1	19	2	19	4	19
3	20	4	20	6	20	7	20	2	20	3	20	5	20
4	21	5	21	7	21	1	21	3	21	4	21	6	21
5	22	6	22	1	22	2	22	4	22	5	22	7	22
6	23	7	23	2	23	3	23	5	23	6	23	1	23
7	24	1	24	3	24	4	24	6	24	7	24	2	24
1	25	2	25	4	25	5	25	7	25	1	25	3	25
2	26	3	26	5	26	6	26	1	26	2	26	4	26
3	27	4	27	6	27	7	27	2	27	3	27	5	27
4	28	5	28	7	28	1	28	3	28	4	28	6	28
5	29	6	29	1	29	2	29	4	29	5	29	7	29
•	• •	7	30	•	• •	3	30	•	• •	6	30	•	• •
Ad2		Nis		Iya		Siv		Tam		Ab		El	

The Muslim calendar

This calendar is based solely on the moon. It begins with the year of the Hegira (622CE in the Julian calendar), when the Prophet Muhammad (BBUH) travelled from Mecca to Medina.

The calendar runs in cycles of 30 years, with leap years in years 2, 5, 7, 10, 13, 16, 18, 21, 24, 26 and 29. It is used principally in Iran, Turkey, Saudi Arabia and other Arabian peninsula states, Egypt, Malaysia and certain parts of India.

The Muslim year consists of 12 months of alternately 30 days and 29 days. In a leap year, one day is inserted at the end of the 12th month, Dhû'l Hijja. This means that common years have 355 days, while leap years have 356 days. The extra day is inserted into the calendar on leap years in order to reconcile the date of the first month with the date of the actual New Moon. Some Muslims register the first of the month on the evening that the crescent becomes visible. The Moon is particularly important in Ramadan, the month of fasting. According to *Qur'an*, Muslims must see the New Moon with the naked eye before they can either begin or end their fast.

Table M1 The Muslim year

1 Muharram (30)	2 Safar (29)	3 Rabia I (30)
1 2 3 4 5 6 7	1 2 3 4 5	1 2 3 4
8 9 10 11 12 13 14	6 7 8 9 10 11 12	5 6 7 8 9 10 11
15 16 17 18 19 20 21	13 14 15 16 17 18 19	12 13 14 15 16 17 18
22 23 24 25 26 27 28	20 21 22 23 24 25 26	19 20 21 22 23 24 25
29 30	27 28 29	26 27 28 29 30

4 Rabia II (29)	5 Jumâda I (30)	6 Jumâda II (29)
1 2	1	1 2 3 4 5 6
3 4 5 6 7 8 9	2 3 4 5 6 7 8	7 8 9 10 11 12 13
10 11 12 13 14 15 16	9 10 11 12 13 14 15	14 15 16 17 18 19 20
17 18 19 20 21 22 23	16 17 18 19 20 21 22	21 22 23 24 25 26 27
24 25 26 27 28 29	23 24 25 26 27 28 29	28 29
	30	

7 Rajab (30)	8 Shaabân (29)	9 Ramadan (30)
1 2 3 4 5	1 2 3	1 2
6 7 8 9 10 11 12	4 5 6 7 8 9 10	3 4 5 6 7 8 9
13 14 15 16 17 18 19	11 12 13 14 15 16 17	10 11 12 13 14 15 16
20 21 22 23 24 25 26	18 19 20 21 22 23 24	17 18 19 20 21 22 23
27 28 29 30	25 26 27 28 29	24 25 26 27 28 29 30

10 Shawwâl (29)	11 Dhû'l-Qa'da (30)	12 Dhû'l-Hijja (29 or 30)
1 2 3 4 5 6 7	1 2 3 4 5 6	1 2 3 4
8 9 10 11 12 13 14	7 8 9 10 11 12 13	5 6 7 8 9 10 11
15 16 17 18 19 20 21	14 15 16 17 18 19 20	12 13 14 15 16 17 18
22 23 24 25 26 27 28	21 22 23 24 25 26 27	19 20 21 22 23 24 25
29	28 29 30	26 27 28 29 (30)

Table M2 1416AH: an ordinary year (of 355 days) corresponding to the Gregorian period 31 May 1995 to 18 May 1996 (part of which corresponds to the year in Part 2)

	95			95			95			95			95			95	
	Muh	May		Saf	Jun		Rb1	Jul		Rb2	Aug		Ju1	Sep		Ju2	Oct
W	1	31	F	1	30	S	1	29	M	1	28	Tu	1	26	Th	1	26
Th	2	1	S	2	1	Su	2	30	Tu	2	29	W	2	27	F	2	27
F	3	2	Su	3	2	M	3	31	W	3	30	Th	3	28	S	3	28
S	4	3	M	4	3	Tu	4	1	Th	4	31	F	4	29	Su	4	29
Su	5	4	Tu	5	4	W	5	2	F	5	1	S	5	30	M	5	30
M	6	5	W	6	5	Th	6	3	S	6	2	Su	6	1	Tu	6	31
Tu	7	6	Th	7	6	F	7	4	Su	7	3	M	7	2	W	7	1
W	8	7	F	8	7	S	8	5	M	8	4	Tu	8	3	Th	8	2
Th	9	8	S	9	8	Su	9	6	Tu	9	5	W	9	4	F	9	3
F	10	9	Su	10	9	M	10	7	W	10	6	Th	10	5	S	10	4
S	11	10	M	11	10	Tu	11	8	Th	11	7	F	11	6	Su	11	5
Su	12	11	Tu	12	11	W	12	9	F	12	8	S	12	7	M	12	6
M	13	12	W	13	12	Th	13	10	S	13	9	Su	13	8	Tu	13	7
Tu	14	13	Th	14	13	F	14	11	Su	14	10	M	14	9	W	14	8
W	15	14	F	15	14	S	15	12	M	15	11	Tu	15	10	Th	15	9
Th	16	15	S	16	15	Su	16	13	Tu	16	12	W	16	11	F	16	10
F	17	16	Su	17	16	M	17	14	W	17	13	Th	17	12	S	17	11
S	18	17	M	18	17	Tu	18	15	Th	18	14	F	18	13	Su	18	12
Su	19	18	Tu	19	18	W	19	16	F	19	15	S	19	14	M	19	13
M	20	19	W	20	19	Th	20	17	S	20	16	Su	20	15	Tu	20	14
Tu	21	20	Th	21	20	F	21	18	Su	21	17	M	21	16	W	21	15
W	22	21	F	22	21	S	22	19	M	22	18	Tu	22	17	Th	22	16
Th	23	22	S	23	22	Su	23	20	Tu	23	19	W	23	18	F	23	17
F	24	23	Su	24	23	M	24	21	W	24	20	Th	24	19	S	24	18
S	25	24	M	25	24	Tu	25	22	Th	25	21	F	25	20	Su	25	19
Su	26	25	Tu	26	25	W	26	23	F	26	22	S	26	21	M	26	20
M	27	26	W	27	26	Th	27	24	S	27	23	Su	27	22	Tu	27	21
Tu	28	27	Th	28	27	F	28	25	Su	28	24	M	28	23	W	28	22
W	29	28	F	29	28	S	29	26	M	29	25	Tu	29	24	Th	29	23
Th	30	29	•	•	•	Su	30	27	•	•	•	W	30	25	•	•	•
	Muh	Jun		Saf	Jul		Rb1	Aug		Rb2	Sep		Ju1	Oct		Ju2	Nov
		95			95			95			95			95			95

Table M2 1416AH: (continued)

	95			95			96			96			96			96	
	Raj	Nov		Shb	Dec		Rm	Jan		Shw	Feb		DQ	Mar		DH	Apr
F	1	24	☼	1	24	M	1	22	W	1	21	Th	1	21	S	1	20
S	2	25	M	2	25	Tu	2	23	Th	2	22	F	2	22	☼	2	21
☼	3	26	Tu	3	26	W	3	24	F	3	23	S	3	23	M	3	22
M	4	27	W	4	27	Th	4	25	S	4	24	☼	4	24	Tu	4	23
Tu	5	28	Th	5	28	F	5	26	☼	5	25	M	5	25	W	5	24
W	6	29	F	6	29	S	6	27	M	6	26	Tu	6	26	Th	6	25
Th	7	30	S	7	30	☼	7	28	Tu	7	27	W	7	27	F	7	26
F	8	1	☼	8	31	M	8	29	W	8	28	Th	8	28	S	8	27
S	9	2	M	9	1	Tu	9	30	Th	9	29	F	9	29	☼	9	28
☼	10	3	Tu	10	2	W	10	31	F	10	1	S	10	30	M	10	29
M	11	4	W	11	3	Th	11	1	S	11	2	☼	11	31	Tu	11	30
Tu	12	5	Th	12	4	F	12	2	☼	12	3	M	12	1	W	12	1
W	13	6	F	13	5	S	13	3	M	13	4	Tu	13	2	Th	13	2
Th	14	7	S	14	6	☼	14	4	Tu	14	5	W	14	3	F	14	3
F	15	8	☼	15	7	M	15	5	W	15	6	Th	15	4	S	15	4
S	16	9	M	16	8	Tu	16	6	Th	16	7	F	16	5	☼	16	5
☼	17	10	Tu	17	9	W	17	7	F	17	8	S	17	6	M	17	6
M	18	11	W	18	10	Th	18	8	S	18	9	☼	18	7	Tu	18	7
Tu	19	12	Th	19	11	F	19	9	☼	19	10	M	19	8	W	19	8
W	20	13	F	20	12	S	20	10	M	20	11	Tu	20	9	Th	20	9
Th	21	14	S	21	13	☼	21	11	Tu	21	12	W	21	10	F	21	10
F	22	15	☼	22	14	M	22	12	W	22	13	Th	22	11	S	22	11
S	23	16	M	23	15	Tu	23	13	Th	23	14	F	23	12	☼	23	12
☼	24	17	Tu	24	16	W	24	14	F	24	15	S	24	13	M	24	13
M	25	18	W	25	17	Th	25	15	S	25	16	☼	25	14	Tu	25	14
Tu	26	19	Th	26	18	F	26	16	☼	26	17	M	26	15	W	26	15
W	27	20	F	27	19	S	27	17	M	27	18	Tu	27	16	Th	27	16
Th	28	21	S	28	20	☼	28	18	Tu	28	19	W	28	17	F	28	17
F	29	22	☼	29	21	M	29	19	W	29	20	Th	29	18	S	29	18
S	30	23	•	•	•	Tu	30	20	•	•	•	F	30	19	•	•	•
	Raj	Dec		Shb	Jan		Rm	Feb		Shw	Mar		DQ	Apr		DH	May
		95			96			96			96			96			96

Table M3 1417AH: a leap year (356 days) corresponding to the Gregorian period 19 May 1996 to 8 May 1997 (part of which corresponds to the year in Part 2)

	96			96			96			96			96			96	
	Muh	May		Saf	Jun		Rb1	Jul		Rb2	Aug		Ju1	Sep		Ju2	Oct
Su	1	19	Tu	1	18	W	1	17	F	1	16	S	1	14	M	1	14
M	2	20	W	2	19	Th	2	18	S	2	17	Su	2	15	Tu	2	15
Tu	3	21	Th	3	20	F	3	19	Su	3	18	M	3	16	W	3	16
W	4	22	F	4	21	S	4	20	M	4	19	Tu	4	17	Th	4	17
Th	5	23	S	5	22	Su	5	21	Tu	5	20	W	5	18	F	5	18
F	6	24	Su	6	23	M	6	22	W	6	21	Th	6	19	S	6	19
S	7	25	M	7	24	Tu	7	23	Th	7	22	F	7	20	Su	7	20
Su	8	26	Tu	8	25	W	8	24	F	8	23	S	8	21	M	8	21
M	9	27	W	9	26	Th	9	25	S	9	24	Su	9	22	Tu	9	22
Tu	10	28	Th	10	27	F	10	26	Su	10	25	M	10	23	W	10	23
W	11	29	F	11	28	S	11	27	M	11	26	Tu	11	24	Th	11	24
Th	12	30	S	12	29	Su	12	28	Tu	12	27	W	12	25	F	12	25
F	13	31	Su	13	30	M	13	29	W	13	28	Th	13	26	S	13	26
S	14	1	M	14	1	Tu	14	30	Th	14	29	F	14	27	Su	14	27
Su	15	2	Tu	15	2	W	15	31	F	15	30	S	15	28	M	15	28
M	16	3	W	16	3	Th	16	1	S	16	31	Su	16	29	Tu	16	29
Tu	17	4	Th	17	4	F	17	2	Su	17	1	M	17	30	W	17	30
W	18	5	F	18	5	S	18	3	M	18	2	Tu	18	1	Th	18	31
Th	19	6	S	19	6	Su	19	4	Tu	19	3	W	19	2	F	19	1
F	20	7	Su	20	7	M	20	5	W	20	4	Th	20	3	S	20	2
S	21	8	M	21	8	Tu	21	6	Th	21	5	F	21	4	Su	21	3
Su	22	9	Tu	22	9	W	22	7	F	22	6	S	22	5	M	22	4
M	23	10	W	23	10	Th	23	8	S	23	7	Su	23	6	Tu	23	5
Tu	24	11	Th	24	11	F	24	9	Su	24	8	M	24	7	W	24	6
W	25	12	F	25	12	S	25	10	M	25	9	Tu	25	8	Th	25	7
Th	26	13	S	26	13	Su	26	11	Tu	26	10	W	26	9	F	26	8
F	27	14	Su	27	14	M	27	12	W	27	11	Th	27	10	S	27	9
S	28	15	M	28	15	Tu	28	13	Th	28	12	F	28	11	Su	28	10
Su	29	16	Tu	29	16	W	29	14	F	29	13	S	29	12	M	29	11
M	30	17	•	•	•	Th	30	15	•	•	•	Su	30	13	•	•	•
•	Muh	Jun	•	Saf	Jul	•	Rb1	Aug	•	Rb2	Sep	•	Ju1	Oct	•	Ju2	Nov
		96			96			96			96			96			96

Table M3 1417AH: (continued)

	96 Raj	Nov		96 Shb	Dec		97 Rm	Jan		97 Shw	Feb		97 DQ	Mar		97 DH	Apr
Tu	1	12	Th	1	12	F	1	10	Su	1	9	M	1	10	W	1	9
W	2	13	F	2	13	S	2	11	M	2	10	Tu	2	11	Th	2	10
Th	3	14	S	3	14	Su	3	12	Tu	3	11	W	3	12	F	3	11
F	4	15	Su	4	15	M	4	13	W	4	12	Th	4	13	S	4	12
S	5	16	M	5	16	Tu	5	14	Th	5	13	F	5	14	Su	5	13
Su	6	17	Tu	6	17	W	6	15	F	6	14	S	6	15	M	6	14
M	7	18	W	7	18	Th	7	16	S	7	15	Su	7	16	Tu	7	15
Tu	8	19	Th	8	19	F	8	17	Su	8	16	M	8	17	W	8	16
W	9	20	F	9	20	S	9	18	M	9	17	Tu	9	18	Th	9	17
Th	10	21	S	10	21	Su	10	19	Tu	10	18	W	10	19	F	10	18
F	11	22	Su	11	22	M	11	20	W	11	19	Th	11	20	S	11	19
S	12	23	M	12	23	Tu	12	21	Th	12	20	F	12	21	Su	12	20
Su	13	24	Tu	13	24	W	13	22	F	13	21	S	13	22	M	13	21
M	14	25	W	14	25	Th	14	23	S	14	22	Su	14	23	Tu	14	22
Tu	15	26	Th	15	26	F	15	24	Su	15	23	M	15	24	W	15	23
W	16	27	F	16	27	S	16	25	M	16	24	Tu	16	25	Th	16	24
Th	17	28	S	17	28	Su	17	26	Tu	17	25	W	17	26	F	17	25
F	18	29	Su	18	29	M	18	27	W	18	26	Th	18	27	S	18	26
S	19	30	M	19	30	Tu	19	28	Th	19	27	F	19	28	Su	19	27
Su	20	1	Tu	20	31	W	20	29	F	20	28	S	20	29	M	20	28
M	21	2	W	21	1	Th	21	30	S	21	1	Su	21	30	Tu	21	29
Tu	22	3	Th	22	2	F	22	31	Su	22	2	M	22	31	W	22	30
W	23	4	F	23	3	S	23	1	M	23	3	Tu	23	1	Th	23	1
Th	24	5	S	24	4	Su	24	2	Tu	24	4	W	24	2	F	24	2
F	25	6	Su	25	5	M	25	3	W	25	5	Th	25	3	S	25	3
S	26	7	M	26	6	Tu	26	4	Th	26	6	F	26	4	Su	26	4
Su	27	8	Tu	27	7	W	27	5	F	27	7	S	27	5	M	27	5
M	28	9	W	28	8	Th	28	6	S	28	8	Su	28	6	Tu	28	6
Tu	29	10	Th	29	9	F	29	7	Su	29	9	M	29	7	W	29	7
W	30	11	•	•	•	S	30	8	•	•	•	Tu	30	8	Th	30	8
•	Raj	Dec	•	Shb	Jan	•	Rm	Feb	•	Shw	Mar	•	DQ	Apr	•	DH	May
	96			97			97			97			97			97	

Roman calendar

The starting date of the Roman calendar is taken as 1 AUC (Ab Urbe [Romanis] condita = from the foundation of the City [of Rome]), equivalent to 753BCE.

Romulus (the alleged founder of Rome) is supposed to have devised a calendar of 304 days divided into 10 months, of which the first was Mars (March).

It is thought that Numa Pompilius (715–673BCE) added January and February, and set the months with alternately 29 and 30 days, making 354 days, and an additional day making a total of 355 in a year. He also ordered an intercalary month of 22 or 23 days in alternate years, so that an additional 90 days would be inserted in eight years. Numa's years thus averaged 366.25 days, which we now know was a day too long, but there is some doubt as to how well his method was applied.

In 46BCE Julius Cæsar decided to take the calendar in hand, and asked the Egyptian astronomer Sosigenes to help sort it out. Results were rapid, and that very year (46BCE – dubbed 'the Year of Confusion') was assigned 445 days to re-align the calendar with the seasons, and the following year saw the inauguration of the Julian Calendar (which we show below in its Roman form).

The fixed points of the month are:
the first day – the Kalends
the fifth or the seventh – the Nones
the thirteenth or fifteenth – the Ides.

Mnemonic: In March, July, October, May,
Make Nones the seventh, Ides the fifteenth day.

The rest of the days of a month were described by counting to the next fixed point. In Table 1, the left-hand column relates to March, May, July and October, and the right-hand column to the rest of the months. We have shown both columns as 31-day months. Table R2 shows a complete year.

Table R1 Roman months

March, May, July, October –
Nones seventh; Ides fifteenth. All 31 days.

Other months – Nones fifth; Ides thirteenth.
They may have 28, 29, 30 or 31 days; we have
chosen 31 days

Day	Arabic	Named	Abbreviated	Day	Arabic	Named	Abbreviated
I	1	Kalends	Kal	I	1	Kalends	Kal
II	2	VI Ante Nones	VI AN	II	2	IV Ante Nones	IV AN
III	3	V Ante Nones	V AN	III	3	III Ante Nones	III AN
IV	4	IV Ante Nones	IV AN	IV	4	Pridie Nones	Prid Non
V	5	III Ante Nones	III AN	V	5	Nones	Non
VI	6	Pridie Nones	Prid Non	VI	6	VIII Ante Ides	VIII AI
VII	7	Nones	Non	VII	7	VII Ante Ides	VII AI
VIII	8	VIII Ante Ides	VIII AI	VIII	8	VI Ante Ides	VI AI
IX	9	VII Ante Ides	VII AI	IX	9	V Ante Ides	V AI
X	10	VI Ante Ides	VI AI	X	10	IV Ante Ides	IV AI
XI	11	V Ante Ides	V AI	XI	11	III Ante Ides	III AI
XII	12	IV Ante Ides	IV AI	XII	12	Pridie Ides	Prid Id
XIII	13	III Ante Ides	III AI	XIII	13	Ides	Id
XIV	14	Pridie Ides	Prid Id	XIV	14	XIX Ante Kal	XIX AK
XV	15	Ides	Id	XV	15	XVIII Ante Kal	XVIII AK
XVI	16	XVII Ante Kalends	XVII AK	XVI	16	XVII Ante Kalends	XVII AK
XVII	17	XVI Ante Kalends	XVI AK	XVII	17	XVI Ante Kalends	XVI AK
XVIII	18	XV Ante Kalends	XV AK	XVIII	18	XV Ante Kalends	XV AK
XIX	19	XIV Ante Kalends	XIV AK	XIX	19	XIV Ante Kalends	XIV AK
XX	20	XIII Ante Kalends	XIII AK	XX	20	XIII Ante Kalends	XIII AK
XXI	21	XII Ante Kalends	XII AK	XXI	21	XII Ante Kalends	XII AK
XXII	22	XI Ante Kalends	XI AK	XXII	22	XI Ante Kalends	XI AK
XXIII	23	X Ante Kalends	X AK	XXIII	23	X Ante Kalends	X AK
XXIV	24	IX Ante Kalends	IX AK	XXIV	24	IX Ante Kalends	IX AK
XXV	25	VIII Ante Kalends	VIII AK	XXV	25	VIII Ante Kalends	VIII AK
XXVI	26	VII Ante Kalends	VII AK	XXVI	26	VII Ante Kalends	VII AK
XXVII	27	VI Ante Kalends	VI AK	XXVII	27	VI Ante Kalends	VI AK
XXVIII	28	V Ante Kalends	V AK	XXVIII	28	V Ante Kalends	V AK
XXIX	29	IV Ante Kalends	IV AK	XXIX	29	IV Ante Kalends	IV AK
XXX	30	III Ante Kalends	III AK	XXX	30	III Ante Kalends	III AK
XXXI	31	Pridie Kalends	Prid Kal	XXXI	31	Pridie Kalends	Prid Kal
I	1	Kalends of following monthl	Kal	I	1	Kalends of following month	Kal

Table R2 The Roman calendar

Note the table below shows both an ordinary February and a leap February. Only one occurs in any given year.

	Jan	Feb	Leap Feb	Mar	Apr	Mai
1	Kal Jan	Kal Feb	Kal Feb	Kal Mar	Kal Apr	Kal Mai
2	IV AN	IV AN	IV AN	VI AN	IV AN	VI AN
3	III AN	III AN	III AN	V AN	III AN	V AN
4	Prid Non	Prid Non	Prid Non	IV AN	Prid Non	IV AN
5	Non	Non	Non	III AN	Non	III AN
6	VIII AI	VIII AI	VIII AI	Prid Non	VIII AI	Prid Non
7	VII AI	VII AI	VII AI	Non	VII AI	Non
8	VI AI	VI AI	VI AI	VIII AI	VI AI	VIII AI
9	V AI	V AI	V AI	VII AI	V AI	VII AI
10	IV AI	IV AI	IV AI	VI AI	IV AI	VI AI
11	III AI	III AI	III AI	V AI	III AI	V AI
12	Prid Id	Prid Id	Prid Id	IV AI	Prid Id	IV AI
13	Id	Id	Id	III AI	Id	III AI
14	XIX AK	XVI AK	XVI AK	Prid Id	XVIII AK	Prid Id
15	XVIII AK	XV AK	XV AK	Id	XVII AK	Id
16	XVII AK	XIV AK	XIV AK	XVII AK	XVI AK	XVII AK
17	XVI AK	XIII AK	XIII AK	XVI AK	XV AK	XVI AK
18	XV AK	XII AK	XII AK	XV AK	XIV AK	XV AK
19	XIV AK	XI AK	XI AK	XIV AK	XIII AK	XIV AK
20	XIII AK	X AK	X AK	XIII AK	XII AK	XIII AK
21	XII AK	IX AK	IX AK	XII AK	XI AK	XII AK
22	XI AK	VIII AK	VIII AK	XI AK	X AK	XI AK
23	X AK	VII AK	VII AK	X AK	IX AK	X AK
24	IX AK	VI AK	VI AK	IX AK	VIII AK	IX AK
25	VIII AK	V AK	VI AK*	VIII AK	VII AK	VIII AK
26	VII AK	IV AK	V AK	VII AK	VI AK	VII AK
27	VI AK	III AK	IV AK	VI AK	V AK	VI AK
28	V AK	Prid Kal	III AK	V AK	IV AK	V AK
29	IV AK	•	Prid Kal	IV AK	III AK	IV AK
30	III AK	•	•	III AK	Prid Kal	III AK
31	Prid Kal	•	•	Prid Kal	•	Prid Kal
	Jan	Feb	Leap Feb	Mar	Apr	Mai

*Dies bissextus = the twice sixth day, or bissextile; the Romans were not always logical.

Table R2 The Roman calendar (continued)

	Jun	Jul	Aug	Sep	Oct	Nov	Dec
1	Kal Jun	Kal Jul	Kal Aug	Kal Sep	Kal Oct	Kal Nov	Kal Dec
2	IV AN	VI AN	IV AN	IV AN	VI AN	IV AN	IV AN
3	III AN	V AN	III AN	III AN	V AN	III AN	III AN
4	Prid Non	IV AN	Prid Non	Prid Non	IV AN	Prid Non	Prid Non
5	Non	III AN	Non	Non	III AN	Non	Non
6	VIII AI	Prid Non	VIII AI	VIII AI	Prid Non	VIII AI	VIII AI
7	VII AI	Non	VII AI	VII AI	Non	VII AI	VII AI
8	VI AI	VIII AI	VI AI	VI AI	VIII AI	VI AI	VI AI
9	V AI	VII AI	V AI	V AI	VII AI	V AI	V AI
10	IV AI	VI AI	IV AI	IV AI	VI AI	IV AI	IV AI
11	III AI	V AI	III AI	III AI	V AI	III AI	III AI
12	Prid Id	IV AI	Prid Id	Prid Id	IV AI	Prid Id	Prid Id
13	Id	III AI	Id	Id	III AI	Id	Id
14	XVIII AK	Prid Id	XIX AK	XVIII AK	Prid Id	XVIII AK	XIX AK
15	XVII AK	Id	XVIII AK	XVII AK	Id	XVII AK	XVIII AK
16	XVI AK	XVII AK	XVII AK	XVI AK	XVII AK	XVI AK	XVII AK
17	XV AK	XVI AK	XVI AK	XV AK	XVI AK	XV AK	XVI AK
18	XIV AK	XV AK	XV AK	XIV AK	XV AK	XIV AK	XV AK
19	XIII AK	XIV AK	XIV AK	XIII AK	XIV AK	XIII AK	XIV AK
20	XII AK	XIII AK	XIII AK	XII AK	XIII AK	XII AK	XIII AK
21	XI AK	XII AK	XII AK	XI AK	XII AK	XI AK	XII AK
22	X AK	XI AK	XI AK	X AK	XI AK	X AK	XI AK
23	IX AK	X AK	X AK	IX AK	X AK	IX AK	X AK
24	VIII AK	IX AK	IX AK	VIII AK	IX AK	VIII AK	IX AK
25	VII AK	VIII AK	VIII AK	VII AK	VIII AK	VII AK	VIII AK
26	VI AK	VII AK	VII AK	VI AK	VII AK	VI AK	VII AK
27	V AK	VI AK	VI AK	V AK	VI AK	V AK	VI AK
28	IV AK	V AK	V AK	IV AK	V AK	IV AK	V AK
29	III AK	IV AK	IV AK	III AK	IV AK	III AK	IV AK
30	Prid Kal	III AK	III AK	Prid Kal	III AK	Prid Kal	III AK
31	•	Prid Kal	Prid Kal	•	Prid Kal	•	Prid Kal
	Jun	Jul	Aug	Sep	Oct	Nov	Dec

The World calendar

The World, or Worldsday, calendar is part of the attempt to bring even more rationality to bear on our everyday lives. Even so, it has to contend with the irreconcilable seven-day week and 365/6-day year. January, April, July and October all begin on a Sunday, and all have 31 days. All the other months have 30 days, so all the quarters are the same with 91 days. The extra day in an ordinary year [(91 × 4) or (52 × 7) + 1 = 365] is known as Worldsday, and falls between 30 December and 1 January. Leap years are those divisible by four as at present, and the leap day is another Worldsday that falls between 30 June and 1 July. As would be hoped, the Worldsday calendar fixes Easter Day for those who require it on 8 April. The dates between 1 September and 28 February, counting Worldsday as 31 December, are the same as those in the present Gregorian calendar.

Table W1 The World or Worldsday calendar year

	Jan	Feb	Mar	Apr	May	Jun	Jul	Aug	Sep	Oct	Nov	Dec	
Sun	1			1			1			1			Sun
Mon	2			2			2			2			Mon
Tues	3			3			3			3			Tues
Wed	4	1		4	1		4	1		4	1		Wed
Thur	5	2		5	2		5	2		5	2		Thur
Fri	6	3	1	6	3	1	6	3	1	6	3	1	Fri
Sat	7	4	2	7	4	2	7	4	2	7	4	2	Sat
Sun	8	5	3	*8*	5	3	8	5	3	8	5	3	Sun
Mon	9	6	4	9	6	4	9	6	4	9	6	4	Mon
Tues	10	7	5	10	7	5	10	7	5	10	7	5	Tues
Wed	11	8	6	11	8	6	11	8	6	11	8	6	Wed
Thur	12	9	7	12	9	7	12	9	7	12	9	7	Thur
Fri	13	10	8	13	10	8	13	10	8	13	10	8	Fri
Sat	14	11	9	14	11	9	14	11	9	14	11	9	Sat
Sun	15	12	10	15	12	10	15	12	10	15	12	10	Sun
Mon	16	13	11	16	13	11	16	13	11	16	13	11	Mon
Tues	17	14	12	17	14	12	17	14	12	17	14	12	Tues
Wed	18	15	13	18	15	13	18	15	13	18	15	13	Wed
Thur	19	16	14	19	16	14	19	16	14	19	16	14	Thur
Fri	20	17	15	20	17	15	20	17	15	20	17	15	Fri
Sat	21	18	16	21	18	16	21	18	16	21	18	16	Sat
Sun	22	19	17	22	19	17	22	19	17	22	19	17	Sun
Mon	23	20	18	23	20	18	23	20	18	23	20	18	Mon
Tues	24	21	19	24	21	19	24	21	19	24	21	19	Tues
Wed	25	22	20	25	22	20	25	22	20	25	22	20	Wed
Thur	26	23	21	26	23	21	26	23	21	26	23	21	Thur
Fri	27	24	22	27	24	22	27	24	22	27	24	22	Fri
Sat	28	25	23	28	25	23	28	25	23	28	25	23	Sat
Sun	29	26	24	29	26	24	29	26	24	29	26	24	Sun
Mon	30	27	25	30	27	25	30	27	25	30	27	25	Mon
Tues	31	28	26	31	28	26	31	28	26	31	28	26	Tues
Wed		29	27		29	27		29	27		29	27	Wed
Thur		30	28		30	28		30	28		30	28	Thur
Fri			29			29			29			29	Fri
Sat			30			30			30			30	Sat
						LYWD						WD	

LYWD = Leap year Worldsday
WD = Worldsday
8 April = Easter Day

Clock striking mechanism invented by Revd Edward Barlow (né Booth, 1636–1716) in about 1676

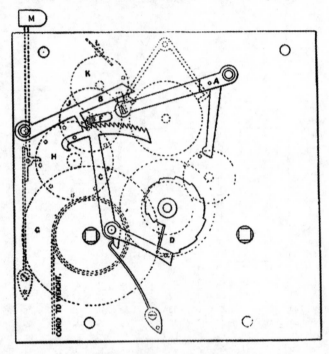

As the time to strike approaches, the lifting-piece A is lifted by a pin on the going train, and raises the rack hook B, which releases the rack C allowing it to 'fall' until the pin in its tail is arrested by the hour snail D. The snail is stepped so that the number of strokes to be sounded on the bell corresponds to the fall of the rack. The striking is now ready, but is held up by a pin on the warning wheel K, which engages with a stop on lifting piece A. The mechanism is adjusted so that when the minute hand is pointing to 12, the pin on the going train releases the lifting piece so that the striking train is set in motion. Pin wheel H rotates so that its pins engage with the tail of the hammer M that strikes the bell; as the gathering pallet F 'gathers' the teeth of the rack, the mechanism strikes one for every tooth of the rack to be gathered, which in turn depends on which step of the snail stopped the fall of the rack. The rate of striking is controlled by the air resistance on the fly L as it rotates.

Admiral Robert Wauchope's Time Balls

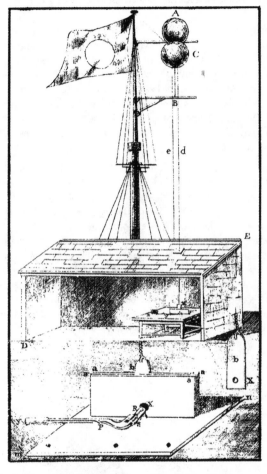

Admiral Robert Wauchope's 'plan for ascertaining the rates of chronometers by an instantaneous signal.' The balls are five feet (1.5m) in diameter, made of black canvas on a wire frame. The top ball is fixed. The lower ball is released by someone watching a clock and pulling a lever four-fifths of a second before the agreed time(!) This is because zero hour is taken as the time when the balls are separated by their own diameter, and this takes four-fifths of a second from release.

From 'About Time',
a work of fiction by Rodney Dale (1995)

Later, Colley had come across a question posed by Arthur Koestler: 'How does a radioactove element know what its half-life is?' He fell to thinking about this statistically at the atomic level, and was drawn to the conclusion that the passage of time is somehow a sub-atomic phenomenon. Atomic masers keep time (at 1.42GHz) correct to one second in 1.7 million years. How you measured this, he didn't know. Once again, he had the feeling that he was on the threshold of a complete understanding of the universe ... and once again the secret eluded him.

Time fast, time slow

Chronos and Kairos; the classical Greek conceptions of time – Chronos constant as the clepsydra; Kairos the correct, the appropriate, time. And yet, experience showed that there was a variable time: 'Where's the morning gone?' ... 'This week seems to have been going on for ever' ... 'Hours crawl; years fly' – Old Chinese proverb.

Time getting faster as you get older ... Colley had found the secret of that one: assume that you develop full awareness at the age of two; then when you are six, you have four years to remember ... so the year between six and seven is one quarter of your aware life. The year between 32 and 33 is one thirtieth of your aware life. The year between 62 and 63 is one sixtieth of your aware life. And so on ... no wonder that the years roll by – on ever-better-lubricated bearings.